I0827132

River
of
Dreams

ISBN: 978-0-9798087-6-0
Library of Congress Control Number:2008926097

Published by Global Authors Publications

Filling the GAP in publishing
Edited by Barbara Sachs Sloan
Interior Design by KathleenWalls
Cover Design by Kathleen Walls
Front Cover Art by Jason Price

River of Dreams

Wildwood Dean

ACKNOWLEDGMENTS

A special thanks to Della, my wife … who for the past 44 years has put up with me romancing Red River.

I thank Mother and Dad for the easy living country life I now enjoy and seeing to it that as a child I received a proper education: in the ways of nature … in the ways of Red River … in the oneness between God, earth, river and man.

I salute Red River; she has given to me freely of her bounty and provided me with lofty dreams.

DEDICATION

I dedicate this book to the “Price Clan.”

Those who are not mentioned in these pages are as dear to my heart as those who are.

INDEX

INTRODUCTION

When Mother and Dad got married, they moved to an upland farm in the Red River Valley. The shadow behind Mother is that of Uncle Lewis Barnett, who owned the farm. He was nowhere on the place when this picture was taken.

"The farm is haunted," Dad proclaimed.

"I don't like living with doppelgangers, and I ain't gonna … no longer than we have to." Mother put her foot down.

Mother and Dad set their hearts to owning a Red River farm.

Red River promised better times. She succored the dreams that sustained my parents. Her valley … a better place to farm; her waters, a better place to fish; her sloughs, holding plentiful fur and game.

Her flowing waters would carry you to the Mississippi and beyond … if you let her carry your dreams.

Mother and Dad continued sharecropping and watched their family grow. They had two sons and eventually bought the farm of their dreams in the farming community of Mulberry, Texas, in 1947. There they overcame every fiasco and circumstance of precarious nature thrown at them. They enjoyed a family bond that came about because of their surviving the harshness of country living after the depression that followed them the rest of their lives.

The family consisted of Joe Price, the withy dad; Sybil Price, the virtuous mother; Delton, the witty baby of the family; and winsome Dean.

~

That family was mine; I am Dean.

It was not until my later years in life, when I reminisced with other people as one will do about their childhood, that I came to realize just how precarious my childhood was. In River of Dreams I have tried to nail down some things about our family that would account for our fortitude, our "strength of mind," Mother and Dad called it.

Our family was a smart family — not educated — just smart. "Eating lots of fish has given us smarts in Nature's Ways," was Mother's philosophy because she read somewhere that fish are brain food.

Mother dreamed of heaven and waited her turn for the preacher to baptize her in the living waters.

She was a Christian woman first, foremost and always, the stabilizing force which kept our family on the correct course. She proclaimed at least once a day: "If you use slang language, the booger man will get you," and she enforced it with lye soap, to the mouth.

Dad had a simple philosophy: "Whatever you want, set your mind to it and you'll be way ahead of those that just have their eyes on it." Dad was a dreamer. He dreamed about how he could get rich on his Red River farm and about taking a trip down Red River to its mouth on the Mississippi River. He instilled his dreams into my mind.

Delton, the baby of the family, had a sense of humor and dry wit that kept many situations from disintegrating into disaster; he always made the family see the lighter side.

Our individual traits, with argumentativeness thrown in as a family trait, gave our family its spice of life.

~

River of Dreams is more than a history of the Price family — it is more than my biography; rather, it captures the essence of the times. It is about us living out our dreams along the banks of Red River following the "Great Depression" and how we thrived in spite of hardships. The dreams of better times ahead were all that held us together during the trying ones. River of Dreams is about a simpler time and the country wisdom of a not-so-distant past — of a time and a river.

1
A COUNTRY BACKGROUND

The old country house had never seen paint; the boards were weather-beaten and cracked. They creaked and groaned with the howling of the wind; it didn't matter from whence it came ... south or north, east or west. The old house carried the name of the farm where it sat: "Uncle Lewis Barnett's home place."

Uncle Lewis Barnett was neither Mother's nor Dad's uncle. As far as everyone knew he wasn't anyone's uncle. He was just a kindly old gentleman whom everyone around the Parker Grove community called uncle.

He obliged Mother and Dad by letting them live with him, rent free, in exchange for taking care of the place and him. They had lived with him through a year of sharecropping, but things were about to get complicated.

One thing, the living arrangement was wearing on Uncle Lewis's nerves. He had batched for many years, and having a woman in the house put restrictions on him, but that wasn't ... *the* whole thing.

Mother discovered that she was with child. Uncle Lewis Barnett was just as excited about the prospects of having a baby in the house as my would-be parents were. That still wasn't ... *the* thing.

Uncle Lewis Barnett had a passel of house cats, barn cats and "just cat cats" as Mother called them. That was ... the thing. Mother couldn't stand cats, and she couldn't keep them out of the house. She stayed on Uncle Lewis's case about fixing the holes in the screen doors.

"Don't you know a cat can take a baby's breath away?" she constantly scolded him. It was more of a combined thing that got on Uncle Lewis's nerves: a woman in the house, his house fixing to get more crowded, and Mother hounding him about fixing up the place.

Ever once in a while Uncle Lewis would up and disappear without saying a word to anyone.

Uncle Clarence and Aunt Helen, Dad's brother and sister-in-law, were coming to visit. Seeing that it was Saturday, Uncle Clarence and Dad took the afternoon off from their cotton chopping.

Two women are more than my nerves can stand, Uncle Lewis thought. He got up and left.

Uncle Clarence and Aunt Helen arrived sometime after dinner, and the four of them spent the afternoon visiting.

When Uncle Clarence and Aunt Helen were getting ready to go home,

Mother decided that she wanted Aunt Helen to take a picture of Dad and her with their new box camera. "It's just got one picture left on the film," she told Aunt Helen.

Uncle Lewis had given Mother an Eastman Kodak box camera and two rolls of film, size 120, that he ordered from Fox Studio out of San Antonio, Texas, so she could take lots of baby pictures.

Mother had used the first roll up learning how to use the camera, and there was only one picture left on the second roll.

Aunt Helen used the last shot to take the picture.

Mother wound the film off the camera and put it in the mailer, which came with the camera, and mailed it to Fox Studio. She could hardly wait for the pictures to come back; neither could Uncle Lewis.

Finally the pictures came, and they all sat down at the kitchen table to view them.

Mother shivered but didn't say anything ... she couldn't.

"What's the matter?" Dad asked.

Mother still couldn't speak and handed the picture to Dad.

He sucked in his breath to keep from losing it and covered his mouth with his hand to keep it in.

"Wahl ... let me see," Uncle Lewis drawled as he reached out and took the picture out of Dad's hand.

"Wahl for goodness sake, that's my shadow behind y'all. How'd that get there? I was gone to Bonham ... I weren't nowhere around. Whoopee!" he squealed with delight. "I got me a doppelganger!" He was so proud of his doppelganger that he bragged to everyone he met for years to come about having one ... "and I can prove it," he would say.

Within a few months after I was born, 1941, I started to crawl. That is when Mother really became worried. The first time I crawled up to the ragged screen door and hunkered there face to face with one of Uncle Lewis's cats, Mother put her foot down.

"It's common knowledge; a cat can, and will, take a baby's breath away," Mother told Dad. "We're moving out of here. I ain't living here with all those cats, afraid every minute they'll get baby Dean's breath away from him."

Dad, Mother and I moved into a sharecropper's house on the Kyle place. Dad sharecropped for the Kyles. Mother was overjoyed. *We don't have to share the house with anyone and certainly not with cats,* she thought.

Delton was born in 1944 while we lived at the Kyles'.

I don't remember my brother Delton being born, but I do remember pushing him around in the house in an old black baby buggy. My job was to keep baby Delton occupied while Mother cooked supper. I remember that Delton liked for me to push the buggy as fast as I could run. Every time the buggy slowed down, Delton would begin to cry.

"Slow down before you tump your brother over," Mother kept reminding me.

Our house had a perfect floor plan that enabled me to make circles through the kitchen, through the only bedroom the house had, through the living room and then back through the kitchen again – around and around we went.

Mother was right in the middle of frying taters for supper and it was the umpteenth time we had made the rounds. As I entered the kitchen and saw Mother's stern look, I slowed the buggy down and passed her. Delton started screaming because I slowed down. After we left Mother behind I peddled my little legs faster and faster to pick up speed and quiet Delton. When we passed through the door that separated the kitchen from the bedroom – it happened.

The front buggy wheel caught the door facing.

Over the thing went.

Delton and all his blankets went sailing out into the middle of the bedroom floor.

There was a hushed silence as Mother left her frying taters and ran to the scene.

"Dean Price, look what you've done. Your brother's probably killed under all that mess," she admonished with a shaky breath.

I've killed my brother!

I chanted, "I killed my brother – I killed my brother – I killed my brother." I danced around and screamed at the top of my lungs.

The buggy was upside down on top of Delton, its wheels still spinning as if it had been going a hundred miles an hour. Delton's bawling screams, muffled by baby blankets and the whir of the spinning wheels, added a sense of urgency to the situation.

Mother clawed at the blankets trying to drag Delton free of the wreck.

The house was filling with burnt tater smoke.

Then Dad walked through the back door. He quietly took Delton from Mother, placed him over his shoulder and went to patting him.

Delton's screams of desperation quickly turned to sniffles.

"Let's all go out on the porch until the smoke clears," Dad said as he cooed to baby Delton. He turned and headed out the front door. Dad gave me a hard look as the screen door slammed and left me inside.

"You're gonna have to peel some more taters for supper," Dad scowled at me, "while your mother collects herself and I take care of your brother."

I was so small and inexperienced with a knife, it took me over an hour to peel enough taters for supper, and I complained.

"I'm hungry. This is too hard. I need somebody to help me."

"You caused the first batch to burn," Mother spoke softly.

I knew what she really meant was don't complain.

Mother and Dad patiently waited, and bedtime came and went before we got to eat the second batch of taters.

~

Little did I realize, as I followed Dad and our mules, Gray and Grady, breaking the watermelon patch with the turning plow, that I was beginning a life in Dad's footsteps.

Dad had me picking up worms as the plow turned them up from the fresh damp soil.

Dad hollered, "No dirt, please," as I filled the Prince Albert tobacco can full of the fat red worms.

When I completed filling the can, Dad quit plowing, turned Gray and Grady out to pasture, and took me to Red River – gone fishing.

That fishing trip was my first with Dad.

On that trip I learned one of the most valuable lessons I ever learned about Red River survival. I got so thirsty, and Dad kept telling me that if I drank Red River water it would only make me thirstier because it was salty. I drank it anyway – and the more I drank, the thirstier I got.

I laugh as I look back. Some people would consider digging worms with a team of mules and plow overkill. To me it was a valuable lesson in efficiency.

I thought we were plowing the field. Dad thought we were going fishing.

I can still smell the fresh dirty smell.

~

The first time I went with Dad to the field to gather corn is one of my earliest childhood remembrances. Fall was in the September air, and as the corn stalks turned a straw brown, Dad made plans for taking me with him to help with the gathering. What Dad didn't plan for was what Mother was worrying about as corn gathering time drew nigh.

"I have this awful feeling something terrible is going to happen," she told Dad, every time the subject came up about me helping him gather corn.

"Old Gray and Grady are good mules; besides, I'll be right behind the wagon, snappin' the corn and throwin' it in the wagon. There ain't nothin' gonna happen to him," Dad reassured her.

"What if he goes to sleep and falls off the wagon seat?"

"No way – my constant hollerin' giddy up, whoa ... giddy up, whoa at the mules'll keep him awake. If I see him noddin', I'll lay him down under the seat where he won't get hit by the flyin' ears of corn and let him sleep."

No amount of reasoning was going to console Mother. She had what she called "a mother's intuition."

It was cool and crisp the September morning we started gathering corn. I went to the barn with Dad and watched him harness old Gray and Grady then hitch them to the wagon. Dad climbed up on the wagon seat and set me down beside him.

For the first time in my life I felt like a man.

I'm gonna tell Mother to quit calling me little Dean, I thought. *Dad doesn't call me that, and Mother has gotta quit.*

"Hang on, Dean," Dad warned. "Giddy up, Gray ... giddy up, Grady.

High on out of here."

The mules moved out a little too fast to suit him. He reined them back a little and hollered, "Hold your taters."

We were on our way.

When we reached the corn patch, Dad headed the wagon down the second and third rows, aligning the team with them.

He handed me the reins and got down out of the wagon.

"What am I suppose to do with these?"

"You just hold 'em. Old Gray and Grady are broke to the voice. I'll handle 'em from the back of the wagon. I'll be gatherin' corn back there, and they'll do whatever I tell 'em to do. When we get to the end, I'll get in the wagon and turn 'em 'round."

I won't ever get sleepy; gathering corn is so much fun.

Dad followed behind the wagon gathering four rows at a time: the one on his left, the two down rows (the ones the team and wagon were running over) and the one on his right.

Everything was going fine – although slow – like a snail's pace.

The slow pace bored me and the warm October sun wasn't helping either. I asked Dad to let me out of the wagon so I could help gather corn.

"I don't think you can throw hard enough to get the ears in the wagon, can ya?"

"Sure," I said, "if you let me gather just the nubbins."

Dad agreed.

However, by noon I was exhausted. I learned that snapping the ears off the stalks and throwing them hard enough so they landed in the wagon was man's work. We took the load of corn to the house – ate lunch as if there was no tomorrow – then lazily dozed for a while.

After we got a short nap, Dad told me, "Rest awhile if you want to. I'll go scoop the corn into the crib and come get you when I get done."

Kids don't need rest.

I was right on Dad's heels as he jumped off the back stoop and headed to the barn.

Dad scooped and I threw corn into the crib until the wagon was empty. Dad left me sitting in the wagon while he went to the house and told Mother that we were fixing to go gather another load. I wasn't about to go to the house with Dad, fearing Mother might talk him into making me stay home.

Somewhere around mid-afternoon, I became drowsy and my head started to nod. I faintly heard Dad holler whoa to the mules and climb over the side of the wagon. He laid me down under the wagon seat so the flying corn couldn't hit me, and then continued with his gathering. I flickered a few times then went out ... like a lamp.

The next thing I knew Dad startled me awake hollering, "Whoa, Gray ... whoa, Grady."

The mules were dancing around and trying to separate themselves from each other and from the wagon at the same time.

Dad was astraddle the wagon's sideboard trying to get his hands on the reins.

Finally Gray and Grady got their efforts coordinated and burst into full speed, dumping Dad onto the ground. He jumped up and chased after the wagon, but he was losing ground.

The mules were making a lot of noise – kinda like a scared-to-death whinny – Dad was hollering, "Whoa, whoa ... whoa!" He even used some words that I didn't recognize. I had never heard them before.

Some of those words sure sound like they would be fun to say.

Dad couldn't keep up with old Gray and Grady, much less catch them. Gradually they ran off and left him in a cloud of dust.

The mules, wagon and I traversed some bedded land that Dad had left laid out. This was land that Dad had prepared for planting the year before but had left unplanted.

The wagon bounced sky high as the iron wheels cut across the beds. First one corner of the wagon then alternating corners bounced as we cut a diagonal path across the bedded land.

I crawled under the wagon seat for two reasons. I didn't want thrown out of the wagon, but mostly I wanted to hide my eyes.

The boards rattled, the iron rims clanked, and on every bounce the wagon strewed corn.

Gray and Grady's whinnies, my crying and Dad's hollering whoa had no rhyme or reason.

We looked like a bad storm coming up. A cloud of dust hung in the air behind us.

Mother heard us coming and ran out onto the front porch just as the team dragged the wagon across the bar ditch in front of the house and headed across the yard.

When the mules reached the barnyard, they turned in without ever slowing down. The wagon didn't make the turn; its big iron wheels grabbed into the dirt.

The wagon flipped over onto its side and stopped the mules.

The two wheels on top were still spinning, and the mules were leaning forward, feet planted firmly, trying to pull the wreck into the barn.

It will never be understood how my parents got there so fast. Almost instantly I heard them tearing through the pile of corn that had me buried. Then just as suddenly as the corn started flying it stopped.

Mother and Dad set to arguing about the accident.

"See, I told you I had bad feelings about this," she said.

"I don't know what happened. They must've seen a snake or something. They ain't ever pulled a runaway before." Dad's excuses fell on deaf ears.

"Well, what they've done before ain't my concern. It's what they've done to my baby Dean that is my worry." Mother cried, and tears mixed with corn chaff ran down her cheeks.

Mother's two words, baby Dean, made me forget all about the wreck. *Now I ain't even little Dean ... and it ain't even my fault.*

In the exchange of heated words, it was as if my parents had forgotten that I was under the wagon of corn.

"Help ... somebody help ... get me out of here," I screamed.

My screams got their attention.

Corn flew again, as they dug toward me as fast as they could. Suddenly I felt Mother's hand clutching at my arm, pulling at me, pulling me free.

She grabbed me to her bosom and sobbed.

I felt warm and woozy ... *I was her baby.*

All was safe, and only minor repairs were needed to the wagon and harness.

~

Some of my warmest childhood memories are of sitting around the sheet iron heater at night listening to Dad spin tales about trapping and night hunting with our family dog, Mickey.

Even though it would be several years before I could accompany Dad on outings, I coveted for that time to come. Running a trapline and going 'coon hunting with Dad and old Mickey captured my imagination.

For the time being I would have to be content – waiting to meet Dad returning from running his trapline – waiting to see how many furs he would bring home.

Most of our family's meals came directly from the land.

In the spring and summer the meals we ate consisted mostly of vegetables from the garden, plants from the woods and nuts that we had harvested the previous fall.

During the winter, we usually had an abundance of meat to eat: quail, rabbit, duck and 'coon.

For two years in a row that wasn't the case, though.

The quail were scarce; Dad thought feral housecats and bobcats were the culprits. There weren't many rabbits; Dad thought that was because there was an overpopulation of coyotes. For the second year there had been very little rain in the fall, no flooded crops left in the fields, no ducks stopping for the winter. The raccoon were thriving, so much so, that those Dad caught were poor and skinny, and he was afraid to eat them.

Late one evening after running his trapline, he spotted a huge fat 'possum in a fence-row persimmon tree. That he was proud of his find was evidenced by his whistling as he stepped in the back door.

"We're gonna have 'possum for supper tonight," he announced.

"Well, my word ... I ain't never! I will neither cook, nor eat, any 'possum

... period!" Mother made her case.

"A possum's nature is whatever he's eatin' on is what he's gonna eat on until it's all gone." Dad held the 'possum up over his head and shook it toward Mother. "See how fat this possum is? He ain't been eatin on no dead cow." Dad made his case.

Mother pinched her nose and gave wheezy nasal instructions to Dad as to just what he could do with his 'possum.

Dad proceeded to dress Mr. 'Possum – out on the back porch – being careful to trim off all the excess fat.

Finally, the fare was ready for the baking dish. He placed it carefully in a roasting pan and piled lots of sweet-taters around it.

The wood cookstove was rocking on its feet and ready.

Dad slid the baking dish into the oven and closed the damper.

Soon the smell of a hardwood fire mixed with that of roasting meat and sweet taters browning filled the house with a mouth-watering aroma.

By suppertime everyone was starving.

Mother ate her helping of Mr. 'Possum so fast and kept going back for more that Dad complained about us not getting our fair share.

"The only reason that 'possum was so good was because we hadn't had any meat in so long," was Mother's claim until the day she died.

Winter wound down to the tune of 'possum for supper many more times after that delicious meal.

After supper Dad popped a dishpan of popcorn. The hours between suppertime and bedtime were really enjoyable for us.

One night in particular Mother was working on a chenille bedspread she and Dad were making.

Dad took time out from working on it to look at a Herters sporting goods catalogue by the light of the coal oil lamp. The catalogue had arrived in the mailbox that morning, and something in it had caught his attention.

Delton and I were lying on some handmade rugs Mother had braided from rags, listening to Dad read from the catalogue.

After he finished reading he laid the catalogue on the wood box, intertwined his fingers behind his head, popped his knuckles and stretched his muscles before he said anything.

"In this winter's catalogue are the first rubber artificial fishing lures I have ever seen. They look so realistic – they sure would save me a lot of skull drudgery work, chasing fish bait this spring – if they work."

Dad knew that in the spring he would again be tending his nets and trotlines to make a living. Finally he had everyone's excitement built to frenzy-level as to whether or not he was going to order the lures.

Then he announced: "I'm gonna order about a dozen – some grasshoppers, frogs, hellgrammites and minnows." With that revelation, it was time to blow out the lamp and go to bed.

Anxiously, Dad checked the mail every day, awaiting the arrival of his "ready made" fish bait.

The mailbox was over a mile from the house, and in late winter it was quite a chore walking to it. I'm sure Mother dreaded the day that Dad's package came because the job of going to the mailbox would return to her.

Finally after 10 days or so, the big day came.

We knew Dad had received his package when we saw him come down the road from the mailbox. He whistled every time his foot hit the ground, and it hit the ground pretty regular.

He rushed into the house and hurriedly opened the box, only to find that the rubber artificial fish baits weren't nearly as lifelike as they had appeared to be in the pictures.

~

Dad spent the rest of the winter rigging lines and nets, building a boat and tending his trapline. All the while he anxiously waited for the day he could begin fishing. Other than running the trapline, building a boat took most of his time.

The first thing Dad did when he decided to build a boat was go to the lumberyard in Bonham and order the material. He ordered a couple of 20-foot 1x12 pine boards.

"I'm telling you ahead of time ... I'm not taking 'em if you get 'em here and they have any knots in 'em," Dad told Earl Cain, the lumberman.

After Dad got the boards home he started the tedious job of sawing them down into the sides of the boat.

"You're my holder downer," he told me. "Set on this board while I saw it with my handsaw." I sat for hours and held boards down while I watched him saw.

"Joe boats," as the river fishermen referred to them, were 4 inches deep on each end. They tapered 8 feet toward the center from each end. There they where a full foot deep in the 4-foot length that made up the center section.

According to all calculations, that required more than 30 feet of sawing with a handsaw.

The finished hull was 2 feet wide in each end, 4 feet wide in the middle and flared the full length of the boat (wider at the top than the bottom). Dad floored the hull with pine tongue-and-groove boards, then tarred the seams and usually painted it with green paint.

Finally the day came; the construction was complete, the paint was dry and the weather was right.

"Let's go launch my new boat today," he announced.

Launching the new boat would cost Dad, but then his theory was, "Anything worth a hoot has a cost."

A 20-foot pine boat with tarred seams and tongue and groove flooring – like would go in a house – is very heavy.

Dad called on his brothers to help with the launch. They showed up one rainy morning and loaded the boat onto the wagon, hitched up the team and headed for Red River.

They were sliding the boat down the high river bluff when Dad stepped into a hole.

His rib cage came down hard against the boat. A cracking sound was heard but nothing thought of it. Everything else went without a hitch.

Dad, his brothers and I all stood around and admired Dad's new green boat.

"It sure looks like it will ride high and dry," Uncle Clarence observed.

The boat was beautiful resting there on the slick water behind the point of land known as "the boat landing."

"I'm gonna take her for a ride and see how she tilts and poles," Dad said as he climbed into one end. He stood on the 2x4 seat with a cedar pole in his hand and shoved the boat away from the landing.

Dad's boats were beautiful and prized by every fisherman up and down Red River. His boats were something he took pride in building.

He stood back many times during their construction and admired his progress. He would sigh and remark, "Looking good."

His boats were known for their maneuverability. A person could stand on the seat in either end of a "Joe Boat," take a long pole and pole the boat around with very little effort.

When we all got back to the house from the launching, Dad couldn't wait to tell Mother about it.

"Boy, that boat went a scattin' up the swift current of Ol' Red. She tilts just right. I don't think water'll ever come over the side ... even when I'm nettin' a hundred pound cat."

"Well, I'd certainly hope not!" That was Mother's only comment as she glanced up from the pan of frying potatoes she was stirring.

The next morning Dad couldn't get out of bed.

"Take a deep breath and tell me where it hurts." Mother did her physical exam.

Dad sucked air then let out an excruciating scream. He grabbed his side. "It hurts all over more than anywhere else."

"Get you another one," she demanded.

Dad screamed, with a half-breath inhaled.

"You got a broke rib or two," Doc Mother pronounced.

"Bind me down, so I won't get phenomena," he submitted.

Mother bound him up in long strips of ducking torn from an old cotton sack, then tied it with fishing string.

Life continued as usual.

~

Dad loved fishing more than any other job. His love of fishing usually caused spring to come early ... in his estimation.

"Fishing season, in the spring, is as soon as you can stick your big toe into Red River and your eyeballs don't pop out." That wasn't the law of nature – that was the law of Joe Price.

The weather had warmed, trapping season was over – everything was almost ready for fishing season.

In those days there weren't many seasons for doing things. There was the "Law of Nature" that the country folks followed. People from the city, even back then, went by open seasons.

Trapping season started in the fall – as soon as the hides weren't blue – that meant they were prime. The law about fur was that when the skin side of the pelt had a blue appearance, the fur would fall out when the hide dried.

"Rabbit hunting season is any month having an R in it. It is closed in May, June, July and August for rabbits to mate and raise their young," Dad explained.

He instilled the laws of nature into Delton and me.

~

The boat was in the river and Dad had plenty of "factory fish bait." It didn't take him long, though, to learn his factory fish bait wouldn't work on trotlines in Red River.

About that time he read in *Fur Fish Game*, the only magazine we subscribed to, about how the lures were working on a device called a "rod and reel." Dad set his eyes on owning one.

That winter had been extremely harsh and wet, and the planting of the crops was delayed. When Dad could get something planted, it was so wet and the ground was so cold, the seeds either rotted or the field mice dug them up before they could sprout. Dad became disgusted.

He stepped up on the back stoop and kicked off his muddy brogans, then came into the house.

"We're moving to California!" he said in a make-believe disgusted voice. His excitement showed through.

"What on earth for? You gonna give up your dream of owning a rod and reel and fishing in Red River?" Mother was shocked. She knew how much Dad loved Red River. She knew trapping, fishing and farming were the things his dreams were made of.

"We ain't ever gonna get anywhere sharecroppin'. We're both gonna work and save our money. We're gonna live with your mom and pop. In time we'll come back here and buy us a farm on Red River – all our own. I want me a sandy-land, river-bottom farm right on the banks of Red River. I want as far away as I can get from this here crawfish gumbo."

Mother knew that Red River held Dad's dreams – whatever it took, she was willing – his dreams were hers.

Red River was Dad's River of Dreams.

2
A FARM WITH A FISHING HOLE

Dad had a favorite saying: "Whatever you want, set your mind to it and you'll be way ahead of those that just have their eyes on it." He was a firm believer in that principal.

Red River, rich in history, was a magnet drawing Dad. He had his mind set concerning owning a farm and living on Red River, and whatever it took, he was willing to pay the price.

We moved to California in 1945 from our upland farm where Dad was eking out a living trapping, hunting, fishing, and truck farming.

I was 4 years old and Delton only 18 months old.

We caught the Greyhound in Bonham bound for Dallas, and there we caught a train bound for Los Angeles.

The other passengers were all soldiers returning home from the war, which had just ended. They took every available seat. Mother got a seat because of having a baby, but other women who didn't have babies stood.

Delton cried, "I wanta bed, Mommy," during the whole train trip.

Dad and Mother worried that Delton's continual screams of desperation were grating on the soldiers' nerves, but the sounds of a baby crying instead stirred their thoughts of home and were welcome.

I felt sorry for Delton and was embarrassed because he wouldn't shut up.

Dad stood up and held me all the way. He never got a seat.

How exhausting that must have been, but Dad had a dream; his mind was set.

We arrived in Los Angeles and found that every seat was booked on the Greyhound going north. It was six hours before the next Continental Bus would leave for Modesto.

We booked passage and waited.

We lived with Grandpa and Grandma Morgan, Mother's mom and pop, in Modesto. Mother and Dad worked in the Stanaslaus Cannery and saved every penny they earned for the next 24 months.

Dad worked the midnight shift because it paid a nickel more an hour, even though it meant he would have to walk back and forth to work. Mother worked the day shift and rode with her mom and pop to work every day.

Eventually Dad found an old bent-up 26-inch bicycle in the trash, and after he gave it a good overhauling with a sledgehammer, he rode it instead of walking. His only complaint was that when he really pushed down hard on the pedals, it would throw the chain off.

A problem that the sledgehammer couldn't fix, he believed. Dad wouldn't spend a penny for anything, so he put up with the problem.

One day he came home with his right britches leg rolled up halfway to his knee. The left leg he hadn't bothered to roll up. His story was that his britches leg had caught in the bicycle chain.

"I was on the bike path, in the middle of the Tuolumne River Bridge. The piece o' junk threw me right out into the traffic ... if there had been any," he complained.

He rolled his right britches leg up to keep it out of the chain and continued home as though nothing had happened.

For the next 18 months he rode his "Piece o' Junk" with his left britches leg down around his brogans and the right one rolled up to his knee.

"You're a sight for sore eyes with one britches leg up and the other one down. Why don't you roll both of them up to match?" Grandma Morgan asked.

"Everyone knows about bicycle chains. I'd look like a yahoo with 'em both rolled up," he claimed.

For exactly two years we lived in California, the longest that Dad had ever been away from Red River, and he hated every minute of it.

"I hate being owned by my job," he complained every day. He would laugh and joke and say, "I want Red River to own me." Deep down in his heart, though, it wasn't a joke and he knew it. Then one Friday Dad came home very excited.

"We have enough money saved up to buy a farm back in Texas," he announced.

The magnetism of Red River and owning a river bottom farm were too much. It meant more to Joe Price than all the money in California.

Gone home to Texas!

~

Dad and Mother started searching for their dream farm as soon as the Greyhound bus pulled into the Bonham terminal. Dad bought a copy of the Bonham Daily Favorite and stuck it in his back pocket. He read in the paper about a farm that the Production Credit Association was about to repossess.

The PCA manager took Mother and Dad to see it.

"One look at that Red River farm in Mulberry is just too much for my bones to bear. We have to own her," he told Mother. Dad had finally found his little dream farm nestled close to a fishing hole in Mulberry, Texas.

My parents assumed the payments and took out some farm-home insurance, which PCA required. We moved onto our new farm in 1947 just in time for Dad to make a watermelon crop.

Dad worried a lot about what he and Mother had gotten themselves into; 113 acres was a lot of land, and $3,957.67 was more money than either of them had ever heard of.

How in Kingdom Come will we ever pay for it? he wondered.

Mulberry became our home and remained so for the next 17 years. The area in Texas known as Mulberry, having rich fertile sandy loam with some areas of red gumbo-clay, lies north of Bonham in a big bend of Red River.

Mulberry was our government's experiment in Socialism. When the Great Depression of the 1930s ended, the Rural Resettlement Administration bought the land from the starving farmers who owned it. The dust bowl days and then the Great Depression had farmers everywhere in starvation's grip.

The government paid them a fair price for their land so they had enough money to move to areas where there was work, like California.

The RRA divided the land into tracts containing from 30 to 40 acres, with a few as large as 50 acres. Two or three tracts were put together to form a small homestead. One of the tracts served as the home place. It contained a small, well-built track house, a large barn and a round outhouse constructed from corrugated sheet-iron and built on a concrete pad. Built in the 1930s, those round, well-ventilated outhouses with concrete floors were state of the art, very modern two-holers.

Each of these working farms eventually sold to a family who would live on them and farm them. One exclusion: Single men couldn't purchase a farm.

The barns were something for the eyes to behold. They were painted barn-red and built on strong creosote poles. They were complete with side sheds, corncribs and mangers with stanchions for holding the milk cow's head. If she kicked, you had to provide your own hobbles.

What most of the Mulberry boys remember about the barns was the fact that they had metal weather stripping fitted between the vertical wallboards. This stripping looked as though it would make perfect sled runners if it was nailed to the edge of a 2x6 board. Delton and I were later to learn that the weather stripping did make good sled runners – if you could endure the switching that robbing them from the barn brought.

Our farm consisted of one 50-acre block for farming, one 40-acre block right on the banks of Red River for pasture, and 23-1/2 acres where a wood-frame tract house sat. The house, barn, smokehouse, hog pen, cow lot, chicken pen, garden and outhouse used up about 3-1/2 acres. That left 20 acres of perfect sandy soil for truck farming. Mother named our truck farm "the Big Twenty."

Our river pasture was directly west of the house and had a really good fishing hole full of flathead catfish. "Apps," country folks called them. Dad was smart; he said Apps was short for Opelousas, and no one questioned him.

However, since we had to walk to Red River and our river pasture was farther from the house, we spent most of our time north of the house. Red River was just a "hop, skip and jump" in that direction, according to Dad's measurements.

The Red River pasture that was north of our house belonged to the Kight family.

The Kight river pasture was the place on Red River that became the playground for all my boyhood friends. It conjures up fond remembrances for me as the meeting place of the Red River Rats.

Kights Point, the name it got stuck with, was where the river quit running north and headed east. It was an area of Red River with high banks, slick shale rock, and deep fishing – or swimming – holes. Fishing or swimming depended upon whether Dad was there. When he was around there was "no swimming." When he wasn't around there was "no fishing."

~

Shortly after Dad bought his Red River dream farm, he decided that his mules were too slow to farm 50 acres of row crop and the 20 acres he planned to plant in truck crop. The only part of truck crop Delton and I heard was watermelons and cantaloupes.

"Never will I pay for this place working those ornery mules – too much cultivatin' land – I'm gonna get me a tractor."

That was Dad's pronouncement, and there was no reason to doubt it. With money borrowed from the First National Bank, he bought an old worn out John Deere tractor, a cultivator, moldboard breaking plow, drag type disk and planter from Audrey Cain.

In a few days a skid tank on stilts was delivered. The big flatbed truck placed it by the smokehouse door and filled it with tractor gas.

Dad spent a considerable amount of time determining where to park the tractor when it was not in use.

"Since the smoke stack is too tall to allow us to park it in the mule shed, the next best place to park it would be in front of our smokehouse. Anyway that's where we'll be keepin' the gas," he finally decided. "Besides ... the only protection from the weather an Iron Mule needs is a tin can over its smoke stack to keep the rain out of its engine." The choice he made as to where to park his "Iron Mule" – in spite of all the careful consideration given – proved a bad one.

Dad was ready to show off his new Iron Mule. Iron Mule was the nickname he used to indicate he liked the tractor better than his old mules.

John Deere tractors were commonly called "Poppin' Johnnys" because of the Pop-Pop-Pop noise they emitted. They had two-cylinder engines and pistons as large as syrup buckets. The gravity feed fuel system, the massive cast iron engine, and a crank – that was nothing more than the engine's flywheel worn slick by repeated crankings – rendered Dad's Poppin' Johnny a mankiller to start.

Getting his tractor started was to be the first fiasco ... of many.

Dad eased the flywheel around to a point where he could feel the compression start to build in the engine. He heaved his whole body and soul into turning the flywheel.

"A pop and a sputter, is that all I get?" He repeated the gut-wrenching process. That time he got a pop and two sputters. "The piece o' junk's flooded ... I think. Blast-it I can't 'member what Audrey said to do."

Piece o' junk was Dad's nickname for the tractor when he was mad at the thing.

"You've cranked that wheel nigh on to a dozen times. Rest a while," Mother told him.

"Well then, tote that bucket over here, and I'll sit and rest awhile and see if I can remember what to do," he said, breathless.

What to do must have come to him right quick like. He jumped up off his bucket and slapped his pants leg with his hand.

"Hot diggety dog, I got it!" he hollered. He grabbed a monkey wrench from his "overhaul" pants pocket and proceeded to take out one of Poppin' Johnny's spark plugs.

"I call them my overhauls because they haul all my freight," Dad explained often.

With the spark plug now out, he reached into his pocket and came out with a kitchen match, heisted his leg so as to tighten the ducking, and whizzed the match up the side of his britches' leg.

The match caught fire.

Dad bent over and peeked into the gas-filled spark plug hole. "So I can watch the engine get 'unflooded,'" he said.

Then he thrust the flaming match into the hole.

Whooiee ... the gas ignited!

Deposited on the ground in a heap, in the fetal position, he clutched at his singed browless eyes.

Everyone was dead serious, except Delton.

"You look like the man they shot from the cannon at the circus." Delton exclaimed.

"Dad-blast-it, I forgot that Audrey said to stand over to one side and don't look down the hole," Dad whimpered with disgust. "One reason I shot so far from the tractor was I had worn the ground smooth from crankin' on the piece o' junk. I had no footin'. Another reason was the blast from the spark plug hole." Dad sputtered and spat soot from his mouth.

Mother daubed the dirt off Dad's arms and face with a wet washrag, lovingly kissed his singed eyebrows and replaced the spark plug for him.

Mother's washrags were literally rags. She made them from old cotton scraps that remained from our old shirts that had been new flour sacks originally.

"She'll crank now ... can't be nary any gas left in her. Did you hear that ka-boom she made? Gosh, she blew me dad-burn nigh-to-he ...."

"Joe Price!" Mother was steamed. "You watch your language; those boys'll be repeatin' you, and I'll introduce the lot of you to a mouth scrubbin' with lye soap."

"Hades ... I mean nigh to Hades."

Two facts unbeknownst to us at that moment were that on the very next rotation of the flywheel the Popping Johnny would start and that getting her started hadn't scratched a dent into all the troubles we would experience before the day ended.

Gathering every ounce of his muscle power, Dad slowly rotated the heavy cast iron flywheel. When he felt the resistance of the compressed energy build to its maximum within the engine, he paused and took a deep breath. Suddenly he lunged into the flywheel, releasing his pent-up energy.

The flywheel spun around.

The Popping Johnny popped once and sent the flywheel around again. Pop-pop twice more sent it around several more times; then a steady pop-pop-pop.

"I pretty near gave my life to that blasted piece o' junk," Dad said as he stepped back and crossed his arms behind his overhaul bib.

"If she hadn't fired off on that crank, I was gonna buy back my old mules. Ol' Gray and Grady need me anyhow." That wouldn't be the last time we would hear him mention Gray and Grady.

Before the afternoon was over he would be talking to them again.

"Y'all jump on! We'll take her for a ride," he yelled over the tractor's pop-pop-pop.

Mother jumped on by Dad's side and held him tight, Delton and I jumped on the axle housing on the other side of the tractor. Dad pushed the clutch stick forward and opened the throttle. He released speed and power none of us had ever experienced before.

"We're off and runnin'... we're gonna go to the watermelon patch. Hang on," Dad hollered, as he opened the throttle wide open. We went tearing down the lane at a breakneck four miles an hour, dodging mud holes from the recent rain.

The watermelon patch was approaching fast.

"How do I stop this dang piece o' junk?" Dad reasoned out loud.

We were smashing juicy red Black Diamond watermelons and had crossed the second row when how to stop came to him.

Popping Johnnys had two brake pedals, close together. To stop, you placed your foot on both pedals at the same time. To make locked-wheel turns, you pushed either the right pedal or the left pedal, depending on which direction you wished to turn.

What Dad wanted first and foremost was to stop. Then he could decide how to get the tractor out of the watermelon patch without destroying the whole kit-n-caboodle.

In his excitement his foot contacted only one brake pedal.

The left wheel locked.

The tractor abruptly halted and at the same time went into a wild, high-speed, circular spin.

For a moment he panicked and shot the gas to her.

We went head over heals into the crushed watermelons.

Not Dad, he hung onto the steering wheel and kept "the piece o' junk" from getting on top of us while the Poppin' Johnny wreaked havoc on the watermelons.

When Dad finally got the Poppin' Johnny stopped he started ranting.

"Now that I have finally killed the piece o' junk, I've got a gut wrenching desire to own my old mules back."

Delton and I were fighting mad. It had nothing to do with the tractor incident ... it was our chance to have a watermelon fight.

I rubbed a chunk of watermelon heart into Delton's face. He returned the favor with watermelon in the hair, and then we started throwing chunks of watermelon heart at each other.

Who knows who threw the chunk that hit Dad in the face. It didn't matter.

Dad seized both of us by our overall straps, lifted us off the ground, stood us on our feet and commanded: "Sybil, take these brats to the house!"

I grabbed a big watermelon heart to eat because I knew from Dad's tone that we were being removed from the scene.

"I'll be along myself as soon as – or should I say, if – I can get this piece o' junk out of this hole she's dug," Dad mumbled through white lips and red face.

He held his tongue, though. He knew it wasn't the time for it.

Mother fixed herself between Delton and me, grabbed us by our hands and off we went.

I thought I heard Dad cuss. *I guess I didn't because, if I had, Mother would have come unglued.*

Two hours later, here came Dad and Johnny – pop-ety, pop-ety, pop-ety.

Mother ran to the door, hollering.

"He's mad, 'cause he ain't sangin', or whistlin', and he's flyin'. Come on, boys, let's go see him come in." Mother said that as if Dad was in an airplane coming in for a landing.

"Why, look at him ... he's standin' up on Ol' Johnny. He thinks he's drivin' Ol' Gray and Grady. Bouncin' round there with his arms out-stretched to reach the steerin' wheel makes him look like he's runnin' to keep up with his mules." Mother had excitedly said all of that under one breath.

Mother's and Dad's mental telepathy was sometime scary; she had just called the tractor "Ol' Johnny" and her nickname would stick, even with Dad.

From that moment on – except in fits of rage – Dad referred to our tractor as Ol' Johnny.

~

Dad made up with Ol' Johnny and the two of them were making good progress breaking up the 50 acres Dad planned to plant in row crops.

He wasn't ready for the calamity that happened next.

First the throttle or the governor stuck. The pop-pop-popping was becoming an audible whine as the mismatched pair approached the parking place by the smokehouse.

The smokehouse was coming to Dad way quicker than he had speculated it would.

Ol' Johnny really flies. This here is a runaway, he thought.

Last but far from least was the matter of his vocabulary. Dad had already learned that giddy up meant nothing to Ol' Johnny. Now he was fixing to find out that Ol' Johnny didn't cipher what whoa meant either.

He grabbed for the clutch lever with one hand and clawed at the gas lever with the other one. He forgot that his "Piece o' junk" even had a steering wheel.

He hollered, "Whoa ... whoa ... w-h-o-a!"

His commands fell on deaf ears.

Something brought Dad out of his hysteria, probably the sound of Ol' Johnny making contact with the smokehouse, and he stomped for the brake pedals.

For the second time that day, Dad put his foot on only one brake pedal.

Just as the first board broke Ol' Johnny went into another mad, circling, hole-digging spin.

The sound of boards bursting as Ol' Johnny rammed its nose through the smokehouse wall caused tears to well up in all concerned.

Ol' Johnny made two fast loops around before Dad could get his foot off the pedal and head the tractor away from the smokehouse.

"What on earth are you trying to do ... tear down the smokehouse with your tractor?" Mother asked as Dad sped by her.

"I did that one-brake, lock-down, turn-around to make her get herself out of the smokehouse – before she grabbed all of our hams and bacon off of the rafters and did 'em in – like she did the watermelons," Dad hollered as he and the tractor headed down the lane.

No one believed that for a minute.

At any rate Ol' Johnny took off back toward the watermelon patch; strewing boards and Dad all over the yard. Mother, Delton and me rushed toward Dad's lifeless body.

He's gotta be kilt.

Suddenly Dad jumped up and went chasing off after Ol' Johnny, screaming.

"Whoa ... ah shucks, whoa ... you piece o' junk!" Other choice tidbits came trailing back from Dad as he ran.

Ol' Johnny tore out the lane fence and headed toward the watermelon patch. Dad finally caught up with her, dispatched her and abandoned her.

I knew not to laugh. I would get my mouth washed out with lye soap just for thinking Dad's slang language was funny.

Mother hung her head in shame, and then she came unglued. "That Joe Price's language ... when he gets mad."

When Mother shook all over, pointed her finger at Dad, pursed her lips and clinched her jaw and called him Joe Price, Delton and I said Mother came unglued. Mother didn't stay unglued for long.

We were all proud the day was over.

In the days to come we all kept hoping Dad would buy back old Gray and Grady.

That didn't happen. Eventually he took up with Ol' Johnny again.

In Dad's and Ol' Johnny's absence from each other, Dad decided his tractor was neither an iron mule; nor a piece a junk. He never called the tractor anything but Ol' Johnny after that.

For years to come, when anyone asked Dad how he caught the tractor he would put on a sheepish twisted grin and give a pat answer.

"I had to. How was I gonna explain the fool thing gettin' back in the watermelon patch? Why, I would've never lived that down." He would wink at Delton and me, then try to change the subject. "Remember all those melons y'all had to eat?"

~

Back in the 1950s, on Saturdays, the school buses went into rural areas, weather permitting, and picked up anyone needing a way to town, a much appreciated service.

Many, possibly most, farm workers back then didn't have automobiles. They had lost everything to the Great Depression. Survival was the first and foremost concern; getting around would come later.

"Come Saturday," Dad announced, "I'm gonna catch the school bus and go to Bonham. I'm gonna buy me a new rod and reel. It didn't take the Red River sand long to eat the bushings out of my wagon wheel reel."

Before we left California, Dad purchased a "Wagon Wheel Reel" and a rod. Those reels are still in production under the name of Alvey, an Australian company specializing in long distance casting gear.

Dad got off the school bus and headed straight to Smith-Moore-Williams, the local hardware company where he purchased himself a new rod and reel. The rod was an octagon steel rod made by the American fork and Hoe Company and the reel was a "Fine Pfluger Fisher," stamped right on the side-plate.

Of course we had to have one, so Delton and I made ourselves replicas of Dad's rod and reel.

A dogwood stick served as the rod, and we used fencing staples for the eyes. A wooden sewing thread spool stolen from Mother's treadle sewing machine drawer served as the reel. I nailed the spools to the big end of each stick with rusty nails that I had encouraged Delton to steal from the outhouse.

Oh, there was always plenty of fishing line to wrap around the spool. The action was hardly that of a bamboo fly rod, but we did catch fish on our homemade rods and reels.

~

There would be no sitting on the porch eating popcorn and watching the setting sun; it was Saturday.

"We gotta get our Saturday night baths ... tomorrow's church day." Mother seemed to live for church day.

To Delton and me, getting ready for church was quite an ordeal. We had to begin preparing for Mother's special day on Saturday night by taking a bath.

"Y'all pump some water before you come in and grab the wash tub on your way, Dean," Mother hollered.

Taking baths for country folks before electricity was skull-drudgery. The end result – questionable to say the least – was everyone had only gone through the motion of getting cleaned up.

I fetched the wash tub from the wall on my way into the house and set it on the screened-in porch.

Delton started cleaning out the tub. Dad pumped buckets full of water, and I carried them into the house and dumped them into the tub until it was half-full, by Mother's measure, not mine.

"Bring a couple of buckets for heatin'. We need hot water to clean this bunch up." Mother thought hot water and lye soap could clean up anything.

Mother always got the first bath.

After some time and with two teakettles of boiling water mixed into the wash tub, Mother was ready to take her bath. Before she got into the tub, she placed two more kettles of water on the coal oil cook stove to heat. When Mother finished her bath, she added a kettle of water to the bath stock and then hollered for Delton to come get in the tub.

He always followed Mother as the next bath taker.

"Wash 'hind your ears and hurry. We don't wanna be midnight gettin' done." Mother always told us to wash behind our ears and then she did it herself, just to make sure the job was done right.

When Delton finished he stretched a towel around himself and went running to Mother as if to gain her approval. He stood there shivering, more from wanting her okay than from being cold.

"Dean, you're next." Mother considered me big enough to heat my own water.

I added another teakettle of boiling water to the stock and then climbed in. The hot water felt good, even though it had a milky appearance from all the lye soap. It was probably getting a little dirty, too, but Dad was the only one left.

When Dad finished taking his bath, the water *was* dirty.

He hollered, "Dean, dip the water out of the tub and be sure to wash the settlings out real good, you can put them on my rose bushes. Delton you hang the tub back on the wall, by the door steps."

We were all cleaned up now – not allowed to go back outside – Mother didn't want us to get dirty, all over again, before church.

After church we always went straight home. Delton and I couldn't go off anywhere before dinner because Mother always cooked a good Sunday dinner and depended on us to kill the frying chickens. After dinner, Mother's law kicked in: "Sunday evenings are for resting."

We usually ate popcorn or had milk with cornbread crumbled up in it for supper.

Late one Sunday evening, Mother popped a dishpan full of popcorn and we all sat on the front porch eating it and admiring the setting sun.

Dad broke the silence. "Boys, I think were gonna like this here farm; someday they say were gettin' 'lectricity and we'll really be steppin' in high cotton."

Mother joined right in. "We can get a new water pump that'll pump water right into the house – right into the wash tub. It'll be a simple matter to heat the bath with some boiling water. We'll take baths ever few days ... at least until the new wears off."

"Everyone can have their own water?" Delton asked.

Mother's eyes twinkled ... "Yeah!"

"I don't know 'bout that," Dad said. "Ever few days and individual baths may make the light bill go too high. Besides we don't wanna burn the pump up the first rattle out of the box ... now do we?"

Dad's reasoning didn't have any effect on Mother.

"Well, I ain't gonna wait till Saturday night. I'm gonna get me a bath any time I see fit." Mother spoke with defiance.

Baths at separate times had never dawned on us, but leave it up to Delton. "Hey ... we won't all have to take baths on the same day."

Dad, disgusted with all the bath talk, looked off toward the western sky – toward the setting sun suspended half above nature's easel, the horizon – and announced the topic for our nightly brainstorming session.

"Do you 'spose, boys, when the sun there starts hittin' bottom, it's causin' all those colors to splash up and paint God's picture for the world to see?"

Dad can ask the best questions.

"Hits bottom of what?" Delton asked.

We were off and running.

The moon was waxing toward a full harvest moon and a chill filled the air.

Mother moved inside and lit the lamp.

Dad, Delton and me followed her inside and finished our nature study.

Another day in Mulberry, living on the Price Family farm, came to a close.

The first growing season had come and gone; replaced by dreams of a Red River winter. Dreams of trapping mink and 'coon and 'possum and of making fishing nets for the upcoming fishing season overshadowed farming.

Hopefully the fun ways of making a living during the wintertime would provide us a living. Hopefully we wouldn't have to resort to the drudgery of making a living by cutting bois d'arc fencepost for the public.

Flailing and picking up pecans, now that was fun, too; but not according to Delton and me. Crawling around on your knees picking up tiny little pecans, fun?

The enthusiasm, the fortitude and the precariousness surrounding the Price family was just beginning.

Mother's and Dad's dream of owning a Red River farm had become a reality. They moved on to other dreams; none of which compared to buying a farm, while memories of the Depression were still fresh in their minds.

Just a few short years back our only dream was getting something to eat, Dad thought.

Mother must have remembered that, too. She shuddered.

3
THE LONG HARD WINTER

Country life on the Price farm revolved around the four seasons. In Dad's mind, each season had a reason; spring was for tilling, sowing and fishing, summer was for enjoying, fall was for reaping and winter was for surviving.

The evening was rather warm for late fall, so we went out on the front porch for a set, before bedtime. We discussed the dire condition we were in and what the winter would bring.

As winter approached, Dad realized that we were ill-prepared.

"Farmin' is different in Red River Bottom. I've been an upland farmer all of my life. I ain't use to land as proficient at producing weeds and Johnson grass as this rank, river bottom land," he grumbled.

There was a difference, to Dad, between grumbling and complaining. Complaining to him was expressing your dislikes. Grumbling was simply stating the facts.

When Mother cornered Dad about his Red River Bottom farming statement, he said, "I wasn't complaining; I didn't say I didn't like it. I was just stating the facts."

"Another thing you ain't use to ownin' a farm with a fishin' hole." Mother poked at Dad. She always knew how to cut right to the facts.

Dad ignored the fishing-hole business. "Our corncrib is less than half full. The corn made mostly nubbins 'cause I couldn't keep the weeds and grass out of it. Ever body will be in the same shape though. Seed corn will be scarce as hen's teeth come spring."

Mother did some grumbling of her own.

"We've got less than a hundred jars of vegetables in the cellar. How's a women 'spose to cook?" She wasn't through. "And you ... Joe Price; without your nets you ain't nettin' any fish for me to pressure can." She still wasn't through. "Firewood is another thing; this river bottom ain't got anything in it but cottonwood, willer, and box elder and swamp dogwood. There ain't a cord a good heatin' wood in the whole bottom."

"Are you through now?" Dad asked.

"Nope ... but yep for now, I guess."

"What are we gonna do for stove wood?" I asked.

"Cow chips if we had a cow." Witty Delton busted us up. Laughter broke out, and the tension was gone ... at least from that conversation.

The spectacular sunset was the subject of the conversation for the rest of the evening, until bedtime.

~

Dad took a job working for Audry Cain, in his sawmill. He worked just long enough to buy a hundred pound sack of pinto beans and accumulate about two cords of cottonwood slab, for firewood and then the sawmill work played out.

It rained so much, the Red River sloughs all filled up with water and it became too hard to get the cottonwood trees back to the open air sawmill. Audry closed the mill.

It rained a lot that first winter we lived in Mulberry. It started in the early fall of 1947 and carried through the spring of 1948. A lot of the farmers didn't get all of their crops out, and the ducks and geese came by in droves to occupy the flooded crop land; that, along with Frank's and Edna's generosity saved us from starvation.

We ate duck and geese prepared every way you can cook them.

Mother baked them, with dressing and without dressing. She fried them and stewed them; she parboiled, roasted and pressure canned them.

"If I have to eat another duck, I'm gonna start quacking and flapping my arms," Delton said.

We all agreed.

Dad knew that if he didn't tie and hoop some new fishing nets, he would miss the flathead spawn and the quillback buffalo run and we desperately needed fish. When we moved to California, Dad gave every last one of his hoop nets to his brothers, Clarence and Bill.

"Our work is laid out for us in the long hard winter to come. There is firewood to cut and haul in, bois d'arc fencepost to cut, fences to build, and a hog pen and hog shed to build for our two sows. Our pullets needed a chicken house – they will start laying eggs come spring – and so far they have no home." Dad tallied up the workload.

"Before you get all that done, you gotta get a cow; you can always stake her out till you get a fence built." Mother added to the pile of chores.

"Get a cow for cow chips to burn?" Delton asked.

"Nope, for milk and butter to fatten up your little bony...."

Dad dropped that word abruptly – Mother interrupted him.

"Joe Price ... you watch your tongue."

~

The very first business in order to get ready for winter was to get in a supply of firewood for heat and cooking.

In years past Mother had helped Dad cut firewood. I was growing up and that was about to change.

A women's place is not cutting wood, Dad thought.

"Honey, I think you oughta stay home and take care of Delton – it'll be too hard on y'all – what with this rain, mud and the cold winter that's on us," Dad said. The thought of cold winter brought a shiver to his voice.

"Delton, you stay home and take care of your mother. Dean and me are gonna spend a few days cuttin' and bringing in our winter wood."

Me, take care of Mother ... Dad thinks I am a little man, Delton thought.

Delton, at his young age, really needed to stay home. I had just turned 6 in July, and Delton wouldn't turn 3 until September.

As Delton grew older he resented Dad's "Stay home and take care of your mother" statements.

Dad converted his old team-drawn wagon from a horse-drawn one to a wagon he could pull behind Ol' Johnny. He always referred to anything pulled behind Ol' Johnny as "she."

"She worked fine for gathering corn behind the team, and she'll be more serviceable for hauling wood with Ol' Johnny pulling her," he said.

After the night chores were done up, Dad loaded the ax and the crosscut saw into the wagon and hooked her onto Ol' Johnny's draw bar.

"We'll make us some splitting wedges out of bois d'arc in the mornin', after we get to where we'll be cuttin' wood," Dad instructed me.

Delton and I woke early the next morning, before sunrise, to the smell of ham and bacon frying and coffee boiling.

Thinking about the day's events sent me bounding out of bed; the aroma probably had something to do with it, too.

I jerked on my overalls and ran to the kitchen.

There Dad sat swigging coffee; Mother hated his swigging sound.

Just as I reached for my straight chair, to pull it out from the table, I heard the all-too-familiar command from Mother.

"Wash your hands first!"

Delton dragged in, rubbing his eyes with his clinched fist, and headed toward the wash basin. I followed him.

I hardly took time to eat, wood cuttin' sounded like so much fun. I ate two biscuits soaked in red-eye gravy, a slab of ham, some bacon and a pile of scrambled eggs and a glob of plum butter as fast as I could cram them in.

"You ate that in one gulp," Mother said in a complaining sort of way, letting me know she didn't appreciate the way I ate too fast.

Dad knew why I ate my breakfast so fast and gave me a bit of advice that added to Mother's complaint.

"Lessons learned from doing things are learned well and remembered long. After today you're gonna remember that wood cuttin' just sounds like fun ... it ain't."

The ride down into Red River bottom seemed to take forever, and then Dad stayed on my case rest of the day for "ridin' the saw."

Riding the saw is what someone does because he is lazy – letting the person on the other end of the cross-cut saw do all the work – In my case, I was riding the saw because I was only 6 years old and trying to do the work of a man. Dad didn't cut me any slack, though.

Dinnertime came and we hurriedly ate our sausage and biscuits then washed them down with boiled coffee from Dad's camp cook set ... a gallon syrup bucket.

When Dad was going to be away from the house all day, the syrup bucket went with him and a pound of coffee. "Water, ah ... you can find water anywhere," he assured Mother.

Dinnertime wasn't necessarily 12 o'clock to Dad. It was when his shadow was so short he could step on the shadow of his head.

Dad would not own a watch. When asked why he never carried a watch, he always answered, "My doppelganger watches me. I never did wanna be watched by a watch."

I tuckered out sometime after we ate.

Dad split the wood that we sawed during the morning, and I piled up in some leaves and grass where we ate dinner and sawed my own wood.

The sound of Dad throwing stove wood into the wagon wasn't what woke me up.

The clinking sound that Dad's axe made, banging against a tree by my head after he finished loading the wood was what woke me up.

"Come on, we gotta cut another tree down."

I loved felling trees and jumped up as ready as a bee.

Dad chopped a "falling notch" to make the tree fall where he wanted it to, and then he started the double-man cross-cut saw on the opposite side of the notch, cutting downward toward it. By the time we got the tree felled and a few blocks cut off, the shadows were getting long.

When Dad had to take a giant step, to step on the shadow of his head he considered it to be the middle of the afternoon. If he couldn't jump to the shadow of his head, the afternoon was finished and evening was setting in. When shadows became so long they started to disappear is when he said dark was setting in.

Seeing dark settling in around us frightened me.

An old lonesome hoot owl let out a hoo-hoo-hoot and I started to whine.

"I'm sceerd, Daddy ... Momma's gonna be worried 'bout us."

"She is Mother to you ... I told your momma not to worry ... not to 'spect us 'fore dark." Dad continued in a voice intended to hurry me. "Help me get the rest of this wood loaded onto the wagon and we'll be on our way."

It was my first time to be down in the river bottom after dark. Dad was driving Ol' Johnny and I was way back in the trailer sitting on the woodpile.

With all the hoot owls, goblins and wompus cats.

By the time we arrived home, well after dark, I was in tears.

Mother and Delton heard us coming. Ol' Johnny was a pop-pop-popping. Dad was whistling and I was crying.

As soon as Dad stopped Ol' Johnny, by the woodpile, he told Mother how I had woke up and said I was sceerd and how I was afraid that she would be worried.

"His little bottom lip was just a quiverin'," Dad said.

"Oh how sweet," Mother said. "What's he crying for now?"

"It's a long story. We were deep in the river bottom and Ol' Johnny was pop-pop-poppin'. The hoot owls were hoo-hoo-hootin'. It was so dark that I couldn't even see Dean back in the trailer. He had a right to cry. He is my little man, though. He'll grow out of crying, and then I can start takin' him 'coon huntin' with me."

I overheard the 'coon hunting part.

Me ... get to go 'coon hunting with Dad and the hounds? Wow!

I might have sniveled a few more times, but I didn't cry another tear.

"Well, I've got supper on the table. Y'all get washed up and come on in."

Mother's thoughts wandered to her little Dean, as her and Dad walked hand in hand toward the house.

Yeah, he is Joe's little man ... all right, she thought.

After supper I laid down behind the sheet-iron heater. The warmth from the wood stove soothed me into a dreamy world.

I'm Dad's little .... I ain't 'fraid of dark ... wompus cat's ... hoo-hoo-hootin'....

The wood cutting continued for a couple of weeks.

I grew quite good at not riding the saw, staying awake all day, loading the split wood into the wagon and drinking Dad's "syrup bucket coffee."

Splitting wood ... no, Dad wouldn't let me even try.

"Why can't I split wood?" I asked.

"Because, you're just too little, that's why."

"But why won't you even let me try?"

"Your britches are too little in the git-along, and your git-along is too little for your britches."

I got more confused. *I got overhauls just like Dad's and they fit.*

"What's my get-along?"

"Your stride, son ... your get-along is your stride."

I didn't know anymore than I did before I asked. I decided that if I was going to figure out what Dad was talking about, I would have to ask Mother.

~

The next thing on Dad's agenda was getting some fishing nets made.

"I need to go to town Saturday and get some cotton string and some coal tar so I can tie me some new fishin' nets. That cotton twine doesn't last long in Red River if you don't tar it," Dad told George Warren in an asking sort of way.

True to blue, when Saturday rolled around George came by for Dad and they spent the day in Bonham.

Late that afternoon here they came. Dad was toting a gunnysack over his back filled with cotton net twine and a block of Coal Tar.

Cutting wood, according to Dad's calculating, was important enough to keep me out of school, but not the net-tying business.

"When you're learning how to tie nets, you're gonna tie a lot of slip knots. Those big flatheads will root right through a slippin' knot. I can ill afford losin' any big flatheads. Your time'll be better spent in school, learnin' your R's. You can help me after school and on weekends."

I couldn't wait for the weekend to come so I could start tying nets. I listened with ears intent as Dad instructed me in the ways of getting a net started.

"First you wrap the net twine, off of your net needle, around a Prince Albert can twice then tie a secure square-knot. Now take the twine off and hang your loop on that nail there in the door facing. Lay the tobacco can under the string there between the needle and the loop. Now run the needle under the can and pick up your loop. As you draw the loop down toward the can, adjust the knot to the middle of the loop. Tie 'er off and repeat the process. Make me a chain of 126 knots, and then I'll show you the next step."

Dad eyed me constantly and kept telling me to keep the string tight and work the knots down tight so they wouldn't slip.

Little did Dad know that I had the patience to tie every knot as it came to me ... he found out soon enough though.

I learned to roll every knot around between my thumb and forefinger and snub them down against the net block with a hard pull on the net needle until they became slip-less knots.

Our next door neighbors, Jim Dad and Ruby Price, found out about my net-tying abilities, and Jim Dad was so proud of me he took it upon himself to carve me a special net-tying needle out of bois d'arc.

I had earned the title of net tier, and Dad laid out the workload.

"Dean, you're gonna be my net tie-er-upper. I'll make the dogwood hoops, hoop the nets and needle down the crow foot throats, and then I'll get you to help me tar 'em. We should have half a dozen nets or so 'fore this winter's over. When next winter comes, we won't be runnin' out of meat like we just did."

It was true: For breakfast we had had our last ham, bacon and sausage. We usually had three meats every meal, and breakfast was no exception.

The next time we sat down at the table, it was red beans and cornbread.

~

The whole week before the Christmas Holidays Dad, Delton and I planned what we would do during my Christmas vacation.

After school turned out for Christmas, all work around the farm would cease. Books wouldn't take up again for two weeks.

Dad planned to run his trapline up on Caney Creek during the early mornings. He was trapping mink and having pretty good luck. While he ran his trapline, I would take off down the river bluff and run my 'possum traps. 'Possums couldn't resist my special made sun-rendered fish oil, and I expected to catch a zillion. During the afternoons Dad planned for me and him to roam Red River Bottom flailing and picking up pecans and walnuts. I had dreams of Delton, Rounder the family cur and me striking off on the trail of some unlucky 'coon as soon as dark settled in. Late nights we planned to reserve for sleeping.

"Boys, speaking of Christmas, we sure are gonna have a big one. With all of the pecans and 'coon hides we're gonna accumulate, we're gonna have a lot of money. We're gonna do Christmas up right."

Dad had a peculiar way of making work sound like so much fun.

The next day after school let out for the holidays it commenced to rain and didn't let up for three whole weeks.

We sure did Christmas up right, all right – house bound – trapped in the house with Mother and Dad.

No outdoor activities and no school ... just net tying, reading, brainstorming, figuring out riddles and scuffling.

Dad's nerves wore thin ... before Mother's did.

"There's just so much of this kind of thing that a fellow can enjoy; then he becomes house whooped." Dad's voice gave him away. He was tired of Delton and me scuffling.

I came up with the perfect solution.

"Can we hitch up Ol' Johnny to the trailer and go to Uncle Frank's and Aunt Edner's?"

Delton realized that we might have to beg and he started to chant.

"Can we, Mother – can we, Daddy – can we, can we, can we? Oh please, can we go to Frank's and Edner's?"

"That is Uncle Frank and Aunt Edna to you boys." Mother butted into Delton's chant with a stern look and a twisted mouth.

Before Delton could commence the chant again Dad spoke up.

"Well ... considerin' all of the rain that we've been havin' I'd have to rig up some dogwood hoops over the wagon so we can put a tarp over it. That's a gob of trouble."

"Hey, I know ... why don't I just make us some popcorn balls?" Mother offered, but she knew that her solution was no solution.

"Ah ... popcorn balls," Delton and I rang out in unison.

That is out of the question. Neither Delton nor I was willing to voice that thought; we commenced begging in earnest.

I ran circles around Mother while Delton clung onto her dress tail and we both chanted, "Let's go. Can we go? Let's go. Can we go?"

What effect the chant had on our parents, we never figured out. We just knew that a chant usually got results. Sometimes good – sometimes bad – but results nonetheless.

It is probably like the squeaky wheel gets the grease.

We got our timing down and got in sync: "Let's go? Can we go? Let's go. Can ...."

"HUSH!" Dad interrupted, "We're gonna go."

We hushed. Things got so quiet you could hear a pin drop.

Dad sighed with relief. *Quiet is good; it's like I zipped those brats' mouths shut.*

He slammed the back door and went outside.

We won. I knew that thought was better left unsaid.

Mother read my mind. "I want you boys to know that you didn't win any argument or get your way. We were planning on going tomorrow anyway."

I heard Ol' Johnny's pop-pop-pop and knew that she was all hitched up to the trailer and raring to go. Delton and I loaded into the trailer, and Mother threw in enough belongings to spend a week away from home. Dad climbed up on Ol' Johnny, pulled the clutch lever back, shot the gas to her, and we were off and running.

The trip normally would have taken a half a day; however, it turned out taking most of the day, due to the toad-strangling rains we had been getting.

When we got to Caney Creek bottom and its black gumbo mud is when the trouble started.

"Hey, slow 'er down. You're throwin' mud in here on us," Mother hollered every time Dad let Ol' Johnny have more gas.

Dad hadn't planned on what Caney Creek's gumbo mud could do; in fact, he had never been across Caney Creek bottom during a rainy spell with anything that had wheels on it.

When we got into that gumbo – no matter what Mother wanted – Dad wanted to sling mud.

"Ever wheel on our rig is growin' bigger and bigger. The stick-tight gumbo mud is collectin' on 'em," Dad hollered back to the wagon. "I'm gonna give 'er some more gas. I hope I can throw some of it off."

Ol' Johnny was a B Model John Deere with a tricycle front end. The two front tires were side by side about 8 or 10 inches apart. Mud had wedged between them, and they were sliding along, skidding toward one ditch then the other.

Dad was getting desperate.

"I'm gonna have to do something," he said. "I can't steer Ol' Johnny 'cause the front tires ain't turnin', and the back tires are gettin' so big I'm fraid they are gonna fetch me off of here."

"The wagon wheels aren't turning either – they're solid mud – they've ground out on the sides of the wagon," Mother hollered.

Ol' Johnny, bless her heart, had all she wanted. If her wheels weren't going to cooperate, she wasn't going to pop.

She died.

Delton and I were wagon whooped and immediately piled out of the wagon. We took two steps before the stick-tight gumbo mud sucked our shoes right off our feet.

"Get back in here ... if Joe Price needs you he'll call you." Somehow when Mother referred to Dad as Joe Price, we knew it meant business.

We threw our shoes in the wagon and politely climbed back in and started prying the mud off our brogans with the new jackknives Santa Claus had brought us.

Dad saw how the mud had clung to our brogans, and he shucked his before dismounting Ol' Johnny.

He rolled up his britches legs, and then waded across the bar-ditch to look for something to pry the mud off the wheels with. He came back with a bois d'arc limb, about 3 feet long, and started prying mud. After a couple of hours he had the wheels clean enough so they could turn.

We were finally on our way.

After making only a hundred yards, it was all to do over again.

Dad complained: "It's the tricycle front end ... mud keeps wedging between the wheels on Ol' Johnny's nose and keeps them from turning. I can't guide 'er with them scootin'. I think it'll work if I take one of 'em off."

Dad's make-do spirit kicked in. He took a monkey wrench out of his overalls' pocket and proceeded to do just that. After he wrestled the muddy wheel off the tractor and put it in the wagon, he looked like squiggles, our old muddy sow.

We crossed the remaining 500 yards and then climbed the bluff out of the bottom and only had to stop once more, to clean off a wagon wheel that had become a skid.

Now that we were finally out of Caney Creek Bottom, Dad stopped Ol' Johnny, climbed off, ran and jumped into the bar ditch and splashed around. He climbed into the wagon, feet first and wiped the muck from between his toes with a gunnysack. After drying them as best he could, he replaced his brogans. Dad never wore socks.

It was well after dark when we reached Uncle Frank's and Aunt Edna's and we had to wake them up. Aunt Edna stoked up the pot belly heater and added some more water and grounds to the coffeepot.

"Let the visiting begin," she said.

Uncle Frank's first words were, "We got us a Radio. If y'all stay through till Saturday night and if I can save enough battery, we'll sure get some good music and that new Dragnet show."

Staying Saturday night means missing church, and Mother ain't gonna go for that.

I knew that we had to come up with a plan – at all costs – because we sure wanted to hear that new Dragnet show.

Wonder why anyone would name a show after a way to catch fish?

"I hope they don't have to drag the net through the mud with a cripple-fronted Poppin' Johnny," Delton quipped.

The laughter soon subsided and everyone started to catch up on community and family news.

Delton and I settled in on the wood box behind the pot belly heater, enthralled by Uncle Frank telling fishing yarns ... one right after the other.

Delton got warm and sleepy and couldn't keep his head straight on his neck.

I cupped my hands together in a megaphone style, put them up to my mouth and whispered in Delton's ear, "Boy, Uncle Frank can sure tell whopper fishing stories; you better wake up."

Delton jumped as if I shot him with my BB gun, and sent post oak bark sailing across the floor.

"No secrets, boys. Dean, you stand up and tell everyone what you said," Mother commanded.

Mother doesn't ever miss anything.

I wobbled to a standup position and made ready to deliver my defense. "All that I said was ...."

Delton jumped up off the wood box, soldier salute stiff.

"All Dean said was, 'Uncle Frank sure tells good fishing stories,' and for me to wake up,' or I'd miss 'em," he blurted.

"Thank you, Delton ... Dean would have probably polished it up anyway," Mother said.

I was off the hook.

By then everyone was yawning, and we all went to bed.

Aunt Edna made Delton and me pallets by the wood heater and told us if we got cold to put another stick of wood on the fire.

The next day Mother and Aunt Edna spent a lot of time in the kitchen, cooking; they did some quilting and did a whole host of gossiping.

If we stayed quiet, didn't cause any ruckus and let the grownups have a good time maybe Mother would forget what day it was. Maybe that was the key to missing church come Sunday, I decided.

After supper Uncle Frank's storytelling broke out again, and after awhile Delton just had to tell me something. It was a repeat all over again except this time it was Delton who started to whisper something to me.

I up and gave him a stiff elbow to the ribcage. I had to stop Delton before we got caught whispering again.

The fight was on.

To our astonishment nothing much happened.

"You boys go to the barn and finish your fightin'." That's all Dad said.

Our brogans were so muddy, we had left them outside the door on the porch. We were fighting mad and didn't take time to put them back on. Just as soon as the bottoms of our bare feet connected with the frozen porch boards, Delton popped his head back in the door and blurted ... "fight's over!"

"Cold feet will cool off hot heads ... works ever time." Aunt Edna, in her bubbling giggling manner, came out with her bit of wisdom.

It is a pretty sure bet, after the ruckus we caused, we're gonna have to go to church.

We settled back to our places on the wood box.

Mother rubbed her eyes and yawned. "I think the boys are getting tired and sleepy. I think we better go to bed and finish this visiting in the morning," she announced.

Uncle Frank held up his hand, as if to say wait a minute.

"Before we go to bed ... Joe, in the mornin' you pick out one of my big killin' hogs. It's plenty cold enough for hog killing. We'll get up early and put on a washpot full of water, for scaldin' and scrapin'. We can have fresh tenderloin for supper and while we're listenin' to Dragnet we can eat fresh rendered cracklings."

"That gets a much-obliged from me," Dad told Uncle Frank.

Uncle Frank had found out about our being down and out, having no meat and running out of canned goods. The Price Clan way was to help each other.

Mother didn't interrupt their conversation – tomorrow night's Saturday night – church is history.

"Y'all can go home with the hams, shoulders and the middlings. We'll get the women to make us some mincemeat pies out of the head meat," Uncle Frank mumbled as he ran his tongue around the outside of his lips. "Man, oh man ... Edna's mincemeat pies are as fine as frog hair."

"I ain't got the spices for mincemeat, and the peddler doesn't come till next week. I got plenty sage and red pepper, though. We'll make the head trimmings up into head cheese." Edna smacked her lips.

So far notta word about church.

~

I woke up early, before daylight. The smells of fresh-killed chicken frying and coffee boiling, mingled in with the smells of frying sausage and bacon, were already wafting through the drafty house. I bounced into the kitchen and found Aunt Edna and Mother standing in front of the stove, preparing the morning's fare.

The wood cookstove danced in its tracks trying to get the kitchen warm and cook breakfast at the same time.

There Dad and Uncle Frank sat, their elbows planted on Edna's new red plaid oil cloth, warming their hands around big crock coffee mugs.

After a "come on in here; breakfast is ready" call from Mother, Delton's pajama clad form showed in the kitchen door. Mother gave him a stern look, and he came back shortly with his britches on.

Aunt Edna and Mother brought the food from the stove, sat it on the table, and Mother offered thanks – like she always did. Everyone thought she prayed so well.

In the middle of the table was a big bowl of white gravy, made with crisp crumbles from fried chicken in it. Beside the gravy, on a stone ware platter, sat a mountain of buttermilk biscuits covered with a freshly laundered floor sack to keep them warm. There was a gigantic cast iron skillet, piled high with fried chicken, sausage, ham and bacon. The trimmings included a quart jar of pear preserves with its bail thrown back holding the glass lid open, along with fresh honey. Uncle Frank and Dad had spent all day Friday down on Brushy Creek robbing honey from a hollow tree where a hive of wild bees had stored their precious nectar. There was a big bowl of fresh-churned, lightly salted butter, too.

"Are you tryin' to kill us?" Dad asked.

"Nope," Aunt Edna said, with her infectious down-from-the-belly laugh. "We just wanna get us a good day's work out of you men. Y'all have not done any work all week 'cept for robbing those bees yesterday and 'coon huntin' your nights away."

We ate all we could and even crammed some biscuits in our overall pockets.

While we finished the last drop of the coffee, Aunt Edna and Mother cleaned up the kitchen and made everything ready for processing meat.

"Y'all better get on with your hog killin'. Sybil and me are liable to decide to go 'coon huntin' and leave y'all with it," Aunt Edna said through rolling laughter.

Killing hogs is a lot of hard work for everyone involved, man, women and child.

Delton and I had plenty of work to keep us busy. We had to keep the fire going under the wash pot, help scrape hair from the hog, and run meat-filled dishpans to the house. The most fun of all was washing the slippery guts out.

Aunt Edna and Mother stayed busy trimming meat; they sorted it according to what they would use it for later, then put it in washtubs. One washtub held trimmings for making sausage and one held meat suitable for head cheese and mincemeat; which included the snout, head, feet and ears. A third washtub held hide and guts, for making cracklings, chitterlings and sausage casings. Yet another one held fat, to render into lard.

The day's work was on a schedule that would take us until bedtime to finish and everyone had starved out.

Mother scooted everything aside and covered things with a clean flour sack bedsheet while Aunt Edna fried up some fresh tenderloin. Everyone ate like there was no tomorrow.

After supper Uncle Frank pushed his straight chair back from the table and cocked it back on its hind legs.

"Let's go see if we can find Dragnet on the dial," he announced.

Finding any station on the dial was a problem because the dial was broken. It spun on the shaft, and a person never knew where a station would be next.

"I found it!" Uncle Frank said, after considerable twisting and turning of the dial, and the talk is strong, so we got plenty battery."

Dragnet was a disappointment – not about fishing at all – it was some sort of detective show. The Grand Ol' Opry was really good, though.

"Earnest Tubb, now he's for real; it ain't like he's putting up a fake name, like that Joe Friday," I said. "Now who ever heard of a man named Friday?"

"Well, I wouldn't wanna be a Tubb either," Delton countered.

I just can't get ahead of Delton's dry sense of humor.

We thought we had skipping church made, we thought Mother had forgot tomorrow was Sunday. Then out of the blue Aunt Edna spoiled it all.

"Sybil, if you're gonna go to church with me in the mornin', we'll get us a spit bath tonight. I'm too tuckered to mess with real baths."

Aunt Edna had to bring up church. Why didn't she mention us going?

Leave it to Delton to hit upon the reason. "I guess Aunt Edna would be embarrassed to take us to her church after we killed that skunk last night, and too, we ain't had a bath all week. You reckon we stink?"

I always liked to have fun at Delton's expense and saw an opportunity.

"No," I said. "If Mother thought we stank, she would have been scrubbing us with lye soap mixed with Brushy Creek sand, and then she would have dunked us in Brushy Creek."

"Even in winter, with it hog killing cold?" Delton asked.

"Yep ... you don't ever want to let Mother know you stink. Once Jerry Overton and I got in a fight with a skunk; after we killed him, Mother said that I stank." I had Delton's full attention. "She stripped my clothes off and commenced scrubbing me with lye soap and sand while holding me under the pitcher pump. She had Dad flush me off with ice cold well water."

"Really?" Delton's wide eyes expressed concern.

"Yeah really ... and then to make matters worse she took my best overalls and buried them."

I knew Delton wasn't likely to believe that big one, but I was in too deep to turn back now.

"You're joshing me."

"Nope ... If you ever suspect you are stinking, you had best leave home for a few days until whatever is stinking lets you be."

After Mother and Aunt Edna got in from church they sent me to the chopping block to kill a couple of fryers.

After a gigantic Sunday dinner of fried chicken and all the trimmings it was time for us to go home. Dad hooked up Ol' Johnny, and we took off down the road to Mulberry. Goodbyes and waving hands filled the air. No amount of begging from Uncle Frank and Aunt Edna could forestall our trip back to Mulberry, even though books wouldn't take up until January 11, 1948, a full week late due to the heavy rains. Mother and Dad were both ready to put "us brats" back in school.

Soon some gardening could be done and soon some fishing. There was still the matter of fencing the barnyard. There was much to do before spring. Little did we know that the spring season was going to be very, very late. There remained a lot of hard winter left to endure. Mother and Dad learned what winters could be like in the river bottom. We had plenty of meat now, and next winter would be different. We had high expectations for the year ahead.

Caney Creek bottom didn't pose as much of an obstacle going home. Taking the front wheel off had solved the steering problem.

Soon after we got home Dad had the hams packed down in the meat box and the sides of bacon hanging from the rafter, and we all retired to the front porch to make plans for the year ahead. We discussed how many watermelons to plant, where to plant the sweet corn, getting tomato seed planted so he would have seedlings to plant when time came. Dad's list went on and on.

"Yeah, Joe Price, we're gonna make a big garden so I can fill up our cellar with cannin' and with turnips, taters and onions. Who knows? I might even make up a barrel of sauerkraut like your Ma does.

Mother planned and she was serious.

Dad continued with his big plans. "I'm gonna do some serious row cropping, too. I'm gonna plant peanuts, popcorn, field corn and cotton. If the Lord's willin', I'm gonna make a good crop. I'll fight those weeds and Johnson grass tooth and nail."

The tension of surviving our first winter was over. The first full year on the Price Family farm, on Red River, in Mulberry came to a close.

Time would prove how serious Dad's plans were. Everyone knew, though, that Joe Price was serious about his fishing. Red River held as many dreams as ever for him. *Where he would set his nets and his trotlines ... he needed a new boat ... where the dogwood grew... would he catch that elusive hundred pound, flathead catfish.* Dad didn't verbalize those dreams – he pushed them to the back of his mind – they were there though, just as sure as Red River runs red.

4
"SPRING HAS SPRUNG"

Spring made its debut, announced by Robins singing, buds bursting and thunder clapping.

"Spring, has sprung," Dad said.

We had entered one of the busiest times of the year; at least for farmers in Mulberry. Dad had what he considered a two-week timeframe to get the garden in. According to him, the accepted time during which to plant the garden was the week of Good Friday.

No sooner than he got the garden in and up and growing, he started fishing; it was time for the flathead catfish to start spawning. When flathead catfish were spawning, they would go into anything that looked to them as though it would give them protection from the swirling Red River current. Dad's fishing in the spring was mostly with hoop nets because they looked especially inviting to flathead catfish, and he usually kept 10 or 12 of them set out.

We always ate the big flathead catfish fresh, and Dad sold what we couldn't eat.

By the middle of June the quillback buffalo started spawning. Quillback buffalo swim in schools, and Dad caught them by the hundreds, which Mother canned.

There was nothing Delton and I liked better than fried fish patties made from canned quillback buffalo.

In addition to it being the time of the year that Mother canned fish, she was in the middle of spring cleaning. It was the time of the year when she took everything off the beds and took the feather mattresses out and hung them across the clothesline to air out. She beat the thunder out of them with her straw broom to fluff the down up. While the mattresses aired, she swabbed the bedframe down with her special creosote-kerosene mixture for bed bugs.

Farmhouses, back in the 1940s and '50s were very small, and ours was no exception; it had two bedrooms, a living room and a kitchen. There was a screened-in porch on the back and a stoop on the front.

Delton and I shared a bed in the bedroom on the southeast corner of the house, and my side of the bed was the side that was about a foot from the east wall. I had just enough room between the bed and the wall to get in and out of bed without climbing over Delton.

Across one corner of the room was a piece of black steel pipe – put there on Mother's orders – to hang our clothes on. She hung a quilt over the pipe and converted the corner into a closet.

"What's the quilt for?" Delton asked.

"I spread the quilt over y'all's clothes to hide 'em," Mother told him.

"Hide 'em ... we're the only people who ever go in there, and we know that they're there. So who are you hiding them from?"

Delton shouldn't have said that ... just like that.

Mother didn't take lightly to Delton's statement.

We could ask questions; so long as we didn't question the grown ups' motives. We were not allowed to tell the grownups what to do, or make suggestions, as to why or how to do something.

"It doesn't make any difference if anyone ever goes in there or not, Delton. Don't sass me, you hear."

Delton heard ... I heard too, she said the sassing part so loud.

The furniture in our bedroom was homemade hand-me-down; except for the steel bedframe and squeaky springs. The steel bedframe didn't have a headboard. Someone sawed it off and just left blunt, hollow iron posts sticking up. At the foot of the bed sat an old pine quilt box that Granddad Price made. Our extra bed linens were stored there. A small desk that Mother's Uncle Jim made from scrap lumber sat against the wall between the two bedrooms.

Our mattress was a goose down one that Great Grandmother Duty made for Grandma. Grandma had passed it down to Mother and Dad when they got married. Great Grandma Duty kept a flock of geese and picked down from them to make feather mattresses and pillows for all of her kids when they got married.

The room's decorations were just as sparse as the furniture the room held. The 9x12 linoleum that covered the floor was well worn and showed the imprint of every pine board under it. Above the door, between our bedroom and the living room, Dad nailed forks from dogwood trees for our Red Ryder BB guns and sling shots. On the wall by the door he nailed another pair of forked limbs for coat hangers. Over the windows in the east wall and south wall Dad rigged old broom handles across forked limbs. Mother hung window curtains across the broom handles that she made from flour sacks. She dressed them up by appliquéing doilies onto them.

The doilies were the prettiest things I ever saw.

In addition to planting time, spring-cleaning time, and fish spawning time, it was tornado time.

My chore was to make the cellar ready for tornado season.

The weatherman on the radio said Red River was in "Tornado Alley," and Dad believed that. He stood in the cellar door and watched too many tornadoes go down Red River not to believe it. He would soon start taking us to the cellar every time the wind changed directions.

There were certain things Dad expected when he went to the cellar. Two things above all else were for the lamp to have a new wick in it and be full of coal oil and for the cellar to reek from the smell of burnt sulfur.

Not only was it tornado season, it was also copperhead snake season.

There was a place by the door for an ax, and I was supposed to get the ax from the woodpile and put it there. If a tornado deposited a tree over the cellar door while we were inside, Dad could cut a hole in the door and make a way for us to escape.

Dad liked for the cellar to have a neat tidy appearance. Taking canned goods off the shelves and putting empty jars back on them always cluttered up the cellar during the winter. Tidying up the storage shelves was Delton's job.

~

The day was muggy and warm, almost hot, but winter still poised in the distant north ready for one last hurrah, evidenced by a long blue/black bank of clouds across the north.

With the strength of a muscle man, the Norther was trying to overpower the warm, moisture-filled clouds that approached from the Gulf of Mexico and push them eastward.

Neither could push the other.

They started to stack and pile up, as they so often did in the spring of the year. The blue Norther and the grey thunderclouds met in the middle of Red River.

Dad, Delton and I had gone down to the backside of "the Big Twenty" to plant watermelons. The backside of anything, to Dad, was the furthest point you could get away from anywhere. It just so happened that the backside of the Big Twenty wasn't that far from Red River.

Eventually the blue northern bank overpowered the thunderclouds and sent them east. All that remained was cold winds blowing down our collars and five more acres of watermelons to plant.

Every time the eastern sky busted open with rumbling thunder, Delton would stand up, throw his hand up to his forehead and salute Mother Nature. The thunder moved farther and farther away, and Delton asked where it was going. Delton wasn't one to let his questions go unanswered, so Dad finally got disgusted and gave him a Joe Price answer.

"Somewhere east of who knows where – I don't know. What I do know is we have three more acres of watermelons to plant before we can go to the house, and it's sprinkling rain."

Planting watermelon seed consisted of first making a mound of chopped dirt and cutting a trench in the mound with a hoe. Then we placed some watermelon seeds in the trench and covered them with fresh dirt. Then we packed the dirt with our hoes. Next we dipped a double handful of chicken manure, from a pail carried especially for that purpose, and sprinkled it around the mound. The final thing we did was take a page from a Sears

Roebuck catalogue and place it down on the mound and put dirt around the edges of it to hold it in place.

I asked Dad why he covered the seeds with the catalogue page.

"Oh ... for one thing and another" is all he said.

As usual I pressed him for an answer.

"Well, the results are threefold. The seeds can read while they wait to sprout, for one thing. Another thing is the field mice can't find the seeds as easy and the third thing *is* the cover causes the manure to generate heat and makes sproutin' happen quicker." Dad's threefold results were no more than twofold, but he would never admit that.

It was mid-afternoon when we finished planting the watermelon patch. When we got to the end of the last row, Dad stood up, straightened his back and wiped the sweat from his brow. He didn't say anything; just listened to the distant rumbling thunder.

Sprinkles of rain had fallen of and on all afternoon; at the moment they were off.

"Whew, that thunder sounds really bad. It sounds like it's coming back," I offered.

Delton's bottom lip quivered. "Coming back to get us?" he asked.

"Nope, that thunder just sounds bad. Nothin' ever comes out of the east. I'm a dyin' if I'm a lyin'," Dad said, with all the wit he could muster.

We piled our hoes, fertilizer pails, seed buckets and Sears Roebuck hot caps on the trailer behind Ol' Johnny.

Ol' Johnny refused to start.

"She's too damp to spark," Dad figured.

We gathered up our tools and threw them over our shoulders for the long walk home.

By that time the cold wind was spitting sleet and rain.

All of a sudden, the raindrops pelting on the watermelon patch weren't sprinkles anymore. They had gotten together and became more like a sheet of rain. The fresh plowed dirt took on a sheen of wet reflections.

"Last one to the house is a rotten egg!" Dad screamed over a clap of thunder.

We exploded into a dead run for home. Each one of us carried two buckets, one filled with chicken manure and one filled with watermelon seeds. Under our arms we carried Sears Roebuck catalogues and over our shoulders our hoes.

We ran with reckless abandon.

The Sears Roebuck catalogues were the first things to go; somebody yelled that Sears makes new ones. Our seed buckets dangled back and forth on their bails strewing watermelon seeds behind us, soon we discarded them too. The trail behind us was marked with footprints in the mud, pages from Sears, watermelon seeds and empty buckets. Our hoes, we left them where they fell. All we had left was buckets of wet, gooey chicken manure and a hundred yards of dirt lane, wet and slick dirt lane, between us and the house.

As to why we didn't drop them: If you drop a bucket full of wet chicken manure, it splatters ... everywhere.

Duck fashion we ran, single file, Dad in the lead, me following him and Delton beginning to smell like a rotten egg.

Between the chicken coup and the washpot Dad ran.

Around the cellar I went.

Twenty-five more yards to go, and it was all downhill – steep downhill – Delton was going to be a rotten egg.

And then Dad and I collided.

When we finally climbed up on the back porch, Delton was already explaining to Mother just how it was that he won.

"Dean was right on Dad's heels. Dad slipped and threw his bucket of chick duke down in front of Dean. He tried to jump over it and fell, on his face ... right in Dad's dookie. Dean's bucket of chick duke went straight up in the air and came down on Dad's head. I was so far behind, I just went around the mess and that's how I beat 'em!"

Delton wasn't exaggerating.

For days to come, every time Delton would see Dad or me he would chant, "Chick duke - Chick duke – Chick duke!"

From that day forward when a race broke out someone would holler, "Last one there is chick duke."

All three of us were wet and cold. Dad and I were humiliated. We wouldn't have to do up the night chores in the rain, though; for the moment it wasn't raining and it looked like it might hold off until we got them done up.

Dad and me shucked our overalls and walked to the well. We took turns pumping water over each other until we got all the stinky manure washed off. We started to run back to the house but thought better of it and slowed to a walk. After drying off we put on fresh overalls.

"Let's get the night chores done up 'fore dark. The storms gone ... gonna be forgotten," Dad said.

Would he eat those words?

We went to the barn to feed the cows, "juice the jersey" and slop the hogs. Juicing the jersey was Dad's way of saying milk the cow.

Delton went with Mother to gather in the eggs and close up the chicken house.

The constant rolling thunder in the east is unnerving. It seems closer than it did awhile ago. I didn't say a word, though. After all, Dad was the authority on the weather, and he said nothing ever comes out of the east.

It was dusky dark and night was coming on by the time Dad and I finished the barn chores. We heard Mother's voice faintly calling us as we walked down the trail from the barn to the house. As we approached the house her voice rang out, “Supper’s ready.”

We hurriedly climbed the steps and stepped inside the back porch.

“As soon as y’all get that milk separated, wash up for supper,” Mother beckoned.

Dad dumped his pail of milk into the separator bowl, washed his hands and face and then left me to do the separating. Before the door could close behind Dad, the smell of taters frying and plum pudding baking came wafting out the kitchen door.

I started cranking the handle. The handle was hard to turn at first but got easier as the separator gathered speed. The whirring sound grew louder as the slow climb to the speed it took to separate the cream from the milk was reached. I cranked faster and faster, spurred on by the whirling of the separator and the smell of taters.

Under the influence of the spinning drum, the milk and the cream began to separate. They couldn’t stand each other’s company. Finally the milk separated itself from the cream; the job was finished. I let go of the handle and as the separator coasted down I made a mad dash for the supper table.

Mother turned away from the coal oil cook stove to bring a pot of beans to the table and caught me in midair.

“Go wash those dirty hands, Dean.” She scowled.

It wasn’t enough of a scolding to kill my appetite, though. I did an about face, accented by a growling stomach, ran to the wash basin, then met the rest of them at the supper table.

Before we bowed, Mother told me. “Dean, you have got to remember never to let your manners get killed by your appetite.” Then we grabbed hands under the table, and Mother said the blessing. She ended it with: “and save us from this storm that’s coming upon us.”

For the umpteenth time Dad made his weather prediction: “Boys, don’t worry. Hardly anything ever come out of the east.”

I noticed Dad’s twist on words; *Mother’s intuition has Dad worried ... now it’s hardly anything ever comes out of the east.*

After supper there was restlessness in the air; the constant rumbling in the east was unnerving. The slackening north winds had an eerie howl. A faint stirring draft caused the lamp to flicker.

Delton and I sat on the wood box behind the sheet iron heater and created shadows on the wall with our hands and fingers. The movement of the shadows in unison with the flickering of the lamp grated on Mother’s nerves.

Dad didn’t let it show but he had a case of jittery nerves, too. He never popped popcorn – except on Saturday night – it was Tuesday night and he had popped a dishpan full.

After we finished eating the popcorn Dad started carving on a net needle. None of us wanted to go to bed; everyone was finding things to do.

Delton and I sensed that something wasn't right. Dad hadn't engaged us in our nightly brainstorming session.

Dad is unnerved by the rumbling in the east, but he ain't about to let it show.

"Let's go out on the back porch and check the cloud 'fore we go to bed," Mother suggested.

Dad grumbled, "Well, okay ... but nothin ever comes out of the east."

We made our way to the back porch and watched as the constant lightning lit up a very ugly, black, boiling cloud, way off in the distance. Every few seconds, a brilliant flash of lightning would light up the edge of the ugly cloud with a yellowish silver fringe.

"Yep ... that's an ominous looking cloud all right," Dad admitted. "If that cloud does come up, we'll probably just get copious amounts of rain. Let's go to bed."

Now Dad is saying ... if that cloud comes up.

By that time we were tired of hearing Dad's weather forecast – tired enough that we agreed with him about going to bed.

We lay in bed and discussed the fact that Dad hadn't brought up a subject for discussion. We loved our nightly brainstorming sessions that Dad put us through and hated missing this one.

"Oh well ... 'nothin' ever comes out of the east' is what it would have been about anyway," Delton said.

We closed our eyes and tried to go to sleep.

"Ominous looking ... copious amount ... wonder why Dad used such big words?" Delton asked.

"Ominous means as mean as the devil, and copious means a toad strangler. Dad always uses fancy talk to confound us when he doesn't know something.

That storm is not gonna come out of the east and get us ... is it, Dean?"

"I wish I knew, Delton."

"You boys settle yourselves down in there and go to sleep," Dad hollered.

Sleep was hard to come.

Delton and I weren't the only ones who were restless; Mother and Dad were having a hard time finding sleep, too. Dad stirred and tossed and turned, and Mother prayed.

"I gotta go, Dean; will you go with me?" Delton asked.

"I'm trying ... just shut your eyes and shut up."

"Naugh, man, I mean go to the bathroom with me ... I'm scared."

There was no indoor plumbing, and the outhouse was 50 yards from the house. Most nights we went outdoors to the outhouse to excuse ourselves. To excuse one's self was Mother's choice of words over "TT," which she thought sounded nasty. On winter nights when it was icy cold, Mother let us excuse ourselves in the chamber pot that she and Dad kept by their bedside. On moonless nights when it was too dark, we never made it all the way to the outhouse. We didn't this time either; the thunder and lightning were too bad. We hurried, and then ran back into the house, jumped in bed and covered up our heads.

The last thing I remembered was Dad grinding his teeth and murmuring something about the east.

Sometime before midnight I roused up; Dad was snoring and grinding his teeth – Mother was snoring and grinding her teeth – everyone was snoring and grinding their teeth.

No ... the Denison Katy Train de-railed! It's crashing through the house.

The house was alive. The walls pulsed in and out.

"Hey, how'd the wall get over here against our bed?" I hollered.

No one answered. I wondered where Mother and Dad were.

Suddenly there was a sickening crashing noise.

Some part of the house left.

Delton screamed from underneath the bed. "Mother, Dad, come in here quick. I think I see lightning flashing in our house."

The tornado left just like it came – suddenly.

Things got deathly quiet .... and pitch black.

The house was no longer Jell-O. It settled back down on its blocks; all I could hear was sheets of rain and Mother and Dad running. We met in the doorway between our bedrooms. Delton crawled out from under the bed and joined us. We smothered each other with tears.

We were in for several shocks in the minutes ahead. We discovered that the drops falling into our faces wasn't tears – we were laughing with joy – they were raindrops falling through the ceiling.

"Joe and I are so thankful; you and Delton didn't leave with the storm. I prayed that he would let y'all stay with us," Mother said with a breathless sigh.

"Delton and I thought you and Dad left with the storm, too." I managed to say through shivers of excitement.

The lightning that Delton thought he saw through the bedroom door, through the living room ceiling and through the roof from his spot under the bed – it was for real. Now sheets of rain were gushing through the ceiling, where lightning had been a few minutes earlier.

Light from the coal oil lamp revealed that the roof was peeled back like an orange rind. Busted rafters protruded through the ceiling. They looked like rib bones sticking through the skin of a dead cow's stomach. The jagged ends of half a dozen rafters seemed to be in midair suspension and were pointing down toward Delton's and my bed.

We all knew there had to be extensive damage to the outside of the house. Dad opened the kitchen door and confirmed our greatest fears.

"Where is the back porch? Our house has completely divorced the back porch," Dad said.

"It must've run off with the storm," Mother said through a simulated laugh.

Morning would tell the rest of the story.

For now, what we needed to do was get the lake of water out of the living room floor. Then we could concentrate on trying to keep the torrential rain out of the house. Dad, true to his make-do nature, came up with a way to get the water out, but he was buffaloed as to how to keep it out.

"Boys, wheel your mother's newfangled gasoline powered Maytag washing machine in here. It's got a pump on it, and if we can keep her tub full, she'll pump the water out for us."

I wheeled the washing machine in and put it directly under the largest waterspout. Dad cranked her off, and as fast as we could dip buckets full of water and dump them into the Maytag, she pumped the water out of the house.

The washing machine belched blue-gray exhaust fumes as it gulped water and spat it out an open hole in the side of the house. There wasn't any danger from carbon monoxide; the roof was gone, a window was gone and the tornado had put a gaping hole where the back door used to be. Anyway, back then folks didn't pay much attention to such dangers.

We were all having so much fun pumping water we didn't notice the pink tint developing in the eastern sky.

Delton was always the wisecracker in the Price family and he seemed to be able to take accurate readings as to how far to go with his wisecracks.

"Well, you can't ever say 'Nothing ever comes out of the east' any more."

I knew that was something Delton shouldn't have said, and I tried to divert attention away from Delton's uncouth statement.

"That thing sounded like the Katy freight train had derailed and was coming through our house."

"I knew it wasn't the Katy freight train," Delton said, "because its tracks are way over in Denison ... 25 miles away."

We all broke up with laughter and then helped each other climb out the back door of the house. The screened-in back porch was the part of the house that left with the storm. When we were all firmly standing on the ground, Mother noticed that Ol' Johnny was gone.

"She's still there; she's hiding under that box alder tree. It came over from its spot by the cellar and got on top of her," Delton said.

The poles to the barn were still standing, and a lot of its siding was still in place. Metal weather stripping from the sides of the barn lay everywhere, even up in the cottonwood tree.

And just think we won't even get a switching for getting it and making sled runners.

The chicken house was gone; it was in the hog pen, and the hogs were in the garden. Only about half the chickens survived, probably because they stayed in the hen house when it blew away. The chickens that blew out of their house, the tornado plucked clean and they were stone dead. The live chickens had abandoned the riddled henhouse and had gathered up in a huddle under the house. A pair of scrounger 'coon dogs, eaten up with the mange, which the tornado had blown in, were eating the dead chickens.

"The only way to cure chicken-eatin' hounds is with a shotgun." Dad headed back into the house to get his.

Mother stopped him. "Joe Price, you can't kill somebody's chicken-eatin' hounds; besides if you don't let 'em eat the dead ones, you're gonna have to bury 'em yourself." Mother commanded, with disgust in her voice.

"Well, you've got a point ... but they better lay off the live ones, or they're dead meat." Dad changed the subject. "One thing's for certain, the next day after a tornado is always a beautiful day to begin rebuilding. Let's get to the chore." Dad spoke with a lighter tone to his voice.

"Where do we start?" Mother asked.

"Well, we'll send to Bokchito, Oklahoma, for your Uncle Jim. He's the best carpenter I know – he and your Aunt Nora can live with us 'til we get things rebuilt.

~

Jim and Nora Duty showed up just as the last picking of wild plums came off. Mother knew that wild plum cobbler (with the seed left in) was Jim Duty's favorite desert; so it was that she went overboard making a plum cobbler for him. She sent Delton and me to Red River to gather her some sandbar plums. There were wild plums growing all around the place, but she thought nothing made cobblers like the sweet tart little thin-skinned plums that grew on Red River's sandbars.

"I don't want any with cracks on 'em or wormy holes in 'em, and don't get any mushy ripe ones or any that's too green."

"What if there ain't any good enough?" Delton asked.

Mother cut her eyes at him and clinched her jaw. "Get!"

While we were gone, Aunt Nora set herself to churning a batch of fresh butter so Mother could make her special, flaky crust.

Mother mixed Gladiola light crust flour with enough rich creamy milk from our Jersey milk cow to make a big mound of dough, then sat the crock bowl over to one side. She placed a handful of flour on the top of the cupboard, then rolled the dough roller through it a couple of times before she worked the pone of dough into a thin crust. Once she rolled the dough thin enough to suit her, she cut it in half and put half of it in a crock baking dish.

While it was browning in the oven, she steamed the plums in a double boiler, just until their skins cracked. Then she dumped them into the crock bowl with a bunch of sugar and fresh churned butter and set them aside to drink up the sugar and melt the butter.

Mother took the browned crust out of the oven and dumped the plum mixture in, which she called the batter. After she cut the remaining dough in strips, she crisscrossed them in a latticework across the plum batter. She sprinkled cinnamon, sugar and butter over the whole thing, brushed it with egg white and set it in the oven.

When it came out, it was picture perfect and deserved every compliment Dad and Uncle Jim gave it.

After gorging himself on a scrumptious dinner, Uncle Jim fished out a bowl full of the bubbling hot cobbler with as many plums as he could gather. He avoided the "batter."

That was fine with Delton and me – that was our favorite part anyway.

Uncle Jim sucked the tart flesh from the plum seeds and then spat the seeds out on his plate.

"If I ever get to be an inventor, I'm gonna invent a bowl that you can turn wrong side out," Uncle Jim said as he ran his tongue around the sides of the bowl and tried to lick the plum cobbler out of the bottom of it.

"We can suck plum seeds when we go to the plum thicket," Delton said.

5
SUMMERTIME FUN

Springtime – although beautiful – was a time of a lot of hard work. The planting of crops, thinning the seedlings and weeding consumed much of the Price family's energy. Fishing also consumed a good portion of Dad's time and energy.

We spent a lot of time in the cellar, time we could have spent sleeping. Spending most of the night in the cellar, hiding from a spring tornado, is a Red River ritual; but spring was coming to a close.

As the summer season approached and spring wound down, the threat of tornadoes subsided.

By summertime the crops had grown to a point where they were too big to nurture any more if they hadn't got beat down by hail. It was time to lay them by. After Dad got his crops laid by, to him, it was summertime.

Laid by is a term used by farmers to indicate that a particular crop is big enough to fend for itself. Dad believed you needed to leave crops alone at that point so they could produce their bounty. There are certain things that are done to a crop before it is considered "laid by."

Those things are what Dad, Delton and I had been doing to the watermelons.

Dad, Delton and I came in from the watermelon patch, ate supper and finished the night chores, and were sitting on the front porch when Dad introduced the evening's topic of discussion.

"Summer's right around the corner, boys. Summer is for takin' up fun, and in the fun season there are certain things boys need to learn. A boy becomes a man when he learns to swim in Red River. When Red River gets through with you boys, you will be men. What you can't forget though is that men can become boys when they're swimming in Red River."

Dad's bit of wisdom, about a boy becoming a man when he learned to swim, made it a sure bet that Red River held my dreams.

"After this summer, after Red River gets through with us, we'll be men," I assured Delton.

Dad ended the evening's conversation and made plans for the next day. "We're about through coyote-proofing the watermelons. We should finish by noon tomorrow and then after dinner we'll go to Red River and I'll start your swimmin' lessons. Teachin' you boys how to swim is gonna be as easy as fallin' off a log. Let's go to bed for now."

I couldn't go to sleep; I was torn twix the two: becoming a man and my fear of water. I hid my fear well, though, because I thought if Dad knew I was afraid of water he might not teach me how to swim.

If swimming in Red River is what it takes to make me a man ... well, then I'm ready.

The next morning after we ate breakfast, Dad, Delton and I headed to the watermelon patch to finish our coyote-proofing job.

Coyotes are very destructive to watermelons because just as the melons are beginning to get ripe coyotes will bite into every one of them, trying to find a ripe one. They can quickly ruin every watermelon in the whole patch.

Dad had Delton and me setting tall willow poles every 50 foot around the edge of the watermelon patch. From the tops of the tall poles we hung binder twine, so that it sagged almost to the ground between the poles. When we finished hanging the strings around the watermelon patch, we suspended tin cans and can lids from them with drop strings. That was a lot of trouble, but dangling cans and lids were the only things that would keep the coyotes out of the watermelon patch.

By the time dinnertime came, we had finished coyote-proofing the watermelons and went to the house for dinner.

We ate dinner and then went to Red River.

We arrived at the boat landing at Kavanaugh's point, and while Delton and I shucked our overalls Dad untied the boat and got in.

Man, that water looks deep and swift and full of alligator gars.

"What if that Indian girl sees us naked?" Delton asked.

"Indian girl ... what Indian girl ... what are you talkin' about?"

"Dean said there were some perty Indian girls living over in Oklahoma and if one of them saw me naked I would have to leave home and marry her."

"Shucks," Dad said.

"I can learn ... while in the boat?" I asked.

"Nope, but I'm gonna take you to where you can learn. Come on in."

We piled in the boat, and Dad rowed us to the middle of Red River. When we reached "our classroom," as Dad called it, he stood up in the boat and instructed us.

"Y'all jump out of the boat."

Delton did ... not me.

Delton quickly got his actions together and headed downstream.

"I can't swim," I pleaded.

"Well, you can't learn how to swim without getting in the water." Dad instructed me in the fine art of flouncing and bobbing and then shoved me overboard.

The saying, "after you go down three times you drown," ... that's false.

I flounced and bobbed and flailed my arms; after going down for the sixth time I began to propel myself forward, to my surprise.

The swift current had swept Delton downstream.

In my panicky state, after I finally got my arms coordinated with my legs, I almost caught up with Delton.

We finally reached the bank about a hundred yards below the boat landing. We laid in the edge of the water at the foot of the high sandy riverbank and panted for air.

"I don't know about you, Delton, but I'm about flounced and bobbed out," I said, as I dragged myself out of the water.

Tearing our way through salt cedars, dogwoods, bull nettles and sand burrs back up to the boat landing wasn't my idea of the way to end a long swim. However, Dad was waiting for us at the boat landing with praises, and he made it all worthwhile. "Y'all have learned yourself how to dogpaddle. Now all you need is practice, practice, practice. Get in the boat, boys, and we'll do it again."

"Hey, wait a minute till we get Red River out of our nose," Delton said as we gasped for air, coughed and wheezed and spat gritty water.

Dad's praise was encouraging; but if practice, practice, practice meant having to jump out of the boat in the middle of Red River over and over and over again, I had my reservations.

"I just wanna dogpaddle, not swim like a fish," I told Dad.

"The remainder of your swimmin' lessons will be rowing you to the middle of Red River – jumpin' you overboard and then letting you swim back to the bank – now doesn't that sound like fun?"

The second time was easier.

Dad instructed us as we swam: "Y'all don't fight the current; let 'er work for you ... quit that flouncing ... reach out and grab you some water."

How to swim in Red River gradually became ingrained in our minds, due to Dad's continual hollering throughout the evening.

Dad continued his lesson as we walked along the river trail to the house in the late afternoon shade.

"Red River's a thing I don't want you boys to be fraid of. You have got to respect her 'cause she delights in taking those who panic. Don't ever fight against her current. Let her have her way with you, and she'll eventually spit you out ... if you fight her, she'll swallow you up. We'll do it again in a few days; after we get through layin' the watermelons by." Dad ended his instructions, leaving us in suspense as to just when we would get to go swimming again.

We both knew that when it came to working in the watermelons a few days might mean more, even a week.

Coyote-proofing the watermelons, was only the first step in "laying them by." The next step was turning the vines, plowing the middles and whitewashing the first crop of melons. Now the real work was fixing to begin.

Dad didn't have any trouble keeping us on the job, though. He just made it perfectly clear that there would be no swimming until the watermelons were whitewashed. Finally after more than a week of working in the watermelon patch, all we lacked finishing was to whitewash the biggest melons, or as Dad called them, "the first crop."

Whitewashing the melons was a method employed by Dad to keep the scorching summer sun from burning sunspots on the watermelons.

"Okay, boys," Dad's instructions were plain, "put about half a gallon of slacked garden lime in three buckets and stir in enough water to make the mess about as thick as your ma's water gravy. While y'all are doin' that, I'll wind some of her worn-out wash rags around sticks and make us some daubers."

We put the buckets of whitewash, the daubers and a bag of slaked lime in the trailer behind Ol' Johnny and went to the watermelon patch.

When we got there, Dad dished out the daubing instructions.

"Ok, boys, start here on the first row. Let's make sure we give every watermelon in the patch, that's bigger than your head, a paint job. Daub 'em real good if they're beginning to show any sunburn."

Dad's melons were the sweetest, prettiest ones grown anywhere, and whitewashing them was only one of his secrets. When he sent his watermelons to market they were perfectly ripe ... vine ripe. He knew how a black diamond melon looked when it had ripened on the vine, and he left them there until they were ripe to perfection. He also knew how a vine-ripened watermelon was supposed to sound when he thumped it. The rich yellow color of its belly and the thud sound when he thumped it had to be just right before he picked a melon. He vowed to pick no watermelon before it was ready, and he never plugged a melon to see if it was ripe.

We finished whitewashing, and Dad drilled us about staying out of the watermelon patch until they started to ripen. He didn't want us traipsing around damaging the vines.

"There's nothin' to do now but to watch that big one that I hid under that Johnson grass over there." Dad pointed to a big clump of grass. "That will be the first one to get ripe."

Yeah ... nothing to do now but swim, Delton and I thought, but neither of us pressed the issue.

"Let's go to the house and eat dinner, boys."

When Dad said that, you could bet it was 12 o'clock.

We were always barefoot in the summertime. The plowed sandy dirt became so unbearably hot that a person with bare feet could not tolerate the heat when the sun was directly overhead. At noon the shade was directly under the watermelon vines, and stepping on them was off limits, so it was time to go to dinner. It always amazed Mother when we showed up for dinner the same time every day ... 12:15.

"I know you don't carry a watch, Joe," Mother declared as we stepped up on the back porch.

We sloshed our hands around in the washbasin and dried them on our overalls (Mother didn't see that); then we headed to the dinner table.

The noon meal was "dinner" to country folks because it was the largest meal of the day. The amount of physical labor put out from sunup until noon made it necessary for a person to take in a lot of food; not only did we come to the table physically exhausted, but we had to eat enough so we could work until suppertime or dark, whichever came first.

"Red beans ... cornbread ... fried taters," Delton said with disgust. "We had 'em yesterday and we'll have 'em again tomorrow and I ain't hungry for 'em today."

"Delton Price!" Dad lashed out. "You apologize to your mom. She has done the best that she could. If you're not hungry for beans, you just sit there and watch us eat 'em."

After several minutes of grueling silence, Dad spoke again.

"I'll put you boys through the mill this afternoon ... them beans will be good come suppertime."

Mother had heard enough talk about them beans.

"I want y'all to know it's those beans ... not them beans."

To my understanding, putting us through the mill meant working. *We aren't going to get our swimming lesson.* Was I in for a shock. Not only were we going to get our swimming lesson, I was to learn swimming lessons like Dad taught *were* work.

"A stuffed belly, tired bones and hot summer days makes me lazy. I'm gonna take a nap 'fore we go back to work," Dad said, as he exhaled a long breath and sprawled out face down on the cool linoleum.

Delton and me headed outside to play a little catch with the baseball, while Dad recuperated enough to put us through the mill.

When we played catch, it seemed Delton always ended up getting hurt.

I designated myself pitcher. "Get ready ... here she comes!" I hollered. I put all I had into my windup and let her fly.

As soon as the ball cleared my hand, I hollered with a slow drawling voice.

"S t r i k e ... one!"

The ball was a rising curve – a real burner – it rose just enough to clear the top of Delton's glove, and then it smashed into his nose. It hit him right where his nose went into his head.

He dropped on crumpled legs.

Stone dead, I thought.

I rushed to his side and bowed on bended knees.

He's dead ... his eyes are gone.

Delton's eyes were rolled back in his head. He was lying on his side and had his hands cupped over a bulging pump knot that was oozing blood.

I looked into his white orbs and slapped him.

He moaned ... "I'm dying."

I was relieved he had some life. "Hey, I'm sorry, man ... I'm really sorry. Don't tell Mother and Dad what happened, or we won't get to play catch ... ever again."

"But I don't wanta play catch with you ... ever again. You throw too hard," he whined, then started screaming, "Dean's killed me ... Dean's killed me ... Dean's killed me!"

Whether it was the pain surging through his head or the gushing blood streaming down his face, or both, I didn't care; he was alive.

Delton's blood curdling screams woke Dad, and he and Mother came running.

Delton kicked with his feet and spun himself around in circles.

"Hold still." Dad examined Delton's forehead. "Well now, we'll have to go swimmin' to doctor that bloody pump knot, and I wanted to start hoeing out the garden."

Dad gathered Delton up in his arms and headed to the water well to draw some water. Mother tagged along petting him and cooing to him.

All the old-timers knew about the healing powers of swimming in Red River. It wasn't unusual for a swim in Red River to cure infected cuts, and usually the wound never even got sore. Old-timers claimed the reason Red River's waters had healing powers was because of the salt on the Salt Fork of Red River and the mysterious minerals that were in Big Mineral Creek and Mineral Bayou which dumped into Red River. It was a common belief that they mixed themselves together into "Medicine water," and it oozed down Red River.

Dad set Delton down on the porch steps after his wash down at the water well, and Mother doctored his nose then hugged him into her arms.

"You're only making him feel sorry for himself," Dad said through a yawn. "I'm going back in the house and finish my nap. When he quits cryin', wake me up and I'll take them swimming."

Eventually, Delton's sobs dried up and Dad woke up, raring to go to Red River and go swimming.

When we got to the river, we jumped in the boat and Dad shoved it away from the boat landing. Dad jumped in and picked up his pole as the boat swung out into the swift current. He thrust his pole into the bottom and turned the boat downstream. It was apparent we weren't headed toward the middle of Red River.

My curiosity overcame me. "Where are you taking us, Dad?" I asked.

"Before I turn you boys loose to the river, you gotta swim the rapids," he said and pointed with his finger downstream toward Oklahoma. "We'll put in to that sand bar over there."

The rapids were an extremely swift section of Red River where the river narrowed down and turned east. The river, after running north for 25 miles or more, hit the Oklahoma bank where layers of shale and slate rock lined the bank. After Red River turned the corner and headed east, it became extremely swift. This was "the rapids."

I hadn't ever given a thought to what caused the rapids, but if I was going to have to swim through them, I wanted to know what caused them. My asking what caused the rapids was all Dad needed; he loved explaining the laws of nature.

"There seems to be some sort of underwater something at the point where Red River quits runnin' north and heads east. Whatever it is, it causes the water to sort of back up, and then the river bottom drops down and creates an underwater waterfall. When the water leaves there it is swifter than Ol' Billy. A 'phenomenon' is what educated people call that sort of thing."

"What you said that caused the rapids makes more sense than a phenomenon," Delton said.

Nothing in my past life was as scary as the scene lying out before my eyes that summer day on Red River. Delton and I lay on the wet sand at the edge the swift water and listened to Dad's instructions. What he said didn't do anything but make matters worse for me.

"Y'all see the whirlpools out yonder in the middle of Red River? I don't want y'all to be afraid of 'em. It's old wives tales that they'll suck you down – I've swum in 'em all my life – they just sort of tickle your belly as you swim through 'em."

Dad is enjoying scaring me.

"One more thing," he said as he pointed toward a caving bank on the Texas side of Red River. Y'all will be down about there, about a couple of hundred yards or so when you get across. Don't climb the bank. Just wade back up to where I'll probably be ... any questions?"

"What do you mean, where you'll probably be?" I asked.

Without an answer, Dad barked final instructions. "When y'all are ready, jump in and start swimmin' across to that caving bank on the Texas side."

"I can't do it," I said.

"Yeah, you can. Just remember what I said about fightin' the current and remember I'll be out there in the boat."

"I'm ready," Delton hollered and dove in.

My heart wouldn't have beaten any faster, or pumped any more adrenaline, if Dad had strapped me on the back of a Brahma bull.

I heard a big splash and looked just in time to see Delton come to the surface and start for Texas.

I gotta go ... Delton will go off and leave me ... I'll be out there with all those big alligator gars and whirlpools.

A hand in the middle of my back interrupted my thoughts.

Dad shoved and hollered – "Go!"

I went.

Red River in my face shocked me into action and, before Delton reached the first whirlpool, I caught him.

We swam, drifted and rested, then swam some more. The whirlpools were fun and true to Dad's prediction, the river spit us out.

What Dad didn't tell us *was* that we would be halfway to Shreveport when the river spit us out. We were way past the cavy bank on the Texas side of the river when we made landfall. He didn't tell us how hard it would be to wade back upstream to where he would be waiting with the boat either.

When we reached the boat, Dad piled the praise on.

"Y'all are swimmin' like a couple of mudhens. You boys are river rats now.

Dad's praise is worth all the squiggles my guts suffered.

"Are you ready to do it again?" Dad asked and then he quickly added a statement, as was his habit when he wanted us to make the choice that he wanted us to make.

"We're gonna make a freezer of ice cream when we get home and celebrate y'all becoming Red River rats."

Dad knew that after he dangled the ice cream in front of us, if we chose to swim the rapids again we would be up to the task.

Now we were in a quandary whether to swim the rapids again or go for ice cream. We knew in our minds what we wanted to do – but our bodies weren't so sure. Dad had just given us an out, though. Now we could discuss what we wanted to do until we rested, and he would never know we were tired. Several minutes of trying to decide between swimming the rapids or going home for ice cream brought Delton to say:

"I know what ... let's swim one more time and then go for ice cream."

"Yeah ... and that'll give your pump knot a little more time to heal." My conscience was bothering me. The blue-black color had spread from Delton's forehead around his eyes and down his nose, and it looked so painful.

I shouldn't have thrown so hard.

The second time was fun, not scary at all, and I even rolled over on my back and let the current have its way with me. By the time we waded back to the boat the second time, Dad could have coaxed us to the house with spinach.

"I hope Mother saved my beans that I didn't eat at dinner," Delton told me on our way back to the boat where Dad was waiting for us.

Just as soon as we hit the back door, Mother called ... "Wash up ... supper's ready." We all sat down around the kitchen table, and Delton hurriedly reached for the beans.

"No, you don't," Mother commanded as she bowed her head.

Mother said blessing.

She had a way of making us feel so sorry for something we had said or done. If there was anything we hated more than a switching with a switch, that we had to go pick, it was for Mother to pray for us, in her presence.

"Dear Lord, help Dean to have mercy on his brother and thank you for healing Delton's head so fast. Oh God, bless these beans that I worked so hard to wash and soak and cook. Please help Delton to like them. Lord, I love him so much, and I want him to love you and to love the things that I cook for him ... Amen."

When we opened our eyes, I expected to find that Delton had crawled under the table.

Quietness settled over the table, like that caused when you throw scratch to a flock of chickens. As the clatter of spoons against stoneware plates faded, the conversation picked back up.

Delton broke the silence. "It's not that I don't love your beans ... it's that I am tired of 'em, but I promise, I'll never not eat them again, Mother."

"Guess what, we're river rats." I changed the subject.

"They both learned real easy. We can turn 'em loose to the river now," Dad said with pride in his voice.

"Can they swim the rapids, Joe?" Mother demanded to know.

"Shucks, yeah, we can, and it's so much fun!" Delton blurted out.

Dad gave Delton a stern look for answering his question but said nothing.

"Has the river ever spit you out, Mother?" I asked.

"NO! And you wanna hear the second verse?"

Mother's second verse wasn't necessary ... her NO was definite.

"Tomorrow you'll have to go see the boys swim, now that the scary learnin' part's over, honey," Dad told Mother.

"We're gonna make some ice cream after supper and celebrate," Delton said.

"Is there enough ice left for that?" Mother asked.

"Yep, we've been covering the ice hole up real good all week long, and Ice Man Pete comes again tomorrow," I said.

Mother felt really lucky to have a good way to keep ice. Most country folks relied on an icebox to keep their ice from melting, and before the iceman came again, all their ice would melt. The iceman came every Monday, and most iceboxes would not keep ice seven days. We always had enough ice left over when the iceman came again to make a batch of ice cream. That is, if Delton and I had done our job of covering the hole back up good and hadn't eat too much when we got into the hole to get ice for tea.

"If you wanna conserve ice, honey, just remind whoever you send to fetch it that if there is any ice left over when the iceman comes, we'll make ice cream." That was Joe's law of conservation.

To make our miraculous icebox Dad dug a hole in the ground in the shade of the big cottonwood tree and lined it with a heavy, cotton tarpaulin.

He placed the ice in the hole, on the tarp, and then wrapped it with one of Mother's old quilts. Delton and I gathered Johnson grass straw and put it over the quilt, then Dad covered our ice hole up with dirt.

When Iceman Pete came – if we had 15 cents – we would purchase a hundred pound block of ice. Sometimes when there was no money in the house, Dad traded a catfish, eggs or a watermelon for ice.

Fresh brown hen eggs and thick cream from the Jersey cows made ice cream worth remembering. The freezer of black walnut ice cream that we made after we swam the Red River rapids was exceptional, not because it had a cupful of hand-picked, black walnut goodies in it, but because it marked a special time in our life: the day we became river rats.

After we learned how to swim in Red River, we could go swimming anytime we wanted to if we had our chores done up. Some of the other boys who hadn't learned how to swim in Red River started slipping off with us and going swimming with us. JD's Mother, Rose, confronted Mother with the problem.

"Sybil, I got a question for you. Have you ever seen Jerry Don's ears clean?"

"Well, I hadn't given very much thought to it. Why do you ask?"

"The only time I've ever seen his ears clean is when we take him to Red River swimming. I know Jerry is slipping off to Red River with Dean and going swimming. He keeps coming home with clean ears after he's got with Dean."

~

The job of teaching Delton and me how to swim, to Mother's satisfaction, had turned into work, and more work was piling up on us. The peaches were blushing, and the tomatoes were turning white and would soon start turning red. Pinto beans were in the snapping stage, and sandbar plums were ripe. Best of all, the watermelons were fixing to start coming off.

Across the breakfast table Dad made his predictions. "The first of next week we'll get a ripe watermelon – I think by Dean's birthday, and then I'll send for the trucks. We have got to spend a few days on Red River and catch some cannin' fish ... 'fore we get too busy."

Nothing sounded better to me than a few days on Red River.

"Goody, we'll swim till we sink," Delton said.

"Wrong ... When I said catch some cannin' fish that is exactly what I meant. The days ain't gonna have enough time in them for swimming. There will be plenty time for swimming when the summertime doldrums set in," Dad said.

"What's the summertime doldrums?" Delton asked.

"Oh, that's another one of your Dad's slang sayings; it's kind of like the dog days of summer. What they are is when he gets so lazy he needs some excitement," Mother explained.

"*We might get in some nighttime swimming.*" Wrong again ... we would be too tuckered out.

After breakfast we fed the cows, milked and slopped the hogs, then spent the rest of the morning rigging trotlines and throw lines, seining the slough for trotline bait, and hooking the wagon to Ol' Johnny.

After dinner Mother helped us load our gear while Dad got his after-dinner nap.

When he woke, he was in an all-out hurry to get to the river.

"We better get a move on ... if we're gonna get our lines set 'fore dark. Hurry up, boys! Why ain't y'all ready?"

Delton and I climbed into the wagon with all the fishing gear, fishing bait and camp necessities. Dad's camp necessities weren't much: a skillet, a couple of milk pails and a syrup bucket which he used for a coffeepot made up our cooking utensils. There were also a couple of number two wash tubs. I had been on fishing trips when Dad took wash tubs and they were not part of his cook set. Our groceries were meager, too: potatoes, bacon, coffee, grease and salt, and a burlap bag full of goodies Mother packed for us.

We had just entered the lane that led to the river bluff when I started in on Delton. "Ask Dad what the tubs are for."

"Nope ... you ask him," Delton countered.

"Nope ... you ask him."

We went back and forth, exchanging "you ask hims" until a fight broke out.

Dad must have heard the ruckus over the pop, pop ... pop of Ol' Johnny. We were kicking the wash tubs around pretty good when Dad yelled out – "Hey, what's the matter with you brats?"

We ignored him.

I had Delton in a headlock, and Delton had my forefinger between his jaw teeth. I was inflicting so much pain on Delton I wasn't about to release my hold. Delton also knew that if he opened his mouth to answer, I would jerk my finger free.

"Hey ... I said, what in the tarnation is the matter with you young'uns back there?"

We knew better than to ignore Dad's second question. We both heard him the second time, but the fury of the moment required our full attention. It didn't matter why we didn't answer. The important thing to Dad was that we did not ignore his questions.

Since the day almost two years ago that Dad ran over the smokehouse, he hadn't misapplied Ol' Johnny's brakes – he hadn't been this mad either.

"Dad-nab-it ... you will answer me!"

We heard that and knew it was too late.

Dad crammed his foot on the brakes. He crammed so hard, in his fury, that his foot slipped off the pedals and caught only one brake pedal.

Ol' Johnny went into her locked-wheel-circling act. She circled so fast the wagon couldn't keep up. By the time Dad got his foot off the brake pedal, the wagon had jackknifed, turned over on its side and spewed us out into a bull nettle patch.

The fight stopped.

Now I'll get me some answers. Dad thought. He killed Ol' Johnny and crawled off her. On his way back to the wagon to see if we were dead, he found the twisted, broken, wagon tongue sticking up out of the dirt. He picked it up and walked swiftly toward us, holding the bois d'arc wagon tongue over his shoulder.

He's gonna finish us off.

We looked pathetic lying there in the bull nettles, with whelps all over our shirtless bodies. The sudden change in course had jerked my finger out of Delton's jaw, and it was squirting blood. Delton looked up through muddy tears, his freckles smeared with blood. "All we wanted to know is what are these wash tubs for?"

Dad couldn't help it: He busted out laughing.

"If you would have only asked ... see the trouble that we could have saved," Dad said with disgust. "The tubs are for the green grapes that we're gonna pick for your mother to can."

No one said anything for several minutes.

Then Dad spoke: "We're gonna miss the rest of the day now and probably several days to come. First we gotta find a good bois d'arc fencepost with no cracks in it, and then we gotta go back home and make a wagon tongue out of it. Dean, you're gonna have to learn how to use a drawknife. Shaving a bois d'arc fencepost down into a wagon tongue is a hard job; they are big and heavy and hard as nails. Delton, I'll figure some sort of punishment for you latter."

I am gonna get to make a wagon tongue? That ain't punishment. That's fun.

I learned pretty quick that thinking about making a wagon tongue and then actually making one are two entirely different things.

After two days Dad got impatient waiting for me to finish the tongue and, although he grumbled a lot about having to, he broke down and put the finishing touches on the wagon tongue for me.

"Son, it has taken you two days; a termite could've chewed a tongue out of a bois d'arc stump by now," were some of Dad's milder grumblings.

Delton's punishment, as it turned out, was to shuck nubbins until he filled the wooden barrel in the corner of the corncrib. I thought he got off easy, because we would have had to shuck the nubbins anyway, as we feed the cows.

Somehow Dad knew I started the fight.

I assessed in my mind – as we carried the new tongue back to Ol'

Johnny – how much our fight had cost us. *Three days and a lot of hard work ... it wasn't worth it.*

It didn't take long to bolt the tongue into place and we were on our way again.

When we finally got to the river, Dad pulled Ol' Johnny's nose up to a big cottonwood tree that sat right on the bank of Red River. The rest of the day we spent striking camp, setting trotlines and throw lines, and cooking supper.

When nightfall came Dad built a campfire right on the edge of the high river bank. We set our rods and reels where we could tend to them and lay around the campfire.

After a supper of fried taters, ham and skillet fried cornbread, we sat around the fire watching our fishing poles and drinking river coffee.

To make river coffee Dad sent me to fetch a pail of Red River water. He set it aside until all the sand and debris sank to the bottom. Then he very carefully poured the clear water into a gallon syrup bucket, added a heaping cup of coffee grounds and set the lid on loosely, so the steam could escape. He set the coffee bucket on the edge of the fire, "So the water and grounds could get warm together," while he raked coals from the fire into a heap. Then he put the bucket over them and left it there until the coffee came to a rolling boil ... "A boil that you can hear." As soon as the coffee was boiling so hard the bucket wanted to walk off the fire, Dad pulled it over to the edge and let the coffee steep.

In the event he wanted coffee after that first batch was all gone, he would add a few grounds and a little water and shove his coffee boiler back on the fire. When he heard bubbles breaking, he had a freshened up cup of coffee, as he called it.

The moon was rising and the fire had consumed all of its fuel; it was nothing more than a dying flickering twinkle.

Dad and Delton had already flickered and twinkled out, but I was wide awake. It was the time of the day I enjoyed most of all. I was by myself, just me, my fishing pole and my thoughts.

I traced imaginary constellations in the star-lit sky. The warmth of boiled coffee seeped through my veins and lulled me into an aristocratic feeling.

This night ... this river ... this time, is exclusively mine.

I played the events of previous fishing trips out in my mind as if they were happening for the first time; time stood still.

If I had a watch, I wouldn't let it take these regal moments from me by sending me to bed.

I looked across the river to the seemingly faraway bank and saw the reflection of the full moon's beam. It cast down from above and fell in a long shimmering finger of light onto river water that flowed swiftly out of its reach.

I was only faintly aware of the moonbeam that cut an arc across the tip of my fishing pole. My fishing pole was immobile for now, but at any moment it was capable of busting into the forefront of my awareness ... if a fish took my bait.

My eye caught a cottonwood log as it slowly drifted across the moon's reflection. In my day-dreamy state of mind, it became a canoe. A limb that stuck up off of the log, covered with dead leaves and cottony panicles, became a warrior standing in the bow wearing a chieftain headdress.

My imagination ran wild.

A pack of coyotes tuned up their wailing voices and brought me out of my trance of historical reminiscing. Their trail ran edgewise, along a slough filled with dogwoods and rattan vines, not 50 yards behind camp. Yips, wails and howls reverberated from the distant riverbank as if a cloned pack was over there, too. Then just as suddenly as their lonesome wailing erupted, the whole noisy pack moved around the river bend and fell silent.

The coffee had gotten cold, the fire was dying and the fish weren't biting. I decided I might as well go to bed.

I'm talking to myself anyway.

I threw a few more logs onto the fire – for light and smoke – to keep the mosquitoes at bay.

The fading embers were proud of new fuel and angrily sputtered in their attempt to draw the logs into a renewed rage of warmth and light.

The coffeepot emitted simmering sounds then came to a full boil from the ever-increasing fire. The wafting aroma of boiling coffee convinced me to have one more cup. Several times throughout the day the coffee had boiled only to cool off again, and what remained was coal black and thick.

Am I gonna have to shake it to get it to pour ... But oh ... it's good.

I took the cup in both hands, then sat down and leaned back against a log and realized how tired I was.

I finished drinking my coffee and banked the fire. I walked down to the boat landing, checked the rope holding the boat, and it was secure. I checked our throw lines, took the fish off and baited them up again.

Dad's gonna be proud of me.

When I returned to the fire I was ready to go to bed and laid down on the tarp. My mind wandered from one thing to another as my thoughts raced through my mind, stacked endlessly on top of each other. I felt my eyelids go limp and then ... all my thoughts became none.

The night flew by and I roused up just as the sky got light enough to wash the stars away. I snuggled deeper into my patchwork quilt that Mother had made from the pants legs of worn-out overalls. I wasn't ready to get up yet. I quit thinking ... dozed back off into a dreamy world.

The colorless landscape held me captive. Night creatures returned home. Creatures of the day waited all around me for Mother Nature to paint color into their world. A tweeting mockingbird waited for the colorless sky to turn azure blue. Eagles waited for the black forest to turn green. A wet slimy snake crawled across my face, headed to his dark den.

I woke suddenly.

Dad was holding a catfish that was so big it took him and Delton both to lift it high enough so his wet tail could slap me across the face.

The catfish flounced.

"Are you awake yet?" Delton asked.

I spat and sputtered, "What do you think?"

After several days of fishing, Dad came into camp one evening and announced: "In the mornin' we're gonna gather green grapes. I spied a good low hangin' muscadine vine a while ago. They are at the perfect stage: Their little teeny seeds are still soft; they ain't started hardening yet."

Green grapes make a sweet, tart pie filling with a taste like nothing else and Mother's delicious green grape pastries; whether cobblers, fried pies or her special deep-dish pies, that she makes are "out of this world good." Just thinking about a green grape cobbler flushed my mouth with saliva and eased the burden of gathering the pea-sized fruit.

The next morning we put the washtubs in the trailer and Dad pulled it right up under the grapevine with Ol' Johnny. He instructed us in the fine art of picking green grapes.

"Just pull them off in clusters and leave them on their stems until we get 'em washed. We just need one tub full."

With zillions of grapes hanging right in front of our eyes and Dad only wanting one tub full, we were lulled into thinking the job wouldn't take long. Soon we learned that there has never been a more tedious job than picking enough pea-sized grapes to fill a number two wash tub.

We picked the "dumb little grapes," as Delton called them, off the vine all morning long. Dad finally called it quits about an hour before it was dinnertime. Back at camp we dumped the grapes out on a tarp, filled the empty wash tub with river water and then started picking the grapes off the stem one at a time, and throwing them into the water.

"If the grapes float, the seeds are too big in 'em. Be sure and throw the floaters out," Dad instructed.

Yeah, there is a more tedious job than picking grapes off the vine ... picking them off the stem.

We had finished eating supper and the moon was rising before we finished the grape sorting and washing.

"We're gonna go home in the morning. I gotta help your mother get these grapes canned. Besides tomorrow is ice day and I'm anxious to see Iceman Pete's eyes light up when he sees our big catfish."

Delton was really excited about getting to go home, seeing his mother and eating some of her cooking.

"I don't like fish cooked on a stick. I want Mother to fry them in a skillet. I ain't even tired of red beans anymore," he added.

We had gotten a few swims in while Dad was out hunting wild muscadine grapevines. For the most part he had kept us so busy chasing after trotline bait that we didn't have time to swim or were too tired when we did have time. We took what Dad called a swim every night before bedtime, but to us it was just a dip. I was too scared to swim in Red River at night by myself, and Delton was too hard to wake up.

We got back home on my birthday. Mother made me a fresh green grape pie instead of a cake for my birthday and put the rest of the grapes in the cellar so she and Dad could can them the next day.

Somehow Mother convinced me it would be a lot of fun if I cooked my own birthday dinner.

It didn't take Delton and me long to run down a couple of our biggest pullets and wring their necks. I soon had chicken frying and potatoes boiling for "smashed taters." After I fried the chicken, I started flour browning in a big cast iron skillet for gravy. I thought there was nothing better than brown gravy with fried chicken crumbles in it.

The watermelon that Dad hid ripened right on schedule; it and Mother's green grape pie were perfect deserts for a perfect birthday dinner.

The big trailer trucks started arriving to carry Dad's watermelons to market. The money that the watermelons brought in was our main income during the summer months. Dad and Mother counted on them to bring in enough money so they could pay last year's grocery bill.

Weldon Doggett carried the bill for our groceries from one watermelon season to the next. Money from the watermelon harvest also bought new shoes and school supplies for Delton and me.

After we finished eating my birthday dinner, we went out on the porch and waited for Dad to start the evening's discussion.

"Well, boys, I guess you know we owe our hearts and souls to Red River. If it weren't for her, there would be no catfish to eat or trade for ice, no green grape pies and no swimming holes."

And no place to daydream – or – get in tune with nature, I thought.

"Living on her sure makes them red beans good." Delton had the last word.

6
FALL ... A TIME OF PLENTY

"I know summer is nearly gone when the mornin' dew sparkles on the grass and the nights become cool and crisp." Dad's sign for the ending of summer was at hand. Summer was winding down.

It was getting hard to find enough good melons to load out a truck, and the truck we were loading would be the last one of the season. After it left, we spent the rest of the day gathering culls and carrying them to the hog pen. We had a pen full of shoats, and we would fatten them on the remaining melons, then take them to market. Dad always kept two or three and fed them out on corn to butcher.

The day winding down and the smell of fried taters had finally gathered us around the supper table. The early morning dew had caused the mosquitoes to hatch, and the outbreak was so bad that we did our visiting around the supper table instead of going out on the porch.

Dad shoved his plate back and started the conversation.

"Fall is right around the corner. We'll soon start gathering all the field crops. The corn is turning brown and the cotton is beginning to open." Dad reminded Mother and us that harvest time was upon us.

Usually – but not always – we made enough money from the field crops to pay for last year's tractor gas, the bill for the seeds and the yearly payment on our Red River farm.

"Everything is looking good. I think this year we'll have enough money left over to buy that new washing machine that you've been wanting, honey."

"Don't go counting your chickens 'fore they hatch, dear ... you know that's bad luck," Mother reminded him.

Fall was the one time on the farm when farmers had enough money to make ends meet, and Dad's expectations for a good harvest was pretty high.

Dad blew out the coal oil lamp, and we went to bed.

The fall season in the country has always been beautiful, and for country boys it is an especially exciting time.

In Mulberry, a different smell filled the air ... the smell of harvest. The musty smell of corn shucks drying in the sun; the sweet, nutty, clover-like smell of peanut digging time and the smell of cotton bolls busting open filled the air.

Dove hunting fields reeked with their own special odor. The bittersweet smell of wild sunflowers drying in the sun joined with the smell that mature bull nettle pods give off when they dry, crack open and spray their seeds. Mixed with the many odors of maturing leaves and grass were the ozone-like smells of mature dove weeds given off as hunters trampled them under their hunting boots. Dad called it a sunshiny smell, like the smell of clothes fresh off the clothseline.

The smell of fall is unlike any other season. Stories of hunts past but not forgotten become the topic of conversation for men. Duck hunts, goose hunts and dove hunts, deer hunts and stories about last year's trapline are the talk of fall.

I sat spellbound for hours listening to hunters talk about the thrill of the hunt and the many things they learned from studying their quarry.

Before I was big enough to go hunting with Dad, I carried my own Daisy BB gun and went on imaginary hunts. I became a good marksman even with a Daisy Air Rifle. By the age of seven I could shoot a .22 rifle better than other boys in 4-H club who were much older than me.

Dad taught me the proper way to handle a gun.

"The muzzle of a gun is like a copperhead snake. It is always loaded and ready to strike ... at any moment," Dad drilled. My first lesson about the damage a gun could do came one cold fall morning when I was hunting with Dad. The first real cold Norther of fall had blown in, and Mother wanted to make some rabbit chili. Her instructions for Dad were not to bring in half-grown fryers. She wanted old fully-grown rabbits for her chili.

Dad took me down on the river bluff where there were a lot of brush piles and brambles and where he claimed that Mr. Burr Rabbit lived.

A big, old cottontail rabbit jumped right from under my feet and darted into a wild rose patch. I raised the single shot .22 and fired. Somehow the rabbit managed to evade my shot. When the rabbit came out the other side of the wild rose bushes, he headed straight for the family trash dump. Mr. Rabbit parked his rump beside a discarded 5-gallon bucket, full of rainwater.

Dad spied the rabbit first and threw up his 12-gauge shotgun. "Watch this." He pulled the trigger.

Kablooie ... he missed the rabbit completely, but the bucket caught the full charge of shot, directly in the middle.

Water went 10 feet straight up in the air, and the steel bucket erupted at the seams and came down in shredded pieces. Dad was a marksman with his old shotgun, and I knew he missed the rabbit for a reason.

"It would do that to you ... if someone shot you in the belly," Dad said, as he bent over and grabbed his belly in mock pain.

After that day I could go hunting – by myself – with the .22 rifle or the 12-gauge shotgun. Every time I left the house to go hunting, though, I got the same warning from Dad.

"Don't kill any 5 gallon buckets, and remember the first thing you do when you get home is unload your gun, clean it and then load it back up. I won't have an unloaded gun in my house."

Dad instilled that lesson in my mind over and over and over again. "Remember our guns are always loaded. If I ever see you handle any gun like it's unloaded, you'll never handle one of my guns again."

"Even the first time?"

"That 5 gallon bucket didn't get a second chance ... you won't either." Dad meant it, and I knew it.

I grew up without ever having the luxury of getting to play with an unloaded gun.

I hated going hunting with city boys because they grew up playing with guns that were always unloaded. They scared me to death because when they finally got to load their guns they were always forgetting they had loaded them. I wanted to hunt with Delton, but so far Dad hadn't allowed that, despite my constant begging.

"Hunting by myself has a lot of drawbacks. Delton and I can turn a squirrel that's hiding in a tree better than I can by myself. While I wait for a shot, Delton can walk around the tree making lots of noise. If one of us gets hurt, the other one can go for help."

No matter how many reasons I gave, Dad wouldn't give in to us hunting together ... not yet.

"Two boys are twice as careless as one," Dad told me. "The way y'all fight sometimes ... why, I'm plum afraid to send both of you out with guns." Then Dad hit a real touchy spot. "When you boys get serious enough about huntin' to give up your fightin' I might consider it."

As my thinking sometimes did, thinking that I needed Delton for a hunting buddy was going to get me into trouble.

~

Dad and I always started trapping on the first day of December. Usually by then we had several cold spells and the furs had reached prime.

The trapping season was less than a week old, but I already had all of my traps set. Every afternoon, when I got home from school, I pulled my school shoes off and grabbed the .22 rifle from over the door and went to run my trapline. I wanted to be able to slip through the woods like an Indian, and that called for going barefoot.

Who knows? I might slip up on a wolf.

"Its winter-time ... you're gonna get phenomena!" Mother yelled as I headed off the back porch.

"I'm going to kill me a wolf and make me some moccasins," I hollered back, as I disappeared into the woods.

Dad taught me the way to make sets for 'coon and mink, but mostly I was catching 'possums. I had my eyes set on catching a mink, though. My set down on Baker's Pond was just the one that would do it, and I couldn't wait to run that trap.

On my way to Baker's Pond, I remembered how miserably cold I had gotten back on a January day last year. Dad and me stood knee deep in Caney Creek, going over the must do's of making a set for a big male mink that was running Caney. Dad was showing me how to make his "Hole in the bank set," as he called it.

"Dig a hole about a foot back into the bank, right at the edge of the water, and curve it up. If you do it right, you'll have a dry place at the back of the hole where you can put a minnow or crawfish. That way if the creek gets a rise on and the water comes up over the mouth of the hole, the bait will stay dry. Dig a shallow place to bed the trap in the entrance of the hole and put a number one and a half jump trap in the hole. Now put a water-logged leaf over the trigger pan to keep mud from getting under the trigger and then cover the trap with soft mud. When Mr. Mink comes along, he won't be able to resist poking his nose up in the hole – wham – you got him. All that's left to do is put a stake, fork down, through the ring on the trap chain and drive it down, out in the creek. By the time Mr. Mink goes around that stake a time or two, he won't be able to get out on the bank and chew his leg off; he'll get hisself drowned."

When I got to Baker's Pond to my disappointment, my mink trap was just like I left it ... empty. I had followed Dad's instructions to a T, but Mr. Mink had failed to cooperate; he hadn't put a footprint anywhere around Baker's Pond.

Tomorrow's Saturday ... I'll have him in the morning.

I loved Saturday mornings during trapping season because I could spend the day running my traps, making new sets and dressing the fur I had hanging in the shed.

I was up before daylight with high expectations and left straight from the breakfast table to go check my trapline.

So far the run had been disappointing. I hadn't caught a thing, but I had saved my two best sets for last.

My mink set on Baker's Pond captured my thoughts. I had dreamed there was a big boar mink in that trap, and I knew when Dad dreamed that he had caught a mink, he usually had.

The mink hadn't put a footprint anywhere around the pool again for the second night in a row. I didn't go right up to my set because I was afraid I would leave too much scent. I left there and headed for my last trap.

I had placed a steel trap in a trail that ran through a tangle of rattan vines on the river bluff, down on the Guffy place, behind Baker's Pond.

Back then there weren't any posted signs in Mulberry or locked gates either. The unwritten law among country folks *was* if anyone posted their land they couldn't hunt on other people's land. All the gates were just barbwire, and the unwritten law was that you left them like you found them: closed ... close them, open ... leave them open.

When I first caught sight of my set I could tell it had something in it. The adrenaline rushed and the thump of my heart filled my ears. Whatever was in the trap had thrashed the ground and scattered dirt and leaves everywhere.

There was no sign of the critter anywhere. A couple of trenches in the dirt, made by the grapple I had tied the trap to, led off into the underbrush.

My heart sank. *He must have twisted out of the trap.*

I bent down on all fours and crawled under the mess of vines, inching my gun along in front of me.

Growling, hissing, spitting sounds, the kind a lion makes when he is fixing to eat you, suddenly erupted right above my head.

I humped my back and flung dirt with fingers and toes getting out of there.

My knees never touched the ground.

Outside, I stood up and sucked in air.

I didn't know if the thump, thump, thump was my knees knocking or my heart pumping.

I'm gonna go get Dad.

I never stopped running all the way home. I busted through the front door hollering and breathless.

"Dad, I got something big in my trap! It's a real mean critter ... you should've heard him growling ... you gotta come help me get him out."

"Slow down and describe him. How big is the critter ... what did he look like?" Dad asked.

"Big and red ... he's got bloody eyes ... giant claws."

"Slow down, Dean," Mother said.

"He was right on top of my head and fixing to eat me up!"

"You've probably just caught yourself a fox squirrel."

"Maybe I caught a bunch of squirrels; just one can't be that big."

"You couldn't have caught more than one. There ain't a way in tarnation that is possible," Dad said, scratching his head.

"What if a bunch of squirrels was mating and they all got in there at the same time?" I asked.

"Impossible ... squirrel breeding season ain't here yet; it happens in January."

Dad grabbed his coat, and we headed out the door.

"Take me to your monster."

"It's down on Guffy's river bluff behind Baker's Pond. Down there where that rattan thicket is." I guided Dad.

"There?" Dad said with a question mark in his voice. "There is your answer; I bet you trapped yourself a fox. Why didn't you shoot him?"

I realized for the first time I didn't have the .22. I left it somewhere.

When we got to the site of my catch Dad had a good laugh. Between me and whatever I had in my trap, we had destroyed a perfectly good rattan thicket.

Dad knelt down and peeked into the tangle of rattan vines; he couldn't see anything. He crept in a little farther.

"I see what you caught ... it's a big red fox and here is your .22 right where you left it. Come on in here. You have to take care of him."

I got nervous as I crawled toward Dad. I didn't want to ruin the hide.

Dad handed me the .22 and told me to make a head shot so it wouldn't ruin any fur and so the fox would have an instant death.

"I didn't know any of them were left in the country. Mostly Grays are all that's left anymore," Dad said as he held the fox up and admired it.

I couldn't wait to get home and show Mother and Delton and see what the pelt would bring.

We all admired the fox for a while before I went to my room and looked at the F. C. Taylor price list.

In a few minutes I ran into the living room where Dad was combing the fox's fur and announced: "Big Red Fox list for $25. If I flesh him good and stretch him proper, I should get $23 for him in Bonham. I hope I can get enough for him to buy me a pair of Indian moccasins and Delton a jackknife. And, Dad ... you can have the rest of it, that is if you'll buy us a stick of bologna. Delton is tired of red beans."

I will catch a lot of fox and buy us a new pickup truck.

"You bet I will ... next Saturday I'm going to town with George, and I'll buy us a stick of bologna," Dad said in a very agreeable voice.

I decided I would set in on Dad right then and by Saturday I would have him wore down enough, so he'd let me go to town with them.

"Dad, can I go with you and George to sell my fox and buy me some moccasins?"

"Well, I guess so. I can't fit 'em to your feet, unless I've got your feet to put in 'em." Dad's answer shocked me; I figured I would have to beg.

I had read about the Indians slipping through the forest in their moccasins, about them walking like cats and about them running like the wind. I was sure it was true. *I can, too, when I get my moccasins.*

That next week I had trouble concentrating at school.

Ever night I brought home a new book from the library about Indian lore or living off the land, and I plowed through all of our old issues of Fur Fish Game. One book that I found especially interesting contained a story about an Indian who had kept a white man pinned down in his smokehouse for two whole days, while the rest of his hunting party carted off all of his family and their belongings. I read the story to Delton, and we decided that when I got my Indian moccasins we would play a game like that in our smokehouse.

"Since I'll be the one with moccasins, I'll have to be the Indian; you can be the white man and I'll keep you pinned down in the smokehouse."

"Okay, but I want to be a cowboy and shoot at you with my pistol."

"You ain't got a pistol," I protested.

"I will have because I ain't gonna play your game unless you make me one. I want a Buntline Special just like Wyatt Earp carries."

I agreed and carved Delton a pistol from the end of one of Dad's tomato lugs.

Saturday morning finally arrived. George announced by the honk of his car's horn that he was fixing to leave. When we got to Bonham we went straight to the creamery. That's where everyone went to sell their farm produce, and during trapping season there was always a fur buyer there.

George had eggs and turnips to sell, Dad had two cream cans of cream and I had a fox hide.

"Furs are up," the fur buyer told me. "That red fox grades extra large, and he's beautiful to boot. He'll fetch you 35 bucks."

We left the creamery, and George went to the courthouse while Dad and I headed to the shoe store.

Cryder's only had two pairs of moccasins. One cheap pair, made from second grade cowhide, had single soles and they fit perfectly.

They had another pair which was quite a bit more expensive. They had double soles and fancy lacing. The leather in them was chrome tanned elk hide, but they were a size too big.

I'll catch more fox ... I'm gonna be rich. Too big ... If I wade water in 'em, they'll shrink.

I settled on the expensive pair that was too big, and we headed across the street to Smith More Williams hardware store so I could buy Delton a jackknife and case trapper knives for Dad and me. I bought Mother a big eggbeater. The salesman grabbed the wheel and spun it, and I watched the beaters whir. He said it would make the best calf slobber topping for pies you ever ate.

We left Smith More Williams and headed to Parson's where we were to meet George for hamburgers. We lined ourselves out on the stools at the bar and ordered the "eight burgers for a dollar special." After we ate, Dad and I headed to Elkins grocery store and agreed to meet George at Roy Phillips' oil company. I bought a stick of bologna, a brick of Elkins homemade Chili and a sack of soda crackers. Mr. Elkins threw in a few pieces of penny candy; then we left to go to the oil company.

Moccasins are hard to walk in, I told Dad, as we strolled across the street hand-in-hand.

"Well, I reckon so; they're a little big on you. If you look where you're going and quit admiring 'em, it'll help."

"Here ... carry the bologna; it'll help get your mind off of your shoes," Dad said as he shoved the stick of bologna into my arms.

I almost dropped it. I hadn't expected it to be so heavy. "There must be a whole cow in here."

"Well, just about – just wait till you read the writin' on the gut – just don't read it to your mother."

Our business in Bonham was finished; we had sold our goods and resupplied. Roy couldn't deliver the tractor gas that George ordered until Tuesday, so cutting cotton stalks on Monday was off.

The weather turned sour over the weekend, and the blizzard caused school to not take up books on Monday.

After we finished eating breakfast, Dad left for Red River to run his trapline and make a few sets for mink.

I got my homemade bois d 'arc bow, Delton took the pistol that I made him and we went to the smokehouse to conjure up some rules for our cowboy and Indian game. The pistol turned out being a crude imitation, but Delton didn't mind; he had something to shoot at the Indian with.

The rules ... they weren't much either.

Many of the boards in the smokehouse had knotholes in them, and they provided perfect portholes for Delton to peek through, or shoot through, and keep track of the Indian. I could keep track of the cowboy by peeping through the knotholes, and I could launch arrows through them.

With the rules in place, all that was left to do was go to the barnyard and gather a bunch of blood weeds for arrows. With Delton helping we soon had a big bundle of them. By the time we finished getting my arrows gathered up it was dinnertime.

After dinner Dad laid down on the floor for his daily nap, and Mother walked over to Jim Dad's and Ruby Price's for a visit with them.

Delton put on the cowboy hat that Irma sent him for Christmas and climbed up the steps to the smokehouse. He took the pistol out of his belt and went inside.

I dropped the door latch. *This is gonna be for real.*

I tiptoed around the smokehouse and peeked in through the knotholes. When I caught a glimpse of Delton, I would stick a blood weed arrow in the knothole, draw my bow, release it and then quickly peek inside to see if my arrow hit the cowboy.

Delton soon figured out which way the Indian was circling the smokehouse.

As soon as my arrow flew in, he would run ahead to the next knothole. He'd poke his gun out and holler, "Bang ... Pow ... I got you!"

The excitement mounted.

The Indian got into a pattern: Peek through the knothole ... shoot the arrow through ... look and see, and then run to the next knothole and repeat the process.

The cowboy got into a pattern, too. As soon as the arrow came in, he'd run ahead to the next knothole, shove his gun out through the hole and holler, "Pow ... bang."

Neither the arrows flying in, nor the bullets flying out, caused the catastrophe. It was the timing that did us in.

I peeked in the knothole and there stood Delton, eyeball to eyeball with me.

I jerked my eye away, put my arrow in the hole and fired in one sweeping motion.

There was no time to look and see. I ran to the next hole.

Delton did too and shoved his gun barrel out.

Eye and gun barrel met.

"Ah–eeeeee!"

Delton peeked out to see why I screamed.

I was wallowing around on the ground clutching at my eyeball with both hands.

Delton bolted against the smokehouse door and sent the latch flying.

He bent over in my face: "Let me see ... let me see." He pulled at my hands.

"I can't open my eye ... it's crippled!" I screamed

"Indian got good reflex. You shut your eye before my gun barrel got there," I think.

"No I didn't shut it ... you put my eye out ... what makes you think I shut it?"

"Because your eyelid has a gun barrel print on it," Delton observed.

I laughed through a face full of tears.

My cheek turned black and blue all around my eye, my eyelid was red and bloody and the white of my eye was red by the time Mother got there. She had heard the blood curdling screams from Jim's and Ruby's and ran all the way home.

Mother looked me straight in my good eye and asked, "What happened? How'd you get that 'coon eye?"

Delton was afraid of my answer and volunteered, "He ran into a stick."

I wore a patch over my eye for a few days, until the swelling went down and I got where I could hold my eye open in the daylight.

Every day after I came home from school I would put on my moccasins and run my traps with high expectations. Except for an occasional 'possum and a few 'coons I didn't catch anything the rest of the week.

When Saturday rolled around again I was in for another shock.

"Dean, you wanna go to Bonham with George and me?"

"Do I have to go?" I asked.

Going into town will ruin my hunting trip, and Saturday is the first full day that I can hunt wearing my new moccasins.

"Nope ... I just asked if you wanted to go."

Mother wasn't feeling good and she was still asleep in bed when George and Dad left.

Dad hollered his finale instructions to me, as George and he took off down the sandy lane in George's old Chevy.

"Don't you go off huntin' and leave Delton here all alone for your mother to take care of ... she's sick."

Dad couldn't have made it any plainer to me; but somehow I misunderstood. "Don't leave Delton here for your mother to take care of" is what I heard.

Mother was running a fever; she ached all over and thought she was coming down with the flu. She slept off and on. She stirred occasionally, for a drink of water, but went right back to sleep.

Delton and I played in the smokehouse and about every hour I would run to the house and ask her if she needed anything and if she felt good enough for me to go hunting.

"Not until Joe gets home. I can't take care of Delton ... I'm too sick," she kept answering. "There's biscuits and sausage left from breakfast in the oven. Y'all make do."

Mother slept through dinner. The fever had her in a semiconscious state.

We didn't go hungry. When we opened the oven door, we not only found the sausage and biscuits, we found a pan of parched peanuts hiding in there. We crammed our pockets full and headed back outdoors.

I started thinking. That was what usually got me in trouble. *Mother is sleeping so good, she won't know if I take Delton hunting with me, and Dad is gone to town; he won't know. Mother will be proud of me for taking care of Delton, and if everything goes smooth – knock on wood – Dad will also be proud of me. He will probably let us start hunting together, all the time. Anyway what he said was don't leave Delton here for your mother to take care of.*

My childhood reasoning was downright stupid. The biggest fallacy of my reasoning was that knocking on wood didn't work. I knew that if I didn't do something quick I wasn't going to get to go hunting in my new moccasins.

The first problem that confronted me was that Delton was afraid to go off and leave Mother sick in bed. He made excuses. "What if Dad comes home and catches us gone with the .22?"

I used older brother persuasion on Delton.

"You know Dad never gets home from town until well after dark, and you know that I won't be caught in the river bottom after dark."

"Okay ... but you slip in the house and get the .22, Dean. I'm afraid I'll make too much noise."

The squeaky screen door was the next problem; I eased it open without it making a noise.

I slipped inside and tiptoed to Mother's bedroom. She was fast asleep, so I went to the kitchen got a straight chair and carried it to the front door and carefully set it on the floor and climbed up in it to lift the .22 rifle from its rest above the door. I gripped the back of the straight chair in one hand and the gun in the other hand. When the leather sole on my moccasin touched the worn linoleum, my foot slipped.

The chair teetered on two legs and I teetered on one.

A breathless voice came from Mother's bedroom.

"Is that you, Dean?"

The chair and I both settled down just as I thought of a perfect answer.

"Yes, Mother ... I was climbing up to get a glass out of the cabinet so I could bring you a drink of water." I laid the gun down and rushed to the kitchen, dipped a dipper of water, poured it into a glass and rushed to her bedroom.

"Thank you, Dean. I'm so thirsty." Mother sighed as I handed her the glass of water.

I was lucky in more ways than one.

As I left the bedroom I spotted a couple of .22 shells lying on the chest of drawers. I politely took them, because the only ammunition we had was the .22 shell in the rifle.

Finally I was back at Delton's side and told him how close I came to getting caught. That was the wrong thing to do. Delton started to back out. I remembered the .22 shells that I had taken and reached in my overall's pocket and brought one out. "Here, Delton, this will soothe your nerves down," I said, as I handed him the shiny, new .22 short. Seeing the brand new Super X shell did the trick. Delton replaced his unsure look with a "count me in" look.

"Let's go," he said.

We weren't out of the barn yard until a rabbit jumped up and ran into his den under a pile of bois d'arc fencepost. I had previously decided that the first shot was mine. We stood dead still until the cottontail stuck his head out; then I nailed him between the eyes. I handed Delton the .22 and told him to put his shell in while I went to retrieve the rabbit.

Delton tried to eject the spent shell. Dad's old worn out single shot had a bad habit of not ejecting the spent shell. Delton jacked the bolt until he gave up, and the hull never offered to budge.

I took my pocketknife, opened the bolt on the rifle and pried on the base of the spent shell – just like Dad had showed me how to do. The .22

hull was really stuck this time. I pried around on the hull, without any luck, until I finally pried the base off the hull.

"What are we gonna do now?" Delton asked.

It was getting late in the day. I knew that if I left the .22 in the shape it was in, Dad would know I had gone hunting and left Mother sick in bed. In desperation my mind started thinking of ways to get the hull out of the rifle barrel.

Delton panicked. "Let's go to the smokehouse, Dean. We can figure some way to get this thing out with Dad's tools."

We were walking back through the barnyard gate when the idea struck me. "Do you reckon we could take your shell, Delton, and put it on top of the broken hull and blow the stuck one out?"

"*No*, not my shell you don't ... I get the next shot ... use your own."

What neither of us knew was there wasn't going to be a next shot ... not with this gun.

When we got to the smokehouse, I placed my own .22 shell between my fingers and laid it on top of the spent one. I eased the bolt down against it and tried to push it inside the lodged shell. It was no use. The new shell was not going to go into the one I pried the back off of.

What I decided was we needed more force.

"Hold this thing, Delton, I'm gonna get Dad's hammer."

I climbed up on Ol' Johnny and retrieved the hammer from the toolbox. I put the hammer in the loop on the side of my overalls and went to the house.

Mother was still asleep. I glanced at the Baby Bin clock. We still had some time before Dad got home.

I strutted off the back porch and there stood Delton holding the .22 in both hands, pitiful looking and scared.

"Dad's fixing to come home and catch us ... you better hurry." Delton's lower lip was quivering and he was white around the mouth.

"Let me see the blame thing." I took the .22 from Delton's hands.

I placed the muzzle down against the porch step and held the rifle firmly in my left hand, then took the hammer from the loop on my overall pants leg with my right hand and raised it.

Something made me hesitate. *Something ain't right.*

Dad had taught me all the safety rules, but at my young age, I didn't quite understand what made guns fire.

We weren't prepared for what happened.

I banged the hammer down on the rifle bolt.

Kablooie ... fire and smoke belched out. Zing ... Brass shrapnel from the hull ricocheted in all directions. A sickening thud ... the bullet hit something.

Through the gray smoke I could see that the rifle was missing its bolt.

What is Delton doing lying on the ground? Why ain't he moving... or screaming ... or something?

Delton was bleeding from a little round, bullet-shaped hole in the center of his forehead – just above his eyes.

I lost it. With the strength of a mother grizzly, I gathered Delton into my arms. His heavy weight ... dangling arms and legs, unnoticed.

Delton is dead!

I climbed the back porch steps and as I grabbed for the screen door it opened.

Mother met us. She noticed Delton's limp form in my arms. "You put him down. What are you doing to your brother?"

"I shot him 'tween the eyes with the .22 ... he's dead."

Mother fainted.

When Mother fainted and crashed to the floor, Delton came unfainted and screamed at the top of his lungs:

"Dean shot me ... Dean shot me in the head ... Dean shot me with the .22." His screaming revived Mother.

I promptly stood Delton on his feet in front of Mother. When she saw the bullet hole in Delton's forehead, his ashen white face covered in blood and his flour sack shirt splattered with spraying blood, she went out again.

"What am I going to do?" I screamed

I was relieved to hear George Warren's old car drive up.

Dad always knows what to do.

The sound of Dad whistling was the most comforting sound I had ever heard. At that point I could care less what Dad knew.

I ran and grabbed Dad by the hand and dragged him toward the back porch. "Mother's gone on ... and Delton is on his way to going on."

By the time Dad and I climbed the back porch steps Mother had come unfainted and she and Delton met us.

I was afraid the picture Dad saw would send him on: Delton's bloody face and shirt, Mother's face, white as a sheet and bloody from hugging Delton. Delton wringing his hands and dancing a jig; unable to get his jaws working to make talk. They just quivered as blood and tears streamed down his face.

"What in tarnation is the matter with this here bunch?" Dad said and looked straight at me.

I knew it would be me that would have to tell Dad what happened – seeing that I was the only one not stuck hog bloody or dead corpse white.

"What in tarnation is going on, Dean?"

"I can't tell you. It's too bad ... I can't tell you. It's too bad." I danced a jig as the tears gushed.

"TELL ME NOW, DEAN!" Dad said, in the most firm voice I had ever heard him use.

"I shot Delton in the head. I shot him between the eyes ... with the .22."

Dad was always very collected during crises. He calmly pulled his shirttail out of his overalls, took Delton's head in his big rough hands and started to wipe blood away from the bullet hole.

"You couldn't have shot Delton in the head with the .22 rifle. He would be dead by now." Dad's calmness was soothing.

There was a long, much-needed pause in the unfolding events as Dad wiped blood and rolled the little blue dot in Delton's forehead around with his forefinger.

"A little piece of brass from a .22 hull is in his head ... I think."

"Dean ... you go and fetch me your mother's tweezers and when you get back, start from the top. I want you to tell me exactly what happened."

I was back in an instant and began telling Dad what happened. Dad listened as he pried around the hole in Delton's forehead with the tweezers, and picked out brass shrapnel.

I expected that I would never get to carry one of Dad's guns again. Dad must have thought I had learned my lesson.

One thing Dad knew was he had failed to teach me how guns fire their shells.

Our nightly brainstorming session, for several nights following that incident, was about how you could fire a gun without pulling the trigger. Inventing a better mechanism for pulling fired .22 shells from a rifle chamber got its fair share of the conversation, too.

Mother voiced her opinion: "As far I'm concerned, I don't think I will ever be sleepy again, especially in the daytime and with those brats around. Another thing ... a mother can't even afford to get sick with kids like y'all," She told me.

We soon put the incident in the back of our minds – never to be forgotten. Delton carried a mark in his forehead for many years. He was around 40 years old when the last of the brass worked its way out of his forehead.

"I have this blue spot in my forehead to show the world how mean my brother was to me," Delton braggingly claimed.

Fall was winding down and wintertime was coming on. Everyone was ready for a change in seasons.

"When Baker's Pond is frozen over in the mornings, it's an exciting time," Dad said. "The ducks and geese will be back in here by the droves ... man, oh man, are they good eating. I don't know about y'all, but I'm ready for a change in diet."

Dreams of hunting and trapping on Red River filled Dad's every sleeping thought ... mine, too.

7
THE DAY ELECTRICITY CAME

It was a cool April day and we had finished eating supper. We retired to the front porch to while away the last hour of the day. We sat silently and watched a thunderhead build in the southwest.

Dad finally broke the silence. "Tornado season is here, boys. Tornado talking ain't gonna be what we talk about tonight, though; what I want us to talk about tonight is history. There are three histories a Texas boy should be concerned with. Two of 'em they teach you in school and the third one I'm fixin' to teach you."

"What history don't they teach in school?" Delton asked.

"Sam Rayburn history," Dad said.

"The only reason they don't teach it is because Mr. Sam hadn't gone down in history yet," I added.

"Well, maybe so ... but he will. You can mark my word on that. Do y'all know what Sam Rayburn discovered that's gonna make him go down in history?"

Delton and I didn't say a word.

Here comes another one of Dad's "We're gonna get electricity" talks.

"Well, I'll give y'all a clue; he discovered something that we're fixin' to get."

"They taught us in school that Thomas Jefferson discovered lightning and that's all that electricity is," I said.

"Yeah, and Edison invented the lightbulb, and we're gonna get us one," Delton added.

"I learned in school that you discover things that God put here and you invent things that you can put here. Sam Rayburn ain't ever discovered anything or invented anything," I said.

"I know the difference between discover and invent," Dad said. "You ain't got anything over on me, Dean – because of your schooling ... not yet anyway. You're wrong about Mr. Sam, Dean. He discovered electricity for country folks. When he wrote the *Rural Electrification Act,* it was back in 1936; country life had changed very little since John Deere tractors took the place of mules."

The Sam Rayburn talk had died down, and everyone expected to hear Dad begin reading from the family Bible when he picked it up. He opened it to the place where he had placed a newspaper clipping. The clipping was yellowed, old and tattered; he carefully unfolded it.

"Mr. Sam made this speech back in 1952, and I've saved it all of these years."

He started to read: '*Prior to the inauguration of the Rural Electrification Administration, in the mid-thirties, rich America had less than one rural home in ten within reach of electricity. Now, in this record-breaking prosperous year of 1952, the reverse is true. She has less than one rural home out of ten without electricity.*'

'*To me the odorous kerosene lamp for light in the home, the musty family storm cellar for refrigerating food, and the wobbly well bucket for drawing all the family water supply are more than mere hearsay. I experienced such handicaps during my childhood, and during my mature years I observed their drawbacks from the great dairy farms of the east to the scattered cowboy bunkhouses of the lonely southwest, and from the fertile farmlands of the middle west to the often dismal tenant houses of what was formerly known as the old south.*'

"Mr. Sam didn't know about us keeping ice in a hole in the ground ... did he?" Delton asked.

"If he thinks musty storm cellars are a handicap, he should try living in tornado alley. He would think that they are a blessing," I smarted off.

Our talk riled Dad. We saw the fire in his eyes as he spoke.

"Mr. Sam knew a lot more than you boys'll ever know ... unless you boys go get you some college learning."

North Texas farmers held their beloved Mr. Sam high on a pedestal. When politics was the topic of conversation among country folks, there were never two sides; everyone was on Mr. Sam's side. One squirish old Mulberry gentleman by the name of Joe Netherly – when asked what he thought about Sam Rayburn – put it this way: "Some people are able to cipher things. People like Mr. Sam are capable of putting the ciphering of others into action."

Bedtime had come, and so far we had dodged the bad weather. Thunderstorms and showers had hung around all week.

"Joe, if what your mom says is correct, 'April showers bring May flowers,' we ought to have a beautiful May," Mother offered.

We went inside, blew out the lamp and went to bed. We slept tight but never knew what the morrow would bring or the rest of the night for that matter.

~

When the mail carrier ran, we had a letter from Aunt Helen, but the day had been too busy to take time out and read it.

After supper and after the dishes were finished we all went out on the front porch to watch the sunset and read the letter. While Dad, Delton and I talked, Mother read the letter. After she finished she clued us into what the letter said.

"Aunt Helen said they heard, on their new battery radio, that *REA* was going to start setting power poles before school starts up again. She also mentioned how happy they were for us. Said she bet all our talk is about getting some of those newfangled thingamajigs that we can run on it. She wants me to write them as soon as we get our new electricity, so they can come and see it. That's all she said in the first part."

"Well, what about the second part?"

"Oh, well, she just said Clarence and Bill had been catching a lot of flathead catfish on their trotlines."

"Well, she could have written more about that," Dad said.

We started talking about fishing and the weather. Mother lost interest when the talk switched away from electricity to fishing, and she dozed off.

A cloud had been brewing in the southwest and with night coming on it looked like it would be worth watching.

"I'm gonna teach you boys how to judge how far away a cloud is. When we first came out on the porch, that cloud yonder was so far off, that after lightning I could count to 15 before I heard it thunder.

"Time your numbers to about a second apart and that is about 15 miles ... over about Ector as the crow flies."

A streak of lightning zigzagged and hit the ground somewhere in the distance, over on the other side of Caney Creek.

"Now count with me," Dad said, "1 ... 2 ... 3 ... 4...." Crashing thunder interrupted the 5.

"Did you say something, Joe ... 'bout 'lectricity in the cellar?" Mother asked with a wild-eyed look.

"Nope," Dad cut her short then turned on me.

"Speaking of cellars, Dean, you were supposed to make sure the cellar was ready for tornado season.

"Did you set that sulfur bomb off in the cellar like I told you to? Those snakes are gettin' bad in there. Did you fill the lamp up with coal oil? I'd hate to be in a cellar full of snakes and have the lamp go out."

I started to tell Dad that I hadn't burnt the sulfur bomb or filled the lamp when another clap of thunder interrupted me.

The cloud had gotten so close that it got real dark and the lightning and the thunder were happening at the same time. A black, boiling cloud; with wind-swept streamers trailing underneath it, spat long zigzagging streaks of lightning across the emerald sky. We went in the house and Mother grabbed a quilt and some pillows, and we headed for the cellar.

I wish I'd burnt the sulfur ... I wish I'd filled the lamp.

We stood at the top of the cellar door and watched the storm brew.

"See the color in that cloud, boys? When you see emerald-black, you can bet there's hail in there."

"Where there's hail, there might be a tornado. Maybe we better go on down in there and shut the door," Mother said.

Just at that instant a bolt of lightning dropped out of the sky, danced around in the yard and then erupted into a tremendous burst of thunder.

Mother went down into the cellar, got the kitchen matches and was ready to light the coal oil lamp when Dad shut the door.

Delton followed her, and then I went down.

I wish I'd filled the lamp.

Dad stood in the cellar door ready to come down, but he couldn't refuse one last look.

Delton and I stood in the middle of the dark damp cellar, holding hands and waiting for Mother to light the lamp so we could see.

I wish I had burnt the sulfur bomb.

It was quiet.

We held our breath as if that would keep the snakes away.

Mother swiped the kitchen match against the sandpaper on the side of the matchbox and the match came to life. She lifted the lamp globe and lit the wick, then turned the wick down a little and replaced the globe. The glow from the lamp filled the cellar with inviting light. I glanced at the coal oil in the lamp.

O*nly a thimbleful in there.*

Dad came down the steps and let the cellar door settle down behind him.

He sniffed ... then inhaled a much longer s-n-i-f-f.

I expected him to say: Dean, I don't smell that sulfur you were s'pose to burn. What he said was worse ... much worse.

"I smell a cottonmouth moccasin! Don't anyone move."

"I ain't movin' ... but I gotta talk," Delton spouted.

"Hush," Dad said, in a whisper. "Put it on hold ... till we locate the cottonmouth."

The light flickered like it was gonna go out.

God help me if it goes out.

It didn't go out; but Delton panicked. *Notta breath of air ... tornado outside ... cottonmouth inside ... I gotta talk.* Delton's lips moved, but not a word came out as he ran up the cellar steps. He forgot that the cellar door was down and rammed his head into it, then tumbled back down the steps and fell into Dad's arms.

"There is that cottonmouth on the step right behind you, Joe; Delton just fell right across him." Mother covered her mouth with both hands and gasped.

Dad stayed calm. "I can't do anything about the snake; if I move to put Delton down the sucker will bite me. Dean, you get the ax off the back wall and kill him."

The lamp flickered and put out a puff of black soot, flickered again and went out.

My heart stopped.

"I know where the coal oil is," I volunteered.

"It was your job, Dean. If I get bit by this cottonmouth, just remember it was your fault."

I filled the lamp and then fumbled with the matches. The first one I whizzed down my pants leg too fast and the head broke off.

"Slow down and do it right, but hurry," Dad encouraged.

I grabbed another match and whizzed it on the side of the matchbox ... it struck ... the wick took the fire from the match.

The cottonmouth moccasin hadn't moved, nor had Dad and neither had Delton or Mother.

I eased the double-bit ax from its perch on the wall and sneaked up beside Dad.

Thanks to my Indian moccasins.

I raised the ax.

"Keep your eyes on his head," Dad instructed.

I swung the ax down with all the force I could muster. The snake writhed off the cellar step – without a head.

The snake-less head still had its jaws open and its forked tongue searched for its predator, in vain. The ax bit sliced and sliced and sliced again at the snake's head, urged on by Mother hollering, "Kill 'em again, Dean!"

Mother and I pushed Dad and Delton up the steps and through the cellar door.

We all stood at the top of the cellar steps and watched a tornado go down Red River, not daring to go back in the snake-infested cellar.

"The reason none of us got bit – was in all the commotion we was causin' – that old cottonmouth couldn't decide which one of us was worth biting." Dad laughed at his wisecrack.

We finished the night sitting around the kitchen table, settling our nerves with cups of strong coffee. We discussed our narrow escape, from the cottonmouth as well as the tornado.

"The first thing we're gonna do is put a lightbulb down there in the cellar," Delton said as he shivered, remembering the cottonmouth.

"NO," Dad disagreed. The first thing we're gonna do, as soon as daylight comes, is Dean is going down there in that snake-infested hole in the ground and burn a sulfur bomb."

Dad wasn't all that sure about putting a lightbulb in the cellar. He didn't think you could put electricity under the ground like that. He thought the wires would get wet and we'd have lightnin' in the cellar with us.

"Maybe lightning would be better than the sulfur that Dean didn't burn," Delton said.

"Up at our school in Ravenna, we got lights in the basement," I told

Dad.

"Yeah ... but a schoolhouse basement is different. Cellars are dank places. They ain't got anything but dirt floors and walls, and logs to hold up a dirt-and-sod roof," Dad said.

~

The days passed, and the tension mounted.

In our minds – we had bought everything electric we could think of – which wasn't much.

Dad wanted a lightbulb for the living room, so we could tie nets at night. Delton wanted a refrigerator with a freezer, so he wouldn't have to go dig ice out of the hole in the ground for iced tea. I wanted a radio so I could listen to the Grand Ol' Opry.

Mother had her wants, too: "No matter what y'all want, the first thing we're gonna get is a water pump so we can take proper baths. I'm tired of all four of us having to take baths in the same water and, at that, only once a week."

Dad and I thought our bath-taking arrangement was just fine.

We counted down the days. Every night after supper Mother marked off the day on the Farmers Almanac as that day went by.

Fannin County REA had already come and set a tall black pole in our yard. School was due to start back in five days, which would be Monday week. Delton and I hoped the electric company would come and get us hooked up to electricity before school started. We wanted to be there to see us get our electricity.

I couldn't imagine how they were going to get the electricity down off the pole in the yard and put it into our house.

Thursday evening was winding down, when a man in a big truck with *REA* printed on the side drove up in the yard. "We'll be there the first thing in the morning to put your meter in," The *REA* man told Dad.

"Well, if you can't make it, we will be here Saturday, too," Dad offered.

"We don't work on Saturday. Friday will be the day."

After the *REA* man left, Delton asked Dad, "What's a meter?"

Dad explained it the best he could: "A meter is a thingamajig that watches you use electricity. You pay it so much a month to watch you – I think 50 cents a month – then if you get any electricity you will have to pay *REA* for however much you get."

"How will it know however much we get?" Delton asked.

"Don't ask so many questions about something I don't know that much about. All I know is they call it your light bill."

We were all up and at 'em by 5 o'clock Friday morning.

We finished breakfast in a hurry, and Dad, Delton and I headed to the barn.

Dad herded the Jersey milk cows into their stanchions. Old Gert was always the first one he juiced. Dad gave her a couple of nubbins to chew on while he did her the honors, then placed his milking stool where he could reach her udder and grabbed a teat in each hand. He pulled down and squeezed a few times to get her milk coming down and aimed a stream of milk at the barn cat. After shooting the cat her breakfast, Dad started to ring the bottom of the bucket.

I shucked nubbins and threw them out through the corncrib window for the cows and their yearling calves.

My 4-H project was the long-legged, grayish-brown bull calf named Buck. He was of a Jersey-Brahma mix, and he reminded me of a deer.

"A Brahma and Jersey cross will give you the best eating beef you will ever eat," claimed Ray Taylor, our agriculture teacher at Bonham High school.

I held an ear of corn out for him to eat, but he shied away. My intentions were: If I could ever get Buck tame enough to eat out of my hand, I was going to jump out of the corncrib window onto his back and ride him. So far that hadn't happened.

Delton dipped the slop bucket into the barrel of fermented barley and took it to squiggles. She was Dad's "super-sow." He called her that because she usually had from 12 to 15 pigs and was in the farrowing pen again, ready to give birth to her umpteenth litter.

"Squiggles'll take to breedin' the first time she comes in after farrowin', and it'll stick every time," Dad boasted.

We finished our morning chores and took the milk to the back porch. Dad poured the milk into the separator bowl for me and went in the kitchen to get himself a cup of coffee. Dad poured a cup for me and brought it out on the porch so he could watch me separate the milk while he waited on the *REA* man.

I was spinning the separator crank and it had almost reached full speed when Mother climbed the porch steps carrying an apron full of eggs.

It was the wrong time to ask her what time it was, but I did anyway.

"Can't you see I've got my hands full – go in and let Big Ben tell you," she shot back.

"I would if I could ... Delton, you go do it."

Delton ran into Mother's and Dad's bedroom. Big Ben showed 7 o'clock. He ran to the back porch.

"Wonder what time city people start to work, anyway? The man said they would be here first thing in the morning, and it's 7 a.m. already," Delton announced.

"They're not coming ... are they?" I asked Dad.

Mother was confident that they would show up. She knew city people didn't start their workday at 5 in the morning like country folks did.

"They'll be here... you ain't giving 'em enough time," she consoled us.

By 9 a.m. Dad and us had given up, and Mother's confidence was waning.

"Well ... we can't just set around here all day waitin' on a bunch of electricity people to show up. Joe, you and the boys go on and gather the beets so I can get to picklin' them."

"But we'll miss 'em," Delton whimpered.

"No, you won't. The beets are just behind the barn, and you can hear that old electric truck comin' a mile off," Mother insisted.

As we passed the cellar Dad told me to go down in it and get a bushel basket to put the beets in.

"Down there with those snakes – you want me to go down there with those cottonmouth moccasins? There's a passel of cottonmouths down in there."

"Yep, I've done told you twice to burn the sulfur bomb down there. The first time you didn't and you almost got me bit. Then I told you to as soon as daylight came ... and you didn't. Those snakes are yours. Delton and I are gonna stand here until you go down there and set that bomb off. Bring a basket when you come back ... if you come back."

"I'll do it now." I said in a ready voice. "Dad, you and Delton go on and start gathering beets. I'll burn the sulfur bomb and come along with the basket in a little while ... okay?"

I lit the sulfur bomb and grabbed a bushel basket. Just as I popped through the cellar door, the *REA* truck drove up. I didn't get a chance to take the basket to the beet patch.

Dad and Delton almost knocked me over as they ran past the cellar door headed to the house singing a made-up song.

"We're getting' 'lectricity ... hurrah!
Oh, we're gettin' 'lectricity today ... hurrah, hurrah!
Everybody get out of our way ... 'cause we're gettin' 'lectricity today!
Hurrah! Hurrah! Hurrah!"

They ran as fast as their legs could carry them, and I joined right in with them, singing their song and running.

The whole family, Mother included, sidled up to the big *REA* truck as the two men got out.

"Hello folks," the driver said. "I'm Bob, and this here is Bill."

"I'm Joe, this is my wife Sybil, and Dean is the oldest boy and Delton there, he's the baby."

"Ain't done it," Delton said under his breath, as he kicked a clod of dirt.

"Are y'all here to give us the juice?" I asked.

The men laughed with a big hearty laugh. "Yeah ... everybody's calling it juice. You boys remember this ... it is electricity," Bob said.

Continuous questions, like Delton and I could throw out, would wear a person's patience thin. Before Bob and Bill were finished, theirs would suffer that same fate.

"What's that glass bowl for?" I asked.

"That will be your electric meter," Bob answered.

"What's a meter?" Delton asked

"It measures how much electricity you use so REA can send you a bill for just the amount that you use."

"Dad said the meter was going to watch us," Delton said.

"No," Bill explained to Delton, "the meter doesn't watch you; it watches the electricity." Between Bob and Bill, they made it so clear that we knew exactly what a meter was when they finished explaining it.

The *REA* men had a bunch of things laid out on the tailgate of the truck. They both got real busy and started to ignore our questions.

Bill took a roll of wire and went to the power pole in the corner of the yard. He laid the wire down at the foot of the pole and put on some of the funniest looking shoes I ever saw.

After he got the shoes on, he held the big creosote pole between his hands and his legs and looked up toward the top. Then Bob told Bill to fasten the wire to the top of the pole, and Bill took off running up the pole. He shinnied right up to the top of the slick, barkless, limbless pole leaving only gouged out holes for tracks.

We saw the way Bill was climbing and leapt into a dead run toward the pole, but he went all the way to the top before either of us could get there.

Man, I have got to get me a pair of those shoes.

"Where did you get shoes like that, Bill?" I asked

"The *REA* gave them to me."

"If I go to work for the REA when I get big, will they give me a pair of shoes like that?"

Bill didn't answer.

My mind was in gear. *If I had a pair of shoes like that, there wouldn't be a holler tree in the country I couldn't check for 'coons and squirrels. Uncle Earl would take me 'coon hunting just so I could jump the 'coons out for the dogs. I have got to get big enough to go to work for REA.*

Bill worked with the wire on top of the pole and finally pitched the coil of wire back down to Bob. Bob took the roll of wire and unrolled it toward the house. Then he climbed up on his ladder and attached it to a steel box that had a big hole in it.

"What's that box for? What's the hole in it for?" Delton asked.

"I'll put your meter in the hole." Bob said and then he ran a wire to another steel box that had a funny looking arm sticking out of it.

"What's that for? Why does it have an arm?" Delton asked.

"Y'all ask too many questions," Bob quipped.

"Looks like y'all have got the boys under control," Dad said. "Don't let 'em get under your skin. I've got to go to the barn and see a man about a horse." That was what Dad always said when he left to go somewhere and either didn't want to give the real reason or it wasn't polite to talk about in those days.

Bob and Bill were getting down to the serious part of their work now and couldn't afford for kids to bother them with so many questions.

They had a solution for little boys with inquisitive minds.

"Come here, boys. I got something that I want to show you," Bill said.

He led the way to the tailgate of the electric truck and showed us a big black box that had two little round posts sticking out of the top of it. Bill climbed up on the tailgate of the truck and picked up a pair of big wires. One wire had red clamps on each end and the other one had black clamps. He fastened the red clamp to one post and the black one to the other post on the battery and then he got a real serious look on his face.

"Here is what will happen if y'all keep distracting us." He held the battery cables at arm's length and shut his eyes, grimaced, then started bringing the clamps together. He cracked an eye open as he brought the clamps toward each other. He had seen little boys run for their lives so many times before, but he had to see it again.

The wires touched. Sparks erupted and sprayed all over Bill.

Sparks started flying and raining down on our heads.

I remembered what Dad had told us about having lightning in the cellar.

Suddenly we were in full flight, and we busted into the barn where Dad was.

"Bill's got sparks flashin' in his hands," I told Dad.

Delton came out with some more of his wit: "Boy ... it put us to flashing out of there."

"Now we can concentrate on what we're doing and finish our jobs," Bill told Bob.

"Yeah, I think we've got every little boy in Mulberry afraid to mess with electricity ... and a good lesson that is," Bob said.

They finished their job, in peace, and left.

Before dark set in, Dad had run a wire to the ceiling in the kitchen and had a lightbulb hanging down from it. Then he went outside and pulled the arm on the steel box down and came back to the kitchen.

"Okay, honey, you and the boys cover up your eyes," he said.

He reached up and pulled the BB chain.

"Open your eyes, now."

We couldn't say a word.

We stared at the light until our eyes throbbed.

"That thing will blind y'all," Delton said. "When y'all look away, all you're gonna see is black spots."

It was a couple of days before Delton or I could pick up enough courage to peek around the corner of the house and see what Bob did with the little one-armed steel box.

~

Things were slow to change after electricity came to the farm. Dad was skeptical of how much electricity our meters would say we used; but the main thing was that just getting a lightbulb in the living room had been such an improvement over a coal oil lamp that country folks were satisfied, for a while at least.

It wasn't very long before Mother got used to having light and wanted running water. Mother constantly dropped hints to Dad about needing water in the house ... for this and that. Dishwater, mop water, bathwater; the list went on and on.

At the supper table one Friday night Dad announced: "In the morning George and I are gonna go to Bonham and get us the makings of a runnin' water system. By tomorrow night you will have your water in the house."

"Is it likely to get them flying sparks in it?" Delton asked.

"Why, no." Mother shrugged.

George came by and picked up Dad on his way to Smith More and Williams Hardware Company in Bonham early Saturday morning before good daylight.

George and Dad bought everything they needed to get the water in the house and had the salesman draw out directions on a brown paper bag of how to do it.

There was no way everything would fit in the back of George's two-door Chevy car, so they agreed to send their pickup out with the water system the first thing after dinner.

Mother, Delton and I were sitting at the dinner table when we heard George's old rattling car coming down the lane. We jumped up and ran to meet them.

"Where is it?" Delton asked. I was peeking in the car window.

"It's a comin'; we couldn't get it in my car. The pipes are too long," George told us.

Before long a pickup delivered the pump and everything it would take to put water in the house.

Dad scratched his head. "I ain't so sure I can remember how to put all this stuff together, and the diagram on the brown paper bag doesn't help that much either; seeing that I don't know that much yet about electrical diagrams or water system lingo."

"Twix the two of us, we're fixin' to learn," George said.

George helped Dad take the old pitcher pump off the well and pull the sucker rod out. Then they attached two black plastic pipes to the foot valve and slid it down in the well. The pipes were 50 feet long, and the well was over 100 feet deep.

"Hurry, Joe, fasten the pipes to the jet pump while I hold them. We don't want to drop the pipes and the foot valve in the well ... a hundred foot ... we'd never get it back. As soon as you get them fastened to the pump, we got her safe." Dad hurried, and George held tight.

In a few minutes they had the pump safely sitting on the well. Next Dad ran electrical wiring from the fuse panel on the wall of the house to the water pump motor while George carried water and primed the pump.

"We're about ready to plug the pump in," Dad announced.

George, his wife Minnie, Mother, Delton and I hovered over the outlet pipe on the pump to see the water come out.

Dad held the electric plug in his hand, ready to stab it in the receptacle and give the pump its electricity.

George started the countdown: "Okay 3 ... 2 ... 1, plug'er in."

The electric pump whirred.

Suddenly, right in our eyes, a drenching gush of water exploded out of the pump.

"Unplug her!" we yelled.

Dad did but not before everyone got soaked to the bone.

"I'm sure glad I know how to swim," Delton said

"I don't know if I want that much water in the house," Mother said.

"We gotta get it *to* the house first," Dad said, as he crawled on Ol' Johnny and backed up to the well. He let the bedding plow down and began digging a trench toward the house. George laid out the pipe, and he and Dad put the pipe in the trench and covered it up.

Dad drilled a hole in our kitchen wall with his brace and bit and ran the pipe up the wall and through the hole. He put a faucet on the pipe so Mother would only get water when she wanted it.

There wasn't any kind of storage tank on the pump, so Dad rigged a pressure switch on it. When Mother turned the water on in the house, the loss of pressure caused the switch to turn the pump on. It amazed Delton and me that the pump knew to pump water when Mother turned the water faucet on.

"We got water in the house, and it doesn't have sparks in it." Delton busted everyone up.

The first time Mother turned the faucet on was a shocker. In her mind she was going to use every bit of the water that came out. Not so ... the floor caught what she didn't.

Dad grumbled, "One thing calls for another." He set a washtub under the faucet to catch the water that Mother didn't use.

Just as soon as we found out it wasn't going to break the bank for us to pay the light bill, Mother decided she was gonna start taking a bath every day. That brought about another problem. With all that water in the house, how to get it back out of the house after you got through with it became a problem.

Taking a bath happened every day for a while, but getting a bath was still pretty hard considering water had to be heated on the coal oil cook stove and then carried out of the house, a bucketful at a time, after you were finished.

Mother complained. "It seems as though I spend all of my time carrying used water out of the house."

A kitchen sink and a bathtub and a drainage system would come later, but we were making progress.

~

I wanted a radio so bad I could hardly stand it. I pleaded and begged, but so far I didn't have anything to show for my efforts.

"Dad, you aren't gonna believe how good the *Light Crust Doughboys* are and the *Lum and Abner* show is; why, you'll bust a gut laughing."

"Yeah," Dad said.

I continued: "And then there is *Gunsmoke* and *Dragnet* and the *Grand Ol' Opry*."

Mother joined the conversation. "Now, there's the real reason you want a radio – the *Grand Ol' Opry*. You've heard that Elvis Presley is gonna be on it, haven't you?"

I saw my chance to get a radio.

"Nah ... all of us boys are gonna go up to Audrey's and Margaret's and watch Elvis on TV with Laqueta and Louise and their girlfriends."

That statement put Mother in a tizzy.

"Whoa ... no you ain't; I'm a hearing he ain't anything but a vulgar site of profanity, and y'all ain't gonna be in mixed company and watch 'em. Joe, you gotta buy Dean a radio."

"I'll buy a radio for the family, and, Dean, you can pay me back out of your 'possum and 'coon hide money that you make this winter."

When Saturday came, we all went to town with George and Minnie. The first store we went to was Britton Hardware.

Mother and Minnie wanted to look at all the electrical appliances. George and Dad needed some new hoes, and Delton and me headed straight for the radios. I picked out a secondhand Crosley radio. The brown bakelite finish didn't have a scratch on it, and Delton thought the big yellow dial was easy to spin.

The first thing I did when we got home was run a wire from the light socket on the ceiling, across to the wall and then down the wall to where I fixed a place to plug in my Crosley. Then I ran a copper wire from the radio to our rooftop for an antenna.

"KFYN up in Bonham comes in loud and clear," I announced, "and if I can find the right spot on the dial, I can cut out most of the static."

I played with the dial the rest of the afternoon.

Delton and I sat glued to the radio on a cold Saturday night in October of 1954 and listened to Elvis Presley sing on the *Grand Ol' Opry*. I accepted listening to Elvis on the radio as my payment for getting the radio in the first place.

I sure would like to be up at Audry and Margaret Cains' seeing him on TV.

Mother and Dad could care less about hearing Elvis sing, but then they couldn't tune him out either. I had the radio turned as loud as it would go. I ignored Mother's protests, and Elvis finished singing before I turned the radio down.

~

During the spring of 1955, Iceman Pete threatened to quit his ice route; he promised it would be his last summer to deliver ice.

"Everyone is getting Frigidaires that will freeze ice for 'em. That and gasoline is fixin' to go up a cent a gallon, Ethel will be 22 cents. I can't afford to drive all the way down to Mulberry just to sell a few hundred pounds of ice."

Delton and I wanted a water cooler for the window. The Bakers had a water cooler, and it was sure nice to sit under during the 100-degree days of summertime. Dad thought a water cooler would just spoil a person into not wanting to do field work, so he ruled it out.

Mother had different thoughts; she thought what we needed was a refrigerator; then Iceman Pete could take his ice and go somewhere else with it.

Most of the time, Mother knew what was best for the family, Dad thought, so they went to town and bought a Frigidaire.

Joe and the boys are fixing to find out that I was right, Mother decided.

The Frigidaire had four aluminum ice trays with little compartments in them for making ice cubes. Mother made two trays of ice, then mixed up a batch of Kool-Aid and poured it into one of the remaining trays; in the other tray she put milk and sugar and tree ripe Alberta peaches.

"Supper's ready." Mother didn't mention the frozen deserts that she had made in the new refrigerator; she wanted them to be a surprise.

After we finished eating, Mother served her frozen deserts to us. We couldn't leave them alone until they were all gone.

Delton got the last Kool-Aid ice cube, and as he reached for it he said, "When I grow up I want to be a Frigidaire salesman."

That was compliment enough for Mother.

~

We had running water, electric lights, a radio and a refrigerator, and we could go to the neighbors and watch TV (if Elvis wasn't coming on). What more could we want? We couldn't think of anything else that we needed in the way of electrical gadgets, until the worst blizzard of the century hit.

We had finished eating supper and had built a big fire in the sheet-iron heater. Delton and I sat on the wood box behind the stove and listened to Mother and Dad talk. They talked about how fast we had gotten used to the ever-day luxuries that city folks took for granted and about the cold snap that was on us.

"I'm worried about the boys. I've put so many quilts on their bed now that they can't turn over, and they're still complaining about freezing to death," Mother hinted.

"Well, then, why doesn't Old Santa Claus bring them an electric blanket?" Dad said.

We perked up. That's what we had been hinting for anyway; we had just been afraid that Old Santa couldn't afford to buy us one.

Old Santa couldn't ... but our old maid aunt in California made sure we got one.

Christmas day an Arctic Norther blew in and enforced the already cold temperatures. Mother couldn't wait to put our new blanket on the bed. The radio said it was proving the coldest blizzard of the century, according to folks back north and out West.

We were going to get to try out our new blanket.

Mother took all our quilts off and spread the new electric blanket on our bed and then put a quilt on top of it to hold the heat in. She was proud that the blanket had twin controls because I hardly ever complained about getting cold and Delton always did.

Delton had come a long way since he asked if the bath water might get electric sparks in it; he never thought twice about sleeping under an electric blanket. It would take some learning, though, on Mother's part before the blanket worked like it was supposed to.

By the time we went to bed, the red in the thermometer had plunged down into the teens and continued toward the bulb.

All night long we were miserable. I kept getting too hot and turning my control down. Delton kept getting too cold and turning his up.

The next morning when we walked into the kitchen and Mother saw me, she knew something was wrong. My hair was sopping wet.

"Dean, what's the matter with you? Have you got a fever?" Mother wanted to know.

"No, my control on our blanket is stuck. I burned up all night long. I kept turning it down, but it wouldn't go down."

Mother glanced at Delton. He was blue and shivering and had goose bumps all over his little arms.

"Oh, baby ... you're freezing. Your control is stuck, too."

"Yeah, I kept turning it up, but it wouldn't go up."

Dad got up from his cup of coffee. “I’ll go check on it; you probably forgot to plug the thing in,” he said.

When he returned he was laughing so hard he was clutching at his side to keep from busting.

“Sybil, you had their controls switched. Delton kept turning Dean’s side up and Dean kept turning Delton’s side down.”

No one had had any idea how electricity would change the lives of country folks – not Sam Rayburn, not Joe Price, not Sybil Price ... not anyone. When electricity came to the farm is when the farm lost its innocence ... forever.

8
THE GODSEND TREE

Our ancestors were very ingenious when it came to making do with what they had. If they had to use something made for one purpose for an entirely different purpose, they excelled beyond measure. Our pioneering ancestors called that "making do with what you have." Many times their lives depended on making do with what they had.

In America's early years, when "Go west young man" was the cry of the day, the more uses an item had, the greater the demand. Early Americans were willing to use a wooden peg in the place of a nail, or a piece of wire instead of a bolt, when a bolt would have worked better. Staple items such as wire, rope and string were always in great demand because of their usefulness.

When our foremothers wanted to bake a chocolate cake and they didn't have any chocolate, they might use cocoa if they had it. One time when Mother didn't have either one she even tried using coffee.

It wasn't bad ... at least it was sweet.

Many times Mother would use honey, cane syrup or sorghum syrup instead of sugar. When a cake recipe called for an egg, Mother assumed that meant any kind of egg. During the molt, chickens quit laying eggs and Mother would send Delton and me out hunting for eggs that our geese, ducks or guineas laid.

Chicken eggs were extra special to Mother, and she insisted they receive proper care, which meant gathering them up three or four times a day during the summer. She didn't want a hen, that had started setting and had a hot body, to spend any time sitting on the eggs. Mother never washed the eggs until she was ready to use them. She claimed that the hen put something special on the shell to keep them from spoiling. For that reason she changed the straw in the nest every time it got chicken manure in it so she wouldn't have to wash the eggs. One thing Mother deplored was eggs with manure on them. Mother stored chicken eggs in the house. "Bird eggs" are what Mother called goose, duck and guinea eggs, and she would never bring them inside until she was ready to cook with them. She thought the birds could find cooler places to lay their eggs than she could find in the house to keep them.

Dad also took a lot of pride in his ability to make do. When he needed a shop, he didn't go build a special building; he converted part of the smokehouse into a shop.

For all the mechanicking that took place on our farm, Dad only had a few tools. His toolbox, which he had made from scrap pine boards, contained a hammer, a pocket knife and a handsaw and an assortment of drill bits ranging in size from half an inch to one big enough to drill a 2-inch diameter hole. The brace he kept hanging on the smokehouse wall.

Along one of the walls in the smokehouse was a workbench Dad built from bridge planks a Red River flood washed out from somewhere. Underneath the bench was a shelf made from a 1x real wide, cottonwood board that he had sawed out of a log at Audrey's sawmill. On the shelf sat a hand plane and a level. Over the years the bench top had soaked up lard from hog killing time, grease from working on greasy farm equipment, and dirt and grime until it was dark and stained.

Dad had saved every washer, bolt and nut, nail, and odds and ends of hardware that he had ever owned. He stored his hardware collection in syrup buckets that he kept on a shelf on the rafters right above his workbench. There was a bucket for machinery washers and one for bolts and nuts; there was one for used nails and still another syrup bucket for "things I might use someday."

Dad owned two big screwdrivers, but only one of them he actually used for a screwdriver. The other one he used for a punch and a pry bar.

"If they keep coming out with these screwy screw heads, we're gonna have to buy another screwdriver. Why don't they leave well enough alone?" he complained after he discovered Phillips head screws.

Dad owned a couple of monkey wrenches that looked like they might have come over on the Mayflower. He said they really were monkey wrenches. Delton and I called them monkey wrenches because when they slipped off the nut and busted Dad's knuckles, he would dance around slinging his arms and go into a painful chant.

"Ugh – ugh – ugh!"

He sounded just like a monkey.

The jaws of the wrenches had frozen into the large size, although they were once adjustable. If Dad needed to tighten or loosen a nut and it was too small to fit the wrench, he would add machine washer shims between the nut and the jaws of the wrench, so the wrench would fit the nut. He didn't make a trip into town to buy the proper size wrench – in fact, he never bought another wrench. He made do with the ones he had.

All else failing, Dad would cut the bolt off with a hammer and chisel, then run enough strands of wire through the hole to fill it. Then he would give the wire several twists with his wire pliers to make the repair secure.

Sometimes Dad would borrow a bolt from another piece of machinery when he thought the bailing wire fix wouldn't do the job or if he didn't have the proper size bolt in his bolt bucket.

"I'll pay you back come first Saturday trade day," he would tell the old piece of machinery he borrowed the bolt from. The first Saturday trade day was when we went to Bonham. Dad always kept his promise to his machinery; he would go home with a pocket full of second-hand bolts.

It seemed that every time Dad wanted to use his hammer, the handle was broken out. When he asked me how the handle got broken, I would just shrug my shoulders and say, "It just happened."

"Nothing just happens," Dad always said as he sent me to the smokehouse with the hammerhead and orders to put a new handle in it.

"Now this time I want a good one that you boys can't break," he would say. "Make it out of a cured dogwood limb or a hickory stick."

It seemed like that was becoming an everyday ordeal, and Dad got tired of it. The next time the hammer showed up with a broken handle, Dad stuck the head of it in his overalls pocket and went to Smith's blacksmith shop. When he returned, he pulled the hammer out of the loop on the side of his overalls and shook it in my face. "See if you can break this steel pipe handle," he demanded. Dad bragged for days about his unbreakable hammer handle. He could never understand why city folks bought a new hammer when the handle got broken out of their old one.

"Well you finally learned that a tree limb ain't much good for handles, with kids like Dean and Delton around," Mother prodded.

"Well, I'll tell you one thing: A tree limb makes a pretty good boat paddle when you're up the creek without one," Dad joked.

When something needed repairing, or Dad needed something he couldn't afford, or he couldn't find what he needed at the store ... Dad had the answer.

"Never fret ... I'll just make do," he'd say.

~

Dad eventually learned how to be a pretty good Red River valley farmer. He learned how to control the Johnson grass and weeds that thrived in the rich bottomland soil, and he learned how to control his urge to go fishing.

He had a beautiful peanut crop in the year of 1949. When he dug and threshed them in the fall, they made a hundred bushels of peanuts per acre. That was the largest peanut crop anyone had made in Mulberry up until that year.

For the first time since we bought the farm, we would have money left over from the harvest after we paid the bills.

In that case, Mother wanted to buy a butane system and a butane cook stove, but Dad wanted a pickup truck.

"You buy me a butane cook stove. I'm tired of soot getting all over the ceiling and everywhere else from that old worn out coal oil cook stove. If you have any money left, then you can buy you a pickup." Mother couldn't have expressed herself any plainer.

Dad bought a butane tank and a cook stove.

There was just enough money left over for Dad to buy a pickup; that is, if he could get Alvey Cain to come off five more dollars on the price of his old '41 Chevy truck.

Dad and Alvey both drove a hard bargain.

"The truck's just eight years old," Alvey claimed.

"But you've put 'er through the mill – besides eight years of Mulberry sand is a lifetime for a truck," Dad insisted.

"Well ... I reckon you've gotta point. I 'spect I could come off of 80 a bit. I tell you what ... I'll take 75 and no less."

"You got yourself a deal, if you'll get me a tag," Dad offered.

They reached an agreement and shook hands on it.

Dad drove up in the front yard, and Mother went running out to greet him. It was plain that she was just as proud of the truck as she had been over getting butane.

"Eight years, these days, is not very old for a pickup truck – that is unless Alvey owned her," Dad told Mother.

Alvey believed in using his pickup trucks, and you could bet before he got rid of his old '41 Chevy, he used it pretty near up. He had rounded up his cattle with it, hauled hay with it and cut out across pastures to check on his herd, and forded sloughs to get to Red River with it. Whatever, whenever or wherever, Alvey did it in his pickup truck, and Dad would not prove any better caretaker than Alvey had.

The first thing Dad did after he purchased the old truck was to load Delton and me in it and begin cutting a road from the house to Red River. He was not one to go to any extra work in order to make the road straight, so it wound around through the rattan and the dogwood thickets and through the giant bottom-land cottonwoods.

Every time we came to a place where the truck wouldn't fit between the trees, Dad would get out and cut one of them down. He made sure he cut the stump off close enough to the ground so the pickup's running gear wouldn't hang up on it.

We finally reached Red River and Dad ended his road abruptly, at the top of the high riverbank in front of a giant cottonwood tree. The tree was right on the edge of the bank; one more flood and it would cave in. From the tree it was 25 feet straight down to Red River.

If the truck loses brakes, I can always use the tree to stop me before I run off into the river, Dad thought.

After we finished building the road, we took a dip in Red River before we went home.

On the way home from the river Dad decided he wanted a smoke.

Delton always got by the window in case he got truck sick, and that put me sitting in the middle by Dad.

Dad reached in his bib pocket and took out his Bull Durham sack with one hand.

I don't know how he's gonna do this, but for goodness sake I hope he keeps one hand on the wheel.

Dad took the string in his teeth and loosened the mouth of the bag. He let off the gas pedal and gave me his instructions.

"Here, hold the steering wheel for me."

I couldn't believe Dad was letting me drive. Dad hurriedly dumped some tobacco into a cigarette paper and gave the paper a few twists. He crammed his finished cigarette into his mouth, beside the string of the Bull Durham sack. He grabbed the sack and pulled down on it to cinch it up and returned it to his bib pocket. He was through using both hands to build a "cig."

He took the steering. "I got her now, Dean. You can turn loose." He steered the pickup through the sharp winding curves between the cottonwood trees with one hand and fumbled in his pocket for a kitchen match with the other. He whizzed the match against the dashboard and lit his cig.

Thank God he's gonna drive with two hands.

He blew a few smoke rings, then hit the tune of *Goodnight Irene.* He eased the words out around the Bull Durham cigarette that dangled in his clenched teeth. Irene was Mother's middle name, and Dad sang that song a lot.

Dad with the help of Delton and me had turned one mile of river bottom into five or six miles of road, and we were very proud of it. Mother's first impression wasn't that good, though.

"Joe Price, your road looks like a narrow, crooked pig trail and the pig that made it must've drunk too much sour mash. Let me smell of your breath." Mother was very good at naming things and thereinafter the road was known as the pig trail.

"Well, that's ok if you think it looks like a crooked pig trail. Now, when your relatives come visiting us from California, we won't have to walk to Red River."

With the creation of new visions, Mother's vision of Dad coming across the pasture, toting a big catfish on his back was gone forever. However, the hundred dollar grin that spread across his face when he came back from Red River with a big catfish in the bed of the truck was a vision Mother would never forget.

~

Dad, Delton and I were working down in the truck patch, staking climbing butter beans. Dinnertime had caught up with us, and we went to the house to eat.

We climbed up on the back porch, skipping the convenience of the steps.

Mother greeted us with a warm, "Hello ... I bet you can't guess what?"

Before anyone could answer her excited guess what question, she answered it herself.

"I just got a letter from my brother, General Russell. Ann wrote it, and she said they are coming from California and that they will be here next week. And listen to what Russell said tell you, Joe." Mother started to read: "'Tell Joe, I'm sure looking forward to doing some fishing with him in Red River. I want him to help me catch a big catfish.'"

"You said they are coming ... who are they?" Dad asked.

"Just the family, you know, Russell and Ann and their kids, Pam and Mike."

"Is Uncle Russell a General?" Delton asked.

"No, General is just his name. Momma and poppa had settled on the name of Russell, but they couldn't think of a name that sounded good with it. My grandma, your great grandma, came up with General."

"The corn is ready to gather. I hope we can get it out before they get here," Dad said.

~

Sure enough we were right in the middle of gathering corn when they arrived. Delton was driving Ol' Johnny, pulling the wagon; Dad and I were following along behind, snapping the ears off the stalks and throwing them into the wagon. We were in the middle of the field, with half a wagonload of corn, when we looked up and saw a big blue Buick pull off the road and into the cornfield.

"Whoa, stop Ol' Johnny!" Dad hollered over the pop, pop, popping.

Delton pulled the clutch lever back and put Ol' Johnny in neutral.

Dad told Delton and me to climb in the wagon, and he climbed up on Ol' Johnny. He put her in road gear and we took off toward the road as fast as the tractor would run, which was about four miles an hour.

Uncle Russell, Aunt Ann, Mike, Pam and Mother stood at the end of the corn patch waving for us to come on in.

Dad locked both wheels when we got there and almost threw Delton and me out of the wagon.

Greetings of hugs, kisses and handshakes flew wildly for a long time before the conversation kicked in.

"Why did you guys drop everything?" Uncle Russell asked, and then he gave his instructions. "You guys finish your work, and we'll see you at the house later."

"Nope ... no way in tarnation," Dad told him. "We're gonna go with y'all. There ain't but two things more important than work: Fishing's one of 'em and family is the other."

"I told Ann you'd say that." Russell laughed. "Y'all climb in the backseat; you can ride to the house with us."

"Nah ... we'll take Ol' Johnny to the house. We're too dirty; besides I bet Mike and Pam would like to ride on a pile of corn," Dad said.

Pam and Mike piled into the wagon with Delton and me.

"I'll lead off," Russell said. "There ain't any way that I can go slow enough to follow Ol' Johnny."

Uncle Russell tore out to the house in their shiny new Buick. When they pulled into the backyard, chickens scattered in all directions and the hounds started barking at the strangers who had come to see them.

Dad and us kids finally got there, and another round of emotional hugs and kisses broke out before the grownups settled down and went inside.

Uncle Russell must've heard about me getting into trouble for smoking grapevines out in the barn. His only instructions to Pam and Mike were, "You guys stay away from the barn. You might get into trouble out there."

Mother made a lot of apologies, because all she had to fix for supper was red beans, fried taters and cornbread.

Ann bragged about how good country cooking was. "No apologies needed. All your brother has talked about for the last month is going to see his sis and getting to eat some of her red beans, fried potatoes and cornbread."

The grown ups visited until midnight, slept till daylight and drank coffee until noon; by then Dad thought it was too late for us to go to Red River.

"Sybil, you and Ann get our sleepin' and eatin' stuff ready, while we take the kids and go seine for crawfish. Then first thing in the morning we'll be ready to go," Dad instructed.

We went to the slough at the foot of Mulberry Hill. Dad parked the pickup out of the road, and we got the seine out and unrolled it. Before we started each drag, Dad pointed ahead to where Uncle Russell and he were going to bring the seine out and told us kids to wait there with the washtub to pick up the crawfish. After two or three drags we had enough crawfish and went back to the house.

Dad and Uncle Russell rushed the women folks around the next morning. "Red River will be as dry as a bone by the time you women folks get everything ready," Russell complained.

"Well, it's easy enough for y'all ... all y'all have to do is load up your fishing gear and climb in," Mother jabbed at Uncle Russell.

After hours and hours of gathering everything up that Mother and Aunt Ann thought we might need and loading it into the pickup, we were finally ready to go.

Dad got in the pickup behind the steering wheel, Mother crawled in next to him and Aunt Ann sat next to Mother.

"I'll set by the window so I can open the gate," Uncle Russell volunteered.

Dad's got other plans about opening the gate.

Delton, Pam, Mike and I piled into the back of the pickup.

Dad delighted in loading city relatives into the pickup and giving them the ride of their lives on the way to Red River. I overheard Dad getting Uncle Russell and Aunt Ann primed for the experience.

"I still hadn't got accustomed to drivin' things with motors in 'em. I liked my mules and wagon better," he said with hesitancy in his voice but loud enough for all to hear.

"Are you kids hangin' on tight?" Mother hollered as she twisted her head around so she could see out the back window into the bed of the pickup.

Mother's question made Aunt Ann nervous, but I think my answer helped. "Yep ... we're all holding on for dear life."

Dad took that to mean all's ready. He put his foot on the gas pedal and crammed it all the way to the floorboard.

Dirt and grass flew higher than the top of the truck.

He stiffened his back and with both hands whipped the steering wheel from left to right and then back again. The pickup careened wildly down the country lane that led from the house to the pasture. Dad busted several mud holes wide open before he got to the end of the lane where the gate was.

The gate in the lane was made out of scrap barbed wire and short bois d'arc limbs. An old single tree that had belonged to our mules hung on the fencepost to wrap around the gatepost and stretch the gate closed.

Dad pumped the brake pedal a few times. If he pumped it too many times he would get brakes, and he didn't want to stop. He wanted to slow down a little and bust the gate down.

Mother hollered to us, "Y'all better lie down in the bed next to the cab ... we've lost our brakes."

We plowed through the gate and sent it over to one side of the road. "Oh, never mind; I'll fix that gate next week," Dad boasted.

From there we went off the river bluff and down into Red River Bottom at a pretty good clip. By then Aunt Ann had opened her eyes again.

Uncle Russell joined in with Dad on his fun and volunteered to help him fix the gate. "Without good brakes on your pickup, accidents like that will happen," he suggested.

Dad wove through the pig trail a little too fast to suit Mother, and she clenched her jaw in a familiar gesture.

"Joe, slow it down. You're gonna hurt somebody."

Dad took his foot off the gas and slowed a little, but he had another surprise for everyone and wasn't going to slow down much.

The passengers in the cab – suddenly – were looking out over Red River from a 25-foot-high bank.

Dad had convinced everyone that the pickup didn't have any brakes and that it was wildly out of control.

Sometimes the Ol' Truck wonders how it is gonna stop short of disaster.

Dad gave the steering wheel a sharp twist and aimed the truck directly toward the tree, All the while pumping the brake pedal and mumbling, "Lord, please give me brakes."

He got brakes by pumping and slammed the pedal hard.

All four wheels locked up, and the pickup started sliding.

It slid to a halt just as its front bumper came up flush to the huge cottonwood tree.

"Whew ... that tree was a Godsend!"

Every one expelled a sigh of relief.

The ancient cottonwood tree would go down in history as the "Godsend tree."

Pam and Mike couldn't believe there wasn't a coke machine or someplace to buy things on Red River. They were ready to go home soon after we got there. We spent the night on the river and the next day, until Mike, Pam and Aunt Ann turned salmon pink from the sun. Aunt Ann threatened to walk home, but Dad promised he would behave.

We finished the week out visiting. Dad and Uncle Russell fished a lot, but Uncle Russell didn't ever catch a big catfish. They packed up and headed back to California on the following Monday.

~

Mother thought we should spend a little money and fix up the pickup or retire it to the family trash dump and buy something else. She pointed out some things about the old truck to Dad that she thought he should fix.

"The pickup's fenders have splits and cracks in them ... in many places. What glasses the pickup has remaining in it look like isinglass. That poor front bumper doesn't know whether it belongs to the truck or the Godsend tree. Those things we can live with, but you really should do away with that maze of wire and fishing line that you're using to hold the bed, cab, motor and transmission together ... you should put some bolts in her."

"Well you've gotta admit, other than the things you mentioned the old truck is in pretty good shape ... don't you think?" Dad said.

~

RFD (Rural Free Delivery) was the greatest thing to come to country farms until the REA (Rural Electric Association) came. However, things were getting difficult; there were getting to be too many people trying to mail letters to each other and too many cities where the mail could go.

Aunt Irma had written to tell us she would arrive in Bonham a little after mid-night, October first, on the Greyhound bus.

The letter didn't make it, but the Greyhound did. The U.S. mail let the Greyhound down.

Most country folks still didn't have telephones – we didn't either – we depended on the mail. The closest telephone was two miles away at Alley Hall's house.

Mother had gone to the back door to throw out the dishwater when Alley drove up with a telephone message from Aunt Irma, Mother's old maid sister. She was waiting at the Greyhound bus station for us to come pick her up.

We all jumped in the pickup and rushed to Bonham to pick Aunt Irma up. As we drove into town Mother and Dad talked about the lost letter.

"The only two towns named Ravenna I know anything about is Ravenna, Ohio, and Ravenna, Italy," Mother said.

"Maybe the letter went to one of those towns," Dad suggested.

When we got to the Greyhound station, Aunt Irma was sitting outside waiting to catch a glimpse of our pickup. She was so proud to see everyone, and everyone her; the lost letter was soon forgotten amongst all the hugs, tears and kisses. The flesh on our cheeks was beginning to get the color back from Aunt Irma's clinched finger pinches by the time we left the bus station.

"Now that y'all have a vehicle, I wanna go to Oklahoma and visit old friends and relatives. That is where your mom and I grew up, boys," Aunt Irma said as we pulled away from the bus station.

"The first thing in the morning, I wanna take you to Red River fishing and then tomorrow evening we'll go to Oklahoma," Dad told Aunt Irma.

"I ain't much on fishing, but I would like to go see Red River and take a picnic lunch. I'll take my movie camera just in case we see a Cardinal; we don't have any red birds in California, you know."

That was all Dad needed; he would introduce Aunt Irma to the Godsend tree.

Uncle Russell must have clued Aunt Irma into Dad's gate-busting trick because she seemed to control her shock.

Just wait till Dad shows her the Godsend tree; she won't be able to control her shock then.

Suddenly there was the Godsend tree right in front of us.

Aunt Irma screamed, "Don't go off into that river! Oh please, Joe, don't go into the water!"

Irma amazed us all because going off the 25-foot bank into Red River was more frightening to her than hitting the Godsend tree.

After the pickup quit shaking, Dad asked Aunt Irma why she was so afraid of going off into the river.

"Because Russell warned me ... 'When you get to the river you'll have a choice of going into the river or hitting the big cottonwood tree.' I knew everyone had survived hitting the tree, and I knew if we went off the bluff into the water, we would all drown ... dead as a mackerel."

By the middle of the afternoon Aunt Irma and Mother were ready to go home and get ready to go to Oklahoma; they could hardly wait to go pop calling on old friends and see their Aunt Nora and Uncle Jim Duty.

Aunt Irma was apprehensive about making the trip to Oklahoma with Dad behind the wheel. She made him cross his heart and hope to die that he would behave.

It was July hot. The temperature was over 100 degrees and had been for several days in a row.

Dad decided it would be best to wait until late afternoon to begin the trip. About an hour before sunset Dad cranked the pickup and we pulled out. When we got into Blue River bottom, over in Oklahoma, the road was country dirt. It didn't have any gravel on it and was very narrow and littered with chuckholes. Both sides of the road had towering trees that overlapped overhead.

Dark overtook us.

Mother had warned Aunt Irma that the old truck's lights had a tendency of going out just when you needed them the most.

Considering how dark it was, Aunt Irma thought it might be one of those times when we needed them the most. *Did you know that you can feel the dark,* she thought.

The old Chevy pickup had one steady headlight and one headlight that spent most of its time searching the roadsides and tree tops for varmints.

We were finding the way just fine with the one good headlight, until a huge chuckhole appeared right in front of the truck.

By the time Dad got the steering wheel wound up enough so the pickup would obey, it was too late. We hit the hole, and it felt like a hog-wallow without the hog in it.

Of course the springs were weak and there were no shock absorbers on the old truck. The chuckhole was all it took to send the sealed beam headlights wobbling around in their sockets. Sparks flew and gray, stinky smoke boiled out from under the dash.

The lights went out.

Not only did Aunt Irma feel the darkness, heavy, thick and black – everyone felt her hysteria; she scratched, clawed and kicked. She was running and trying to get out of the truck at the same time.

"Whoa!" Dad screamed.

Aunt Irma froze.

Dad's whoa saved the ol' truck's door; she was fixing to bust it off the hinges.

Dad let the truck coast down, and it stopped in a grove of towering red oak trees.

"With all of us crowded into the cab of this little pickup, your actions were less than tolerable." Dad laughed as he tried to calm Aunt Irma.

"I ain't one to tolerate trucks with no brakes and no lights, especially with drivers like you, Joe Price." Irma wasn't ready to be calmed.

The shock of Dad striking a kitchen match and asking Aunt Irma for a piece of "factory chewing gum" seemed to take the tension out of the situation.

"What do you think happened to the lights?" Aunt Irma asked, as she dug in her purse.

"The thingamajig that controls the electric juice and keeps the sealed beam lights from burning out – it burned out." Dad gave her a typical Joe Price explanation.

Aunt Irma set everyone straight when she told Dad that the technical word for the thingamajig is a fuse. She pulled a piece of Juicy Fruit gum from her purse and passed it to Dad. "Here we are stranded in the jungle, it is pitch-black dark and you wanna chew gum ... what on earth for?"

"Just you wait and see."

By then the match Dad struck was burning his fingers and he tossed it in the floorboard, squished it with his foot and lit another one. He put it in a crack in the dashboard.

Without saying a word, he removed the wrapper from the Juicy Fruit and handed the gum to Delton. "Share it with Dean," he said.

Dad separated the aluminum foil from the paper gum wrapper and retrieved the burned out fuse from under the dashboard. He wrapped it with the aluminum foil and then put it back in its holder.

Hallelujah – there was light.

The rest of the trip was uneventful except for all the bragging that went on.

Aunt Irma bragged about Dad's ability to make do, and he bragged about how smart he was when it came to the electrical circuitry of automobiles.

We were so excited about the first factory chewing gum we had ever chewed that Aunt Irma felt sorry for us.

~

The long lost letter finally arrived, two years late.

The problem was the address Aunt Irma put on the letter. All she put was: Joe and Sybil Price, RFD, Ravenna. No route number and no state.

The letter had first gone to Ravenna, Ohio, then to Ravenna, Nebraska. The next postmark on the letter was Ravena, New York, and then it went to Ann Arbor, Michigan. It seemed there was someone in Ann Arbor who lived on South Revena Road. The long lost letter finally made it to Rowena, Texas, then to Joe and Sybil Price in Ravenna, Texas.

"You can't get a better ride than that for four cents," Dad remarked.

9
FISHING FOR COWS

George and Minnie Warren had a good collection of 33 1/3 RPM records and one of the best windup Victrola record players RCA made. Even though it had been in the family since 1922, it was in mint condition. Minnie kept it wrapped up in a pillowcase and only got it out on special occasions.

It was Saturday night and the Grand Ol' Opry was coming on the radio, but the special occasion *was* it was George's birthday. Minnie had invited us over to listen to the Victrola and eat supper with them. After supper we were gonna eat cake and homemade ice cream and listen to the Grand Ol' Opry.

Delton and I were really enjoying keeping the Victrola wound up and listening to records.

Mother and Minnie listened to the Victrola playing in the background while they cooked supper. Minnie hummed and Mother tapped her toes to the tune of Roy Rogers singing a lively campfire song.

George and Dad went out on the front porch to discuss me.

Dad had helped me make a soap tractor out of a big wooden spool that Mother's sewing thread came on.

Dad showed me how to put soap on both ends of the spool; then he ran a rubberband, which he made out of a red car innertube, through the spool. He had me put a nail through the rubberband on one end of the spool and a lead pencil through the band on the other end of the spool.

Dad notched the rim of the spool so my soap tractor would have good traction.

I held the pencil and wound the rubberband as tight as it would wind with the nail before turning it loose on the floor. It made a loud clicking noise as it pulled itself along because of the notches in the spool clawing against the floor. It wasn't as loud as the pop, pop, pop of Ol' Johnny; but it was loud enough to get me in trouble.

My troubles started when I took my tractor to school ... which I wasn't supposed to do.

I wound the thing as tight as I could get it and turned it loose in the metal book bin under my desk. As the rubberband came unwound, it sounded like the rat a tat-tat of a Tommygun. Not only did it unnerve Mrs. Gladys Hall, our teacher, but it alarmed her whole room full of first, second and third graders. It had taken Mrs. Gladys until break time to get things under control again.

Mrs. Gladys paddled me for the interruption I caused.

I smarted off and told her she should paddle the whole class because they had got just as much fun out of it as I had.

Dad punished me again when I got home: for taking the tractor to school; for turning it loose in my desk; and for smarting off to Mrs. Gladys.

I felt in my bones Dad and George were talking about the incident, so I left Delton with the Victrola and slipped out the back door. I crawled under the house right up to the porch where Dad and George were discussing boys and their troubles.

"I'm sure proud Mulberry still has its little two-room school. If Dean went to that big Ravenna school, with all of them boys to run with, I'd probably lose him to the law."

George broke off a new cud of chewing tobacco and placed it in his jaw.

"Joe, let me tell you something about boys."

He forced the cud over into his cheek with his tongue and saturated it with saliva before he continued. "If a boy doesn't have enough grit in his craw to get in trouble once in a while, he probably ain't gonna 'mount to a hill of beans."

"Yeah, I know that," Dad agreed.

Things fell quiet, while Dad fumbled with a book of cigarette papers and a sack of Bull Durham tobacco. He built himself a cigarette and then continued.

"George ... do you remember back when we were doin' our growin' up? We weren't allowed to even think out loud. We were almost grown by the time we figured out we had a brain. By then our brain wanted to go fishing ... not do learning."

Dad whizzed a match up his pants leg and lit his new cigarette, settled back and drew several long drags.

"Yeah Joe ... why, I was a teenager before I was allowed to talk. Speaking of losing Dean to the law – have you heard on your radio lately how many laws those Washington bureaucrats of ours are passing?"

"Yeah ... I guess they're trying to keep people out of trouble. If you want to know what I think ... I think they could pass just one law that would work for everybody."

"Oh ... what's that?" George asked.

"They could pass a law that it is against the law for anyone to break the law." Dad accentuated his answer with a down from the belly laugh. As if to punctuate his bit of wisdom, he cast his head back and blew a few smoke rings.

While Dad was blowing smoke, George offered his own bit of wisdom.

"If our forefathers were alive, their solution to the problems the teachers have with the school kids would be divide and conquer. Instead of throwin' all the kids from the whole country into one school, they would send them back to the little one-room country schools like the ones you and I went to."

Minnie called super, and I made a mad scramble to get to the wash basin and freshen up. Everyone had gathered around the table by the time I showed up, and all eyes turned to me.

"Where have you been, Dean Price? Just look at you."

"I went to get a drink out of the well and fell off the porch." My answer seemed to suffice for the moment.

Just wait until I get you home, was the thought I saw in Mother's eye.

After supper Dad and George got the ice cream freezer going and put me to cranking it. Delton liked salty ice and kept bothering me for another piece of it. Before long I couldn't turn the crank and George packed the freezer down and put a blanket on top of it.

The wait was on.

By the time the Grand Ol' Opry came on, it was ready and we all enjoyed ice cream, cake and the radio.

Delton fell asleep, and Dad had to carry him home after the program went off.

~

The trouble Delton and I got into wouldn't have happened if I had continued to feed the cows by myself, and if Delton had continued to feed old Squiggles without my help.

Dad said many times: "Two boys can get into three times as much trouble as one boy, three boys can get into 10 times as much trouble as two boys, and as you add more boys, the trouble gets out of hand."

Every day after we finished our chores, I told Delton how much fun I was having trying to catch Buck with an ear of corn. I told Delton about my plan to jump out of the corncrib window onto Buck's back and give Buck a riding that he wouldn't ever forget. I made my chores sound like so much fun, purposely, that Delton became jealous.

Delton's chore was to slop old squiggles and her litter of pigs. After listening to me, he thought he had the dirtiest and most degrading chore there ever was and he was tired of it.

One night after we finished supper Delton lit in on Dad.

"Why does Dean always get the fun chore and I get to slop the hogs?"

"I don't know. Maybe it's because of Dean's winsomeness."

Dad was good at using words like that when someone got him cornered. Delton had no idea what winsomeness meant; neither did I.

I never expected that Delton would bring it up to Dad, but now that he had it was time to unruffle Delton's feathers.

I wanted to help Dad soothe Delton's anger, so I volunteered to help

Delton slop Squiggles and her pigs. I thought by doing that, Dad might let Delton help me. I was willing to do anything to keep from having to switch chores with Delton and to get Delton to help me.

"Boys, how would you like to help each other with your chores?" Delton agreed and I agreed, and all was hunky-dory.

That seemed to cool Delton off and get Dad off the hook with Delton at the same time. It had played out just like I thought it would.

Now I can put some excitement into slopping old Squiggles for Delton.

There was a little time left to play after supper before the night chores had to be done up. Delton and I jumped off the front porch and started pushing our old car tires down the pasture lane.

I decided to have some fun at Delton's expense. Just as soon as we were out of Dad's hearing, I laid out my plan.

"Delton, you know what I think would be fun? I'll lure Squiggles away from her pigs, and you sneak and grab one of them and we'll pet it." Delton's eyes lit up.

"Hey, boys ... it's time to go get the night chores done," Dad called.

We heard Dad calling and let our car tires roll out of the lane and go under the fence, before we headed to the house.

Dad walked toward the barn. We followed, walking hand in hand.

Dark was coming on pretty fast, and Dad decided to have us wait until the next morning before we teamed up together on the chores.

I finished feeding the cows first and stopped by the hog pen. Delton had just dumped a bucket of sour mash slop in the hog trough, and Squiggles was squealing and rooting the pigs out of the way for her share.

"Ain't her pigs beautiful, Delton? That little fat spotted one is the one that I would like to pet."

Dad came up about that time, and the pig petting talk stopped.

"Both of you boys help your mother tend to the chickens. Dark is right on us, and she don't have time to do it by herself before it gets dark. I'll separate the milk while y'all help her."

We brought the eggs to the back porch just as Dad finished putting the cream in the milk cans.

We were all too pooped to go to any trouble over supper, so buttermilk and cornbread got the call.

A fight almost broke out between Delton and me as to which one would get to pull the chain and turn the lightbulb on.

Mother had to settle it. "Its Delton's time, Dean ... you can turn it on next time. Y'all better hurry and get your homework, boys; it's about bedtime."

Mother made sure we were all in bed before she pulled the lightbulb chain. She pulled the chain, then made her way, groping with both hands, and got in bed with Dad.

I lay in bed, mulling over the events of the evening in my mind.

Man, this played out just like I had it planned. Delton can help me tame Buck ... if he can outrun old Squiggles.

I had to put my hand over my mouth to stifle a laugh.

"What are you sniggering for? Don't you think I can outrun Squiggles?" Delton asked.

"Sure you can. You just leave Squiggles up to me," I assured him.

I decided that if I scared Delton just a little bit, it would be good insurance against him telling Dad about our plan to catch one of old Squiggles' pigs.

"Delton, don't you dare tell Dad that we're going to catch one of the pigs. Dad don't want them being petted, and he's liable to put a stop to us doing chores together."

We went to sleep after that and dreamed happy dreams.

I dreamed that I rode Buck down the streets of Bonham. Everyone wanted to buy Buck; he was a beautiful stallion with silver wings and a weird looking tail. Instead of running ... Buck flew.

Delton talked in his sleep. He kept calling the pigs. "Here, piggy ... here, piggy, piggy ... here, piggy.

We woke up in the dark of a beautiful, crystal clear and youthful day. The stars were fading from view when we stepped out of the kitchen door onto the back porch. Dad was returning from emptying the chamber pot; we still didn't have indoor plumbing.

Dad was in one of his philosophical moods.

"Each day reminds me of the miraculous cycle of life. Mother earth gives birth at midnight to a brand new day and then as morning twilight blooms, the day becomes a teen-ager, full of energy and life. The cycle of life is swift; by noon the day has reached middle age. Sundown comes and the day enjoys the twilight of its minutes; then darkness falls. That's when old age sets in. By midnight the day is in a state of coma."

Dad set the pot down and sighed when he saw the satiny, salmon pink clouds billowing in the eastern sky. He thought for a long moment before he spoke again.

"In the hustle and bustle of a big city, like Dallas, no one notices a day having a cycle of life at all. At night the stars are dim, if you can see them at all, because the light from the street lamps drowns them. Midnight is just as busy as any other part of the day. In the country, where one can observe nature, the period around midnight takes on an eerie silence. The old day's actions are grinding to a halt and the new day's actions burst forth, just like a newborn babe."

Mother's voice came ringing from the kitchen.

"Joe, if you're through spreading it on the boys, y'all wash up and come on in. Breakfast is ready."

After breakfast Delton and I made our way toward the barn to do up the morning chores. Doing the morning's chores had taken on a new meaning for Delton. He could hardly wait to pet a pig.

"If you will help me shuck nubbins and feed the cows first, then I'll go help you catch one of Squiggles' pigs to pet," I promised

We climbed the ladder on the corn-crib wall and dove through the pigeon-hole window into the corncrib. Once inside the corncrib, I started scratching through the ears of corn and showed Delton how to tell a nubbin from a good ear of corn. I explained to Delton that the big, perfectly shaped ears were for seed corn and the little ears were for cow feed.

"Throw the nubbins in a pile over by the window and put the ears of corn that we are going to save for seed corn in the gunny sack. After we feed the cows and Squiggles, we have to take the seed corn to the shelling machine and shell it," I instructed.

After we completed the sorting, we shucked the nubbins and threw them out through the crib window to the cows. I showed Delton how I could lure a cow up to the crib window with an ear of corn and then jump out on her back.

"The cow riding fun will have to wait until this evening, though, while Dad is resting," I told Delton.

We finished feeding the cows in a hurry, but I stalled helping Delton with his chores because I wanted Dad to leave first.

"Dad just went to the house; let's go do your chores. I wanna see you pet one of squiggles' pigs," I urged Delton.

Delton dove out the corncrib window and ran toward the hog farrowing pen. *Getting to pet one of Squiggles' pigs will be the most fun thing I ever did,* Delton thought.

When we got to the pigpen, Delton gave the orders.

"If you're going to lure Squiggles away from her pigs, then go get a bucket of mash out of the barrel that's in the side shed ... and hurry back."

When I got back to the pigpen, Delton had draped himself over the fence and was sweet-talking Squiggles. She was up in her trough, squealing and rooting around, begging for the slop. I knew that as soon as I dumped the slop in the hog trough, her piglets would come running. The last thing I wanted was for the piglets to come join their mammy.

I sat the bucket down right outside the fence to tease Squiggles, then I picked up a stick and punched through the fence at her.

I gave the command ... "NOW! I've got her attention. Jump the fence and hurry."

Delton tried to scramble over the fence, but his big toe hung in one of the meshes of the hogwire fence. I didn't let that stop him. I placed a hand on Delton's butt and shoved as hard as I could.

Delton hit the ground running.

I screamed, "Run and get a pig before Squiggles catches you and eats you, hair, hide, guts and all."

Delton had seen Dad throw a rabbit into the pen for Squiggles. He knew what I meant ... hair, hide, guts and all. His eyes got as big as saucers, and he dug into the mire with both hands and his toes as he spun off toward Squiggles' bed, where her pigs were. He dove into the sow's bed headfirst and grabbed a pig.

The pig squealed ... for its momma.

I reached over the fence with the slop bucket and dumped the slop in the trough; some of it went in the trough ... some on the ground. It didn't matter. Squiggles wasn't hungry anymore.

She headed to the rescue.

My mind was in a whirl.

Delton needs ... gotta run faster. If Squiggles gets him, I'll have to fight her off ... If I can. Oh ... Squiggles is fixin' to get 'im.

I panicked and tried to yell ... nothing came out.

Delton didn't panic: "*Drop her pig ... Drop her pig and run ... Oh God, run fast,*" he thought.

Old Squiggles was gnashing at the seat of his overalls.

I came unfroze and started beating Squiggles over the head with a big stick. It wasn't helping.

Delton made a mighty bound for the fence just as Squiggles grabbed the seat of his overalls with her long, razor sharp, tusk.

She started squealing. Her blood curdling squeals pierced the air. She shook her head violently and backed up.

I saw my opportunity to save Delton's life.

I grabbed Delton by the arm with one hand and released his suspenders with my other hand. Squiggles snatched Delton's overalls off faster than you could blink an eye. She thought she had her culprit and ran toward her squealing piglet, shaking her head.

I grabbed a handful of Delton's flour sack drawers and hurriedly dragged him over the fence.

Delton was shaking like our old 'coon dogs did when they had eaten too many peaches that had fallen off the tree and were trying to pass the seeds.

"You weren't in any danger. I was going to save you if old Squiggles started eating you," I tried to console Delton.

No amount of comforting ... nothing I said kept Delton from running to the house screaming at the top of his lungs, "Dean let old Squiggles eat my britches off of me!"

Delton was a sight to behold; standing in front of Mother and Dad with his head, arms and feet covered in hog mire. Everyone couldn't help laugh at the sight of him standing there in his flour sack drawers, crying big muddy tears and protesting, "Dean let old squiggles eat my britches."

Delton never figured out that I got him into all that trouble, and we remained good buddies.

Mother and Dad were happy and thanked God that I saved Delton's life.

Delton and I lay in bed that night and tried to go to sleep, but neither of us could get sleepy. Delton wondered whatever possessed him to want to pet a dirty ol' pig anyway. I wondered why I ever wanted to convince Delton to try and pet a pig that belonged to Squiggles.

"Tomorrow will be another day – if it ever comes – then we can have us some real fun riding Buck."

"Yeah ... if we can ever get rid of today," Delton agreed.

"I can't wait until tomorrow to see if we can lure Buck up to the corncrib window."

We talked and giggled a long time about Squiggles, until our nerves let us go to sleep.

I didn't smell the coffee, nor did I hear Mother calling that breakfast was ready. I didn't hear her call the first time or the second time, and usually there was no third time.

I woke up with Dad standing over me yelling, "The cows are hungry!"

Delton sat up surprised. "Yesterday just went away." He stretched his arms to the sky. "Is today here already?" he whimpered.

We slopped Squiggles first. Then we went to the corncrib and piddled around sorting corn and shucking nubbins.

Dad finished milking and went to the house.

I threw a nubbin out on the ground. The cows were ready; they pushed and shoved until one of them got the ear of corn and walked off to the corner of the lot. The rest of the cows crowded the corncrib window.

"Watch this," I told Delton. I pitched a nubbin out right in front of a Jersey cow and made ready to jump on her when she picked it up. I gave Delton instructions how I was going to do it. "When she reaches out to get the ear of corn, she'll turn her tail to the window. It will be pretty easy to jump out on her."

The Jersey cow turned her tail to the window and was in perfect position. I reached out and grabbed her by the tail and bailed out on her. I rode the cow around the lot, complaining that cows weren't much fun to ride because all they wanted do was walk.

"Are you going to tell me when one of them cows gets into the right position so I can bail out on her?" Delton was convinced he could do it.

"No ... You're liable to get thrown off, and if you broke your neck you'd blame me and go bawling to Dad that I broke your neck."

"I wouldn't fall off, and if I broke my neck I wouldn't go running to Dad."

"Okay ... I'll see to it that you get to ride a cow if you promise to help me ride Buck."

Delton soon learned that riding gentle cows wasn't all that much fun.

A week had passed, and we had tried everything we knew to get Buck up close to the corncrib window. I became so irritated with Buck that I nicknamed him Dumb Ass, "Because Buck is dumber than Overton's old Jack Ass," I told Delton.

All the other calves had tamed down and were eating from our hands; however, we hadn't tamed down to the point that they wanted me to ride them.

They bucked so hard and ran so fast that I couldn't stay on long, but it was fun trying.

Delton kept begging, "I'm tired of riding walking cows. I want to show you that I can ride one of them calves."

I gave in, without Delton having to beg too much.

Delton's calf bowed his back, twisted his rear end and came down stiff-legged. On the calf's first jump, Delton was off there. He didn't cry, he laughed ... tears.

We had just about given up on riding Buck the Dumb Ass; he was just too skittish to ever get close enough to the corncrib window to let anyone jump out on him.

"Mark my word," I told Delton, "Buck's time is coming ... I'm gonna think of something."

~

Now that we had a pickup truck and could go places, we started going to Granddad and Grandma Price's on Sunday afternoons. Dad didn't call them his mom and dad; they were Granddad and Grandma Price to everyone, even him.

One Sunday Delton and I were especially anxious to make the trip. It had rained all day on Saturday and filled the bar ditches full of water. Us kids (Delton, Patsy, Melba and me) loved to go crawdad fishing, and the grownups loved for us to go. Not only did it keep us out of the house, but come Monday morning Dad had plenty of fish bait.

After church we didn't even go home; we headed straight for Grandma and Granddad Price's.

As soon as the pickup truck rolled to a stop, we went in and hugged Grandma and Granddad Price. Then we asked Grandma if we could have some fat meat for crawdad bait. She took us to the meat box and cut each one of us a chunk of pork belly.

"We gotta eat first ... before y'all go fishing," Grandma said, "but you can get rigged up while we're getting dinner on the table."

Burley helped us rig our fishing poles. Burley was our uncle, but he wouldn't hear of us calling him anything but Burley. "I'm just as big kid as y'all," he maintained.

All the men folks fixed their plates and took them out under the big bois d'arc tree in the front yard to eat. Us kids couldn't go outside and eat because our mothers were afraid we couldn't keep the flies off our food. Mother gagged at the thought of a fly lighting on food. She claimed they puked on food.

The big bar ditch in the front of the house was always a hot spot, so that was where we headed as soon as we finished eating. Everyone was having a good time crawdad fishing except me. I was a little preoccupied; I couldn't keep my mind off Buck and how I could catch him.

"I got it ... Hey, Delton, I got it!"

"What have you got?" Patsy asked.

"Got it figured out ... how we can catch Buck."

"What do you wanna catch Buck for?" Melba asked.

"We don't wanna catch Buck. Dean wants to ride him," Delton said and then asked, "How are we gonna catch him, Dean?"

"Ummmmh," Melba put her hands over her mouth. "I'm gonna tell your daddy."

"Shucks, he doesn't care. Buck's my calf," I bragged.

Delton had waited as long as he could stand it. "Come on out with it, Dean. How are we gonna do it?"

"We're gonna take one of Dad's long fishing poles and tie a short piece of string on it and then tie an ear of corn onto it and fish for Buck."

Patsy and Melba were enjoying fishing for crawfish, but as for me, I couldn't wait to go home and fish for Buck.

I was tickled pink when it finally got time to go.

Back at home, around the supper table, Mother's and Dad's small talk revolved around Granddad Price's state of health. He wasn't well, and it had Dad worried.

We fidgeted around a lot.

It wasn't that we were bored with the small talk, and it wasn't that we weren't hungry. We had other things on our minds.

"What's wrong with you boys? Did you eat too many of Grandma Price's popcorn balls?" Mother asked.

"Nah ... we wanna go feed the cows and get our night chores done up. Can we be excused from the table?"

Mother cut her eyes in Dad's direction with a wondering-what's-up look on her face.

"Your Cousin Doyle didn't give you boys some smokes did he?"

"No ... mother," I said with a disgusted sigh.

"Just remember the rule; you boys can't go botherin' your mother for somethin' to eat after while. Now, for goodness sakes, skedaddle on out of here and tend to your doings," Dad said, then added, "Since you're going early, you can milk for me."

We grabbed some string off the back porch, then fetched Dad's longest fishing pole out from under the house on the way to the barn.

We shucked a few nubbins and threw them out of the corncrib window and then the cows started coming into the barnyard.

Buck stood in the foreground. He seemed more skittish than ever.

"You don't reckon he suspects something, do you, Dean?"

"Nah ... animals can't suspect ... it's just his nature."

I held a big ear of corn up where Buck could see it and called, "Here, Buckee, Buckee ... here, Buckeeee." Buck took a few nervous steps toward the corncrib window and balked.

It's time for the fishing pole.

I tied a good-looking nubbin onto the pole with a few feet of string and dangled it out the window in Buck's direction.

Buck took a few steps toward the window.

I jiggled the ear of corn up and down a few times.

Buck took another step. He looked at the ear of corn and ran his tongue out to catch the drool that dangled from his chin.

"Choke up on the pole, Dean, and ease the nubbin in toward the window."

I did, and Buck followed. *It's working.*

"Here Delton, you take the fishing pole. When you get Buck right in front of the window, maneuver the corn around until Buck gets his tail right here in front of us. Then all you gotta do is lay the pole down, place your feet against the wall on each side of that big, cracked-out knot hole and grab Buck's tail. Pull it down in that crack and hang on. That will give me time enough to jump on him."

Everything was going just like I planned. I climbed up on the windowsill. I was perched and ready to go as soon as Delton grabbed Buck's tail.

My heart chugged like a freight train going straight up Pike's Peak.

Delton eased the pole down and grabbed Buck's tail. He pulled it down in the crack and hollered, "OKAY ... GO."

I heard Buck give out a bloody, bawling, wailful sound.

I hesitated.

"What are you waitin' for, Dean? I can't hang on any longer."

I bailed out on Buck's back.

Buck's ear splitting bawls drowned everything else out. He lunged away from the knot hole and hit a running stride, unlike anything I had ever seen. He never bucked, not even once.

Imagine a calf named Buck that doesn't know how to buck. I should have named him wind. That's what he runs like.

Buck was slinging his tail around and around like it was on fire. Blood and messy stuff was getting in my eyes, on my face and in my hair.

Delton bailed out the corncrib window and struck out running after Buck and me. He knew the what and the why behind Buck's problem.

Delton held the skin from Buck's tail in his hand.

I had had enough. I hadn't figured out just exactly how I was going to end my wild ride, though. I quickly took inventory (in my mind) of the damage Buck had done. *Busted the barnyard gate down, let the cows out, trampled down a row of beets, stomped one of Squiggles' pigs to death, and only God knows what else.*

Buck was headed straight toward the screened-in back porch.

Whoa ... Please God. I remembered Mother saying, "Scared prayers don't get answered."

There Mother and Dad were standing on the back porch.

Buck dodged the porch.

As we whizzed past the porch Dad yelled: "Dean, what have you done to Dumb Ass? His tail's skinned off and bleedin', and he's squirting. You jump off ... come back here and tell us what you've done to Dumb Ass."

Dad's voice faded fast ... Buck was in a laid-out run.

Go on ... take me as far as you can run.

I knew Buck couldn't run far enough to get me out of harm's way. Mother knew about Buck's nickname.

I baled off.

Before Dad gave me his drilling, he hosed me off with the pressure hose from the electric pump.

"Come on in, boys ... you have got some explaining to do. Set down at the kitchen table," Dad ordered.

We sat there in silence, almost forever it seemed.

"What are y'all waiting for?" Delton asked.

"Joe wants to calm down and quit shaking before he begins his questions. He's afraid that if he flies into Dean in his fit of rage, Dean would wind up bloodier than Buck's tail. I've got a question that I want answered though, Dean. Where did you get that filthy name that you nicknamed Buck?"

I knew not to get smart with Mother, but I also knew I had to shoot straight with my answers.

"Jack Ass ain't a filthy name. It's in the Bible, and Buck is as dumb as Overton's old Jack Ass. That's where I got it."

Finally Dad asked his first question. "I wanna know how Dumb Ass wound up with a bone for a tail?"

"Joe Price, don't you say that filthy name."

I knew I hadn't heard the end of the filthy name business. I could taste lye soap already.

Delton reached into his overall's pocket and brought out a long piece of skin with a switch of grayish brown hair on the end. He held the skin up and shook it so Mother and Dad could get a good look.

"This is what happened. Do you want it?" Delton asked.

I knew that Mother and Dad were dead serious. I also knew that even if Delton could lighten them up, nothing was going to lighten the punishment that they would dish out.

Dad, with resolve in his voice, said, "No ... I don't wanna see Buck's tail skin. I want you to tell me how you got it off of his tail and into your pocket."

"Well, uh ... see, uh"....

Dad interrupted Delton. "Don't hem haw around. Come on out with it, boy."

"Okay ... Dean told me to brace my feet against the window sill and grab Buck's tail and hold him so that he could jump on him. I grabbed his tail, but he was about to jerk loose so I pulled his tail down into that cracked knot hole in the windowsill."

"Did Dean tell you to put Buck's tail in that crack?"

"Uh huh ... and when I did, Buck went bawling-crazy-mad and lunged out of there. Next thing I knew Buck was gone and I had this rawhide Buck skin."

Delton's uh huh sealed my fate. Now the punishment's coming.

"Dean ... you know that Buck was gonna to be a prize winnin' bull. Your mother and me, and all of your friends, are sure gonna be embarrassed for you when you show him in 4-H competition next month at the county fair." Dad hung his head.

Mother added ... "You *are* gonna show him."

Dad's final statement on the subject cut deeper than his razor strop would have. "You're gonna be laughed out of the show. Your prize winnin' bull, with a bone for a tail, ain't gonna win any kind of ribbon."

I spent many a sleepless night worrying, worrying about what I would do when time came for the Mulberry 4-H Club to show their projects at the county fair.

I could leave home.

Old Mother Nature saved the day for me. *Maybe scared prayers do get answered ... if you're serious.*

Buck's tail got infected – screwworms took over – Dad had to cut his tail off.

"There is some kind of rule that says bob-tailed calves, calves that have had to sacrifice their tails, aren't eligible to show," Dad explained.

Boy, I got off easy.

I didn't escape my punishment; I had to show rabbits. *Was I ever wrong about getting off easy.*

In my eyes I was a hunter ... I hunted rabbits. To me, showing a rabbit was more degrading than if I had had to show a bob-tailed calf.

The lye soap ... I've eat it before, and I'll probably have to eat it again.

10
SOME DAY I WILL FLY

Dad and his brothers' gathering up at their home place got to be a regular event. Grandma and Granddad Price looked forward to Sunday evenings; not only they, but Dad and his brothers and their wives and the cousins did, too. Counting Dad and his brothers and their wives, there were 14, and if Alice, their sister, and her husband came, there were 16. Aunt Alice and Uncle Carroll lived in Oklahoma City and didn't get to come home very often. When you added the cousins you had what Grandma called "a herd of offspring."

When anyone asked one of the boys how many kids there were in his family, he would say: "Us boys are one short of a baseball team, and we all have a sister apiece. Now you figure that one out."

The usual answer was ... 16. In reality there were eight boys and one girl, Alice, but they all claimed her as their sister, so that made nine. The Sunday gatherings had their ups and downs, though; not all of them were like family reunions. Grandma dreaded the times when the weather kept them inside because she hated to hear them argue, which they enjoyed almost as much as playing ball.

Dad and his brothers looked forward to the baseball games that broke out in the side yard when the weather permitted.

After everyone finished eating dinner, the men from around the neighborhood would come over and form a "visiting team" to take on the Price team. Oscar and Carnie had a son named Max who was a senior in high school and the baseball team's star pitcher. He was also the pitcher for the Price team. Needless to say, the Price team very rarely lost.

Normally a lot of bragging by the Price team, about last week's win, would get mixed in with the bragging by the neighborhood team of "We're gonna slaughter y'all today." Pretty soon someone would holler, "We'll just see who whips who today," and the game would get underway.

Most of the time there were enough young neighborhood men to have a real two-sided baseball game. In the event, though, not enough young men showed up to form a complete team, they would scrimmage, or the womenfolk would fill in for the neighborhood team.

The baseball field's name, "Our ballfield," got its name from Granddad himself.

It was a grassy area, bounded by the log barn and the cow lot behind the catcher's mound. The county road in front of the house was the boundary of centerfield. Left field was bounded by a fenced-off blackberry patch. Anything that went over the house was in deep right field.

When the sluggers came up to bat, the left fielder would crawl over the fence into the berry patch, in hopes of catching a high fly. The center fielder would run across the road in case a high fly came his way. One time the right fielder from the neighborhood team ran around behind the house in case a high fly came over the house. Sure enough one of the Price boys laid wood into the ball and sent it sailing over the roof. The lucky right fielder ran out from behind the house with the ball in his glove and claimed he had caught it.

A fight erupted.

Everyone decided a new rule might prevent a killing. *After that*, when a high fly went over the house, it was a home run.

~

Arguing became the sport of choice, in the later years. Whether they grew up, or they outgrew playing ball, no one remembers.

Uncle Clarence said – and Dad agreed with him – that as you get older running your mouth becomes much easier than running your legs.

I loved to listen to the grownups argue.

The way their discussions, as they called them, played out *was* while the women folks did up the dishes and cleaned up the kitchen, one of the boys would chose a subject, which was either politics or religion. One thing they agreed on was that there wasn't anything else worth arguing about and they never argued about both at the same time.

Things would get a little scary when they all got mad at each other, which happened almost every Sunday. I feared sometime that a fight would break out.

When they argued about politics, by the time everyone had to go home, the whole bunch would be fighting mad. Before they left to go home they would call a truce and vow, by handshake, never to argue about politics again.

The next Sunday religion would be the focus of their arguing, and the same chain of events would take place. They would end up the day mad, vow never to argue about religion again and shake on it. By the following Sunday the topic would be politics again. That vicious circle never found an end.

A common complaint among the Price womenfolk was that their men would argue that a white fencepost was black and then if it changed to black they would argue that it was white.

The brotherhood of Price boys had a complaint as well.

It didn't pertain to their women, though. It was Uncle Rob's tall tales. Dad called them air castles. Dad wasn't sure if Uncle Rob's tales were tall or just stretched truths. What concerned him was the way I sat and soaked up every word Uncle Rob said.

Uncle Rob and Aunt Kate lived in Dallas, and they only came to Granddad and Grandma Price's once in a while. When they did come home, Uncle Rob brought tales from the big city that were hard to believe.

One Sunday as Uncle Rob started telling one of his tales I was sitting on the wood box behind the pot-belly heater, all ears.

"I guess y'all know they are building skyscrapers in Dallas just as fast as they can build them?"

Uncle Rob let that soak in while he pulled a new pack of Camels out of his starched khaki shirt. He packed the end down on his knee, peeled the top back and took a factory cigarette out of the pack. He lit up and waited to see if someone would bite.

No one said a word.

"I bet y'all don't know what keeps those skyscrapers from falling over?"

Still, no one said a word.

Here we go again, everyone thought.

"They've got this big drill bit that they call an earth auger. With one of those earth augers they can drill a hole in the ground plumb to rock; then they pour the hole full of concrete. That's the kind of foundation the 40-story Republic Bank building has got under it. I watched 'em pour it." He puffed on his camel and blew smoke rings.

That sounds reasonable enough, Dad thought, but he still didn't say anything.

"Now here is what y'all ain't gonna believe. The earth auger drills a hole that's bigger around at the bottom than it is at the top. If the hole is a foot across at the top it may be 4 feet across in the bottom."

That did it.

Uncle Clarence lit in on Uncle Rob. "Why, that's a ridiculous absurdity, Rob. That couldn't possibly be true, and you know it. Don't you know that you have got young ears listening to everything you say?"

Dad motioned for me to come with him, and we left Uncle Rob to his yarns and joined Mother in the kitchen.

"I can't believe Rob tells those tall tales for the truth. He ain't anything but a windbag," Dad told Mother.

When the arguments heated up too much, or in this case, Uncle Rob's tales got too ridiculous, our parents instructed us kids to go outside and play.

We usually went to the branch, out to Granddad's log barn or to the old chicken house that Uncle Earl had converted over to a hay barn to play.

We went to Uncle Earl's hay barn.

One of my favorite things to do was build hideouts in the hay barn. Patsy and I moved bales of hay around and placed them in two parallel rows. Then we stacked bales of hay on top of the rows to create a long tunnel. The tunnel twisted and turned and climbed to different levels in the hay barn until it reached the top of the haystack. At the very top of the stack was Patsy's and my hideout.

Delton and Melba tried their best to crawl through the tunnel and reach the hideout. I waited until they were about halfway up, then I growled and took off down the tunnel to meet them. The growling sounds drifting down the tunnel made Delton and Melba mad enough to fight a hornet and sent them scrambling to get out of the tunnel.

Melba complained, "I'm gonna go tell your mothers that y'all won't let us play with you."

We learned that Melba wasn't going to go tell unless Delton went with her. Delton joined in the complaint, so Patsy and I knew it was getting serious. We changed the game to the mommy and daddy game.

Patsy was the mommy, I was the daddy, and Delton and Melba were our kids. Patsy and I never called them "our kids"; we called them "our mean brats."

Our mean brats were always doing something that mommy or daddy didn't approve of; sassing, disobeying or failing to get their homework all brought severe punishment. Sooner or later – sooner, most often – one of our mean brats wouldn't like their punishment and would threaten to go tell on us.

Patsy and I would have to change games again to keep Delton and Melba from running to the house and telling.

Each time we changed the game, the new game got a little scarier, and after the mommy and daddy game we started playing wild animal games.

Delton and Melba got to be the mommy and daddy, and the hayloft hideout became their cave. Patsy and I hid until Delton and Melba got real scared. When they started crying and threatened to come out of the cave, Patsy and I would turn into wild hyenas and attack the cave. When we overran the cave and attacked the cave-dwellers, things got downright brutal.

That game didn't last long, and before long we would have to switch to another game. By that time our patience with Delton and Melba had worn thin and we switched to the spookhouse game. As the games got more and more scary, it got more and more difficult for Delton and Melba to enjoy, which was our goal from the start.

When we switched to the spookhouse game, it was for one reason only and that was to scare the living daylights out of Delton and Melba so they would go running to the house. Spookhouse games involved goblins, witches, ghosts and black cats, and always sent them running to the house to tell Mother and Aunt Dovie. By that time, Patsy and I could care less.

If we had been at home, the punishment would be "take a nap." Since we were at Grandma and Granddad Price's, "y'all go in the back room and play with Burley and rest awhile" was the punishment.

Burley is the most fun, most perfect uncle anyone could ever have, I thought, and those were the sentiments of all of Burley's nieces and nephews. He was just a big kid himself. He stood 4 feet 10 inches tall, had snow-white hair and stooped shoulders. He was the spitting image of a little bitty Santa Claus; from his fat round belly and his blushed round face to his jelly belly laugh. Burley's laughs came from deep down in his little round belly, and when he laughed his belly squiggled around like Jell-O.

You couldn't help but expect him to holler: "Ho, ho, ho."

It was hard to pin Burley down about why he was so short. He would always laugh his jelly belly laugh and say, "I guess I'm tall enough ... my feet hit the floor." When *and if* you did get him pinned down, you learned that when he was a young boy he was helping roof the house and slid off the roof and broke his back.

"I never grew an inch after that. The fall caused my back to go humped and my feet to drag the ground."

The longer we played with Burley, the rowdier we got. our roughhousing climaxed in: "Okay, you kids let Burley rest awhile. Y'all go outside and play some more."

"I know what, Dean ... why don't you and Patsy build you an airplane in the chinaberry tree? Y'all have been talking about doing it for a long time, and I'll help," Burley suggested.

The big chinaberry tree in Granddad's and Grandma's backyard was a favorite place for Patsy and me to play. We loved to climb, and according to Burley we could climb like monkeys.

Burley got me some tools from Granddad's tool room, out on the back porch, and then went to his room to lie down and rest.

The work got underway.

I climbed up into the tree with Granddad's hammer and a pocketful of assorted nails from his nail can.

I locked my legs around one of the big limbs, and Patsy handed up scrap boards as I nailed them into place. I built a seat for the pilot and a seat directly behind the pilot's seat for the copilot. The seats faced the tree trunk where I planned to build the instrument panel.

"The pilot's gotta have an instrument panel," Delton suggested. "Melba and me will go to the trash dump down on the branch and get some tin can lids."

While they were gone, I placed two long boards across the big limb that held the seats ... the plane had wings.

When Delton and Melba got back, they had their hands full of aircraft instruments. Patsy climbed up and brought them to me. I drove nails through the soda pop caps and a big syrup bucket lid to fasten them to the tree trunk. They served as the airplane's instrument panel. The big syrup bucket lid made a perfect air speed indicator.

Patsy and I took turns flying the airplane.

I was "Snake Reeves" when I was at the controls. Our first cousin, Glen Reeves, was a premiere test pilot for Lockheed Aircraft and had acquired the nickname "Snake Reeves." He was Aunt Alice's and Uncle Carroll's son.

When Patsy was flying the airplane, she was Amelia Earhart. She wouldn't fly long before she would hand the controls back to me and start laughing.

"I don't want to fly it long enough to crash," she would say.

Patsy really liked being the gunner.

Finally Patsy and I had found a way to get away from Delton and Melba. They couldn't climb the chinaberry tree, even if they wanted to. The amazing thing was – that for the time being, anyway – Delton and Melba were happy with that.

Then things changed; for one thing they didn't like Patsy bragging about how much fun we were having.

The real trouble happened when Patsy and I started flying over them and dropping make-believe bombs on top of their heads.

Patsy taunted, "Hey, lookeee there, standing on the ground ... It's the enemy."

"Yep, open the hatch ... bombs away!" I tormented.

Delton and Melba started grabbing sticks and clods of dirt up and throwing them at us until their temper tantrums grew into rages of madness.

The airplane game was Patsy's and my favorite game to play; not so with Delton and Melba.

Burley ended our fun.

He felt sorry for Delton and Melba because they couldn't climb up in the tree and he nailed steps on the trunk for them.

"I'll help them up and see to it that they don't fall," he told Mother, Aunt Dovie and Aunt Helen.

Playing airplane wasn't as much fun after that – passenger planes aren't as much fun to fly as fighter Jets.

Patsy and I started playing another game, a game that Burley didn't like to play that much: crawdad fishing. Burley thought fishing for crawdads was play-like fishing and was for kids only.

We slipped away from Delton and Melba and headed to the smokehouse. We cut a couple of cubes of fat from the pork belly Granddad kept hanging from the rafters. Our plans were to go to Uncle Earl's pool on the other side of the branch. We were crossing the branch when Delton spied us and hollered, "Where are y'all going?"

"We're headed across the branch to Daddy's crawdad pool, and y'all can't come with us," Patsy replied.

"Uh huh," Delton said. "I'll go ask Mother." Delton and Melba ran to the house to get permission.

We crossed the branch and ran as fast as we could toward the pool. We knew that Delton and Melba would get scared after they crossed the branch and would give up long before they made it to the pool.

"I gotta stop here in the shade and rest awhile; my side's hurting," Patsy said when we came to a giant old oak tree on the hillside.

"Let your side rest ... I'll climb up and see if Delton and Melba are coming."

The tree trunk was so big around, the only way I could climb the tree was to start climbing one of the long limbs that hung almost to the ground. When I got up in the tree I was amazed at how big the limb was and how big the tree was that it grew out of.

"Patsy ... come look; there's a perfect airplane up here."

Patsy quickly climbed her way up the drooping limb to the huge limb I was standing on.

"Look. Yonder they come." I pointed toward the house.

Patsy placed her hand over my mouth to put a quietus on me.

"They'll never find us up here," she whispered.

Delton and Melba passed under the tree and continued on to the pool. They never saw Patsy and me. We sat down on the huge limb and planned how to build another airplane while we waited for Delton and Melba to go back to the house.

We could hear Delton hollering from the crawdad pool.

"Dean, Patsy ... where are y'all hiding?"

"Y'all had better come on out. We're gonna go tell on you," Melba hollered.

Leave it up to Delton to think of something, which not only got our attention but brought us down out of that tree pronto.

"Daddy said to tell y'all that you could have them old crawdads. Him, Uncle Earl and Burley are gonna take Melba and me to Red River. We're gonna do some real fishing and some swimming." With that they left the pool and continued to holler at us as they headed back toward the house.

When they passed under our tree they were both bawling and rubbing their tear-filled eyes with dirty hands. It wasn't funny, but it looked like Delton and Melba were crying mud. Patsy and I felt sorry for them; besides that, if we were going to get to go to Red River with them, we were going to have to smooth things over ... and real quick. We bailed out of the tree and ran to catch up with Delton and Melba. By the time we reached them we overheard Delton bragging about how he had pulled the wool over our eyes.

Before the fight could break out, Mother, Dad and Burley came out on the back porch, hollering that it was time to go home. Delton and I set in on Mother to let Burley go home with us.

"Y'all better ask Burley if he wants to go home with us first, and you better talk it over with your dad, too."

Burley did go home with us.

We spent the day Monday gathering fish bait, and that night it commenced raining. We didn't get any fishing done all week; we spent the whole time playing checkers.

Burley was a man of passion, he claimed of himself. He claimed that he had a passion for fishing and playing checkers. Before the week was out, I decided that Burley liked playing checkers even more than he did fishing. He had a worn, tattered book about how to play checkers, and it had become that way from his reading it again and again and again; until he had memorized it.

After supper, every night, Burley took Delton and me on in a game of checkers, and he wasn't going to let us win just because we were little. We would play until one of us lost our patience.

"No one can ever beat you, Burley," Delton complained. Finally we would give up and go to bed.

If Burley wanted to, we could go to the river fishing; it ain't rained that much.

~

Patsy and I worked on our new airplane the next three Sundays in a row. We could have finished it sooner, but we didn't want Burley helping us. We were afraid he might nail steps on the tree for the Delton and Melba.

The new airplane had some of the makings of a real airplane that the old one didn't have. I was especially proud of the long sticks I nailed on each side of the limb that the pilot's seat was sitting on. They controlled the imaginary ailerons; the pilot pulled back on the sticks to go up ... pushed forward to go down.

When the pilot sat down on the pilot's seat he was looking at real instruments. I robbed them from an old car someone had abandoned. The car was coming off the red clay hill by Patsy's house, and the driver ran off the road and crashed in the gulley and just left it.

Just as we finished nailing the last nail in the tree, Mother and Dad hollered that it was time to go home.

"Shucks ... do we have to go now?" I could hardly wait to fly the airplane.

The week dragged by.

Burley kept all the pools in the neighborhood free from snakes and turtles. He went around to the pools with his automatic .22 and shot every snake and turtle he could find. During his ramblings, snake and turtle hunting, he found our new airplane. It amazed him how far from the ground the airplane was. It was at least twice as high as the old chinaberry tree airplane.

That Patsy and Dean, they're hiding from the little ones. I'll fix 'em, he thought. He knew it wouldn't be safe for Delton and Melba to climb up in the oak tree, but he had an idea how they could take part in the fun.

I thought Sunday would never come but it finally did, and everyone gathered for Sunday dinner just like usual. As soon as dinner was over, Patsy and I slipped out the back door and took off for our new oak tree airplane.

Flying the new and improved oak tree airplane proved much more fun than flying the old chinaberry tree airplane.

Then Burley showed up with Delton and Melba.

"I'm determined to help the little ones join in the fun. Maybe they can throw stuff at y'all and you can play like they are shooting at you," Burley said.

"Why hadn't we thought of that?" Patsy said. "Let the fun begin."

Burley helped Delton and Melba throw sticks and clods of dirt up at us in the tree.

Happy with himself, he went to the pool to shoot snakes and turtles and left the throwing to Delton and Melba.

Delton soon found out that he couldn't throw nearly as high as the airplane, and he got mad. The harder he tried, the madder he got. With every throw, his temper boiled higher and higher.

Delton's tears were streaming down his cheeks, and he picked up a long stick and swatted the air in his attempts to throw it. In his blind, stumbling madness, he lost his balance and went to his knees. I saw the fury in his eyes.

His stick went into an almost dry cow patty.

When Delton regained his legs he was no longer mad; he was in a horrendous rage. He slung the stick with all his might – in my general direction – in an attempt to dislodge the ripe cow patty.

It left the stick with whirring speed. Splat ... it stuck ... right underneath the airplane.

The face that Patsy made when she grabbed her nose erased Delton's tears – they turned to laughter.

Delton quickly realized the predicament he had us in.

He rustled around and found Melba a stick and showed her how to load it ... and sling it. They both were firing cow patties as fast as they could reload.

Delton screamed as he flung another cow patty, "I will fly someday, and I won't take y'all with me."

The whizzing cow patties were getting closer and closer with every swing Delton and Melba made. Delton loaded up again and screamed as he let go.

"Someday I'll fly, and it'll be a real airplane, just you wait and see."

Patsy added coals to the fire with her taunting. I maneuvered the control sticks back and forth.

Patsy talked on the radio: "We're in a steep climb, 10, 15, 20 thousand feet. Cut her to the left; we're dodging enemy fire. Come in, base ... come in, base."

As far as Patsy and I were concerned, we were in a pretend battle. However, for Delton and Melba, the battle was real; they were flinging the cow patties closer and closer, and they were real, and they slung with every ounce of might they could muster.

"Ha, ha, you missed," I chanted as a ripe patty whizzed by my head.

My taunting gave Delton the power he needed ... he swung with everything he had.

Delton watched his patty sail ... watched Patsy's face disappear behind it.

CURR SPLAT.

Delton's tears quickly turned to laughter when he heard Patsy's announcement on the airplane's radio.

"We've been hit ... the copilot has taken a direct hit to the face ... OVER ...." She took time out to gag and then continued ... "OVER and OUT!"

Melba's patty landed in my lap, and the battle came to an abrupt end.

Patsy and I ran down the long limb and to the stock tank and dove in. The muddy water was green with scum, but it tasted better than the cow patty Patsy claimed.

Delton went on to become an Air Force Pilot. He did fly real airplanes and eventually flew the giant C-5.

I thought about him a lot when he was flying those big C-5s in Vietnam and wondered if in the seriousness of it all, he ever thought about the cow patty incident.

Delton took me flying in a real airplane only once, and as far as I know he has never taken Patsy.

11
BOOM TO BUST

The 1940s brought good times to the Price farm and to other farms in Mulberry as well.

"The Dust Bowl Days," or the "Dirty Thirties," as some farmers had called them, were behind us, gone and forgotten.

Cotton farmers were enjoying their "heyday" in Mulberry. Long staple cotton (the kind you picked) grew taller than a man's head in the rich fertile soil of Mulberry and sometimes made as much as a bale per acre. Cotton farmers' overall breast pockets were bulging; that's where they carried their pocketbooks. They still didn't put much trust in the banking system and liked to keep their money close to their heart. Almost everyone who lived in Mulberry claimed that things were just "hunky-dory." Things *were,* except for the bedbug problem, and they were horrendous.

The boll weevil epidemic of the Texas coastal plains hadn't spread north. There were a few boll weevils in Mulberry, but what few there were, Dad and the other cotton farmers controlled them by spraying with calcium arsenate.

However, there were bad omens on the air. Dad and all the Mulberry farmers were worried. Government reports were that the boll weevils were marching north. They were coming.

More pressing than the approaching boll weevils were the bedbugs. What to do about bedbugs was a main concern. Calcium arsenate was too dangerous to use in the bed.

"What are we gonna do?" became the cry of everyone in Mulberry.

If the '30s were the dirty '30s, then this is the buggy '40s, Dad thought.

There hadn't been any improvements in getting the bedbugs out of our beds, or anyone else's bed for that matter, since 1943. *The American Journal of Nursing* published an article that year devoted to the control of bedbugs. They had sanctioned the use of a mixture of crude oil and creosote, or powdered unslaked lime and kerosene. That was the only thing they knew to use. The stinky solution helped control bed bugs; however, it didn't do much to eliminate them.

"Well ... calcium arsenate will outright kill us ... bed bugs will suck us to death, and what they recommend doing will stink us to death," Dad complained.

The government declared a bed bug epidemic. "Sleep tight and don't let the bed bugs bite" became the national slogan of country folks. By the time everyone in Mulberry got their bed swabbed down, here came the boll weevils.

The warning came from the County Agent. "Boll weevils have developed a tolerance to calcium arsenate, and now they are marching toward Mulberry from the coastal plains of Texas," he said.

When Dad got home from the meeting, he broke the news to Mother. "By 1949 those boll weevils down south got so tough that arsenic wouldn't kill 'em anymore. Now they're on their way here. We're supposed to get something called DDT, though, and we can use it in the house to kill bedbugs, too."

"Well, I ain't worried about the boll weevils coming. Those chemical companies will come up with something. What I wanta know is when can we get some of that DDT to kill the bedbugs? They are sucking my babies to death ... and us, too." Mother was desperate.

Dad's cotton crop in 1950 had a rain at the right time, just before it bloomed, and it hadn't got any hail on it. It was beautiful and in full bloom ... a virtual 50-acre garden. Then the boll weevils arrived. They infested every cotton field in Mulberry. Every square and cotton bloom had a weevil in it; which meant that every cotton boll was going to have a bollworm.

DDT came but not in time to save the 1950 crop; the boll worms were already in the bolls, out of reach of the DDT.

Mulberry's air turned rancid with the smell of DDT. Dad hated the awful smell.

By the next year the farmers were depending on DDT.

"We have to use DDT or we can't make a cotton crop. Makin' cotton ain't the only good that's come from it, though. There ain't a bed bug left in all of Mulberry; so I reckon I can put up with the smell," Dad said.

Mother agreed. "Yeah, me too, even though it stinks worse than creosote or kerosene. I'd rather smell it than to have bed bugs in the covers."

Dad put up with "the stinky stuff' until one day in 1951 when he came home from the cotton patch disgusted.

"There ain't anything alive in my cotton patch," he told Mother. "Why, I even found some dead quail and the grasshoppers are dead by the millions. I'm afraid me and the boys will be next."

Dad and a few of the other cotton farmers got together and invited the County Agent to join them. In the meeting they decided that enough was enough ... no more DDT. The County Agent came up with a plan: import some natural enemies for Mr. Boll Weevil.

It was working other places; it might work in Mulberry, George Warren thought.

Gallon upon gallon of insects (lady bugs and praying mantises) were turned loose in the cotton fields but to no avail. When harvest time came, it seemed that every cotton boll was shriveled and hard and failed to open.

They all had little round holes in them where the cotton bore had entered the boll.

That fall, cotton prices went above a dollar a pound; more than $500 a bale. *But* it was just like Dad said: "A bunch of money for cotton, if you ain't got any, don't pay the light bill."

Dad, George and Audry switched crops. They all planted peanuts in the spring of 1952.

The soil was new for peanuts, the rains came on the right schedule and everyone's peanut vines turned to nuts. Dad made over a 100 bushels of peanuts per acre. There weren't that many peanuts around the country, and prices at harvest time were extremely high.

Dad's, George's and Audrey's pocketbooks bulged again; this time they went to the bank with it.

The next year everyone planted peanuts and flooded the market.

"That's the way it is with farmin' ... farming's a boom or bust business," Dad said.

The government announced that they were going to tell the farmers how many peanuts they could plant, to help stabilize the prices. They issued a "peanut allotment" to each farm based on its past production or potential to produce.

The farmers' complaints were all the same.

"Yep, leave it up to the government to get their hands into our profits," George said. It wasn't long before the government started letting farmers buy and sell their peanut allotments to other farmers. It got to where a person could make more money buying and selling peanut allotments than he could planting peanuts.

Dad wasn't a person who enjoyed the government having that much control over how much of anything he could plant or selling the right to plant something he didn't want to plant.

He sold his allotment "for now and forever" to Audry Cain.

~

Carl and John Baker came to Mulberry in the fall of 1952 and bought the Copeland place. The two brothers came from west Texas and brought new blood and new ideas to Mulberry. John moved into the Copeland house, and Carl returned to west Texas to set things in order to make the move to Mulberry.

By the fall of 1953 John had bought another Mulberry farm and moved out of the Copeland house. Carl, Nickie, Kenneth and Johnny moved into their new home.

The "Copeland house" soon became "the Baker Place."

Carl dreamed of starting a dairy, and there was plenty of Red River water for the dairy cows to drink and plenty of lush pasture in the river bottom, even during the severe drought, which had Mulberry in its grip. Carl knew if his dairy herd was going to give down lots of milk, the cows would need a good high protein supplement. He knew corn silage was the best there was; however, to raise corn during the drought he needed to irrigate it.

Most of the Mulberry farmers were up again hard times.

When they had the money to dig irrigation wells, they didn't know they weren't going to have any rain. Now that farmers were out of rain *and* out of money, they couldn't borrow a penny to drill irrigation wells. Irrigation wells, which may or may not provide enough water to irrigate a peanut crop – when it might rain anyway – weren't on any banker's list of things that they wanted to invest in.

One family gave up hope and sold out; some thought there would be other families to follow.

The Baker brothers had brought enough money with them from their west Texas farming operation to get Bonham's bankers to sit up and pay attention. Financing wasn't going to be a problem, and Carl knew what he needed.

The face of Mulberry was about to change, but it wouldn't be because of families moving out. It was because of a new family, the Bakers, that moved in and the new ideas they brought.

Carl Baker dug the first irrigation well ever dug in Mulberry, and when it came in it was a gusher. It was plain to see that there was enough water to irrigate 50 acres of corn. A canal dug across the end of the corn patch supplied each row with enough water to flood the whole field.

There wasn't a need to conserve water or the energy needed to pump the water out of the ground. There was plenty water in the ground, and there was plenty gasoline to run the pumps and get the water up out of the ground.

Carl was in a quandary; which would be cheaper ... a gasoline engine or an electric motor to run the pumps on the well.

Electricity was a pretty good choice, Carl thought. The REA could hardly give their electricity away. They had to make a lot of it, and about the only thing farmers used it for was the lights. *On the other hand, gasoline was five gallons for a dollar.*

Carl planted the corn thick in the row and the rows close together and poured the fertilizer to it. His irrigated corn would have made well over 100 bushels per acre, had he not cut it for silage. Dry land corn did good to make 20 to 30 bushels per acre when there was plenty rain and during this severe drought ... zilch...zero.

All the farmers in Mulberry knew now that the solution to their dilemma lay in digging irrigation wells. The farmers saw the light, and the money lenders did, too.

Yeah ... Mulberry was changing.

Little sheds with irrigation pumps in them sprang up all over the landscape. Mulberry was proving to be a dairyman's dream come true. Dairy barns were almost as thick as irrigation wells.

The plentiful waters of Red River played a big part in saving the farmers of the Red River valley from extinction.

~

Dad never saw his way back into row cropping. Gardening and truck cropping captured his heart although his garden was suffering ... from lack of water.

Ol' Mother Nature is puttin' the screws to me. It's just so hard to raise vegetables in the scorchin' heat without water. Raising something to eat is the key ... everybody's gotta eat," Dad told Mother.

So it was that I questioned Dad's motives when we struck out to cut fencepost at the bois d'arc thicket that grew on our river pasture.

"How is it that people are gonna eat bois d'arc fencepost?" I asked.

"You watch me trade 'em to Weldon up at the Grocery Store for beans, flour, sugar and maybe a stick of bologna and then ask me that." Dad had a way of making me feel so small.

I knew that Dad was scraping the barrel to keep us fed. I was sorry I had asked that sly question. I promised myself that I would never question Dad's motives again.

I thought about something Dad had told me, another time, when I had said something I regretted. "Words that you're sorry you said are like food. Once you've spat it out and looked it over ... you can't stand to put it back in your mouth and eat it. Words are even harder to eat after you've looked 'em over."

Dad planted his cultivating land – all 50 acres of it – to watermelons. Year after year they continued being the breadwinner.

Dad held his breath and joked with Mother about being afraid the government would find out about watermelons being a good crop. "If they do, they're liable to regulate the profit out of 'em ... on second thought, if they do that I'll just sell somebody else the right to not make a profit on 'em," he'd say.

After the last big truck left in the fall, Dad would buy a bunch of shoats and turn them loose in the watermelon patch to eat the leftovers. The shoats would fatten in a hurry, and he would rush the bloated pigs off to market as soon as they ate the last watermelon. He could count on them to pay the operating loan and the land payments that came due every fall.

By 1954, Dad had worn the soil out for raising melons, and it was bust again. He would never admit that he wore the soil out; he blamed the bust on the drought.

~

The winter of 1954 broke the drought. The drought years of '52, '53 and '54 were gone and now the farmers faced severe flooding. During the winter of 1954 rain happened almost every day, and Dad had a saying for that, too:

"When it rains, we either get too much or too little."

Rains continued during the spring of 1955, and the farmers couldn't get their crops planted.

Things were getting serious, unless you were a rice farmer and there weren't any of those in Mulberry. By July the rains had stopped, and it never rained another drop the rest of the summer nor in that fall or winter. There wasn't enough moisture in the ground to sprout seeds when planting time came in 1956.

"In fact they might even blow away with the sand storms," Dad said.

By the time planting time came, many of the farmers had their backs against the wall. The farmers who didn't had their backs against the bank. Bankers were getting skittish about pouring more money into the farmers' operations; unless rains came ... which they didn't.

Dad was one of those farmers whose back was against the wall. His faith in the fact that people had to eat would bring him through the trying times, though.

"Before I had a farm there was Red River, and back then we made good with our garden and our trappin' and fishing. I'll be dad-gum if I'm gonna let Mother Nature do me in," Dad told Mother.

~

Each year the drought worsened until Dad's truck cropping was on the brink of extinction.

I finally came to the rescue and pulled Dad's truck cropping operation from bust to boom.

It was my first year of high school, and I took FFA like all my other country buddies. The first period of FFA was classroom studies, and the second period was shop work. I had to have a project, and I had never followed the trend of the crowd. I was looking for something different to build, not a hog trough and definitely not a pasture gate.

Why not build Dad a sand point so we can irrigate the truck patch.

I mentioned it to Dad, and he thought my idea would work, so he encouraged me to talk it over with the Ag Shop teacher.

Come Monday I didn't hesitate. I walked right into the Ag class and asked Mr. Taylor, the teacher, if building a sand point would be an acceptable project. He looked puzzled and said we would talk about it after class.

After class Mr. Taylor approached me.

"Now let's hear about this sand point project."

"Well ... Dad can't afford to have an irrigation well dug and then buy one of them expensive irrigation pumps. What I plan to do is get a 6-inch iron pipe and some brass screen wire and build him a sand point. We're gonna dig a hole, by hand, until we hit water and then drive my sand point down in the water sand. Down under the bluff, where our truck patch is, the water can't be more than about 10 feet deep. Centrifugal pumps are pretty cheap and they can lift water 10 feet. I wanta make us an irrigation system out of cheap garden hose and lawn sprinklers."

"If you think you could have a little tomato patch for a project and keep real good records on it, you've got yourself a deal ... I think it'll work." Mr. Taylor patted me on the back and sent me on my way.

Dad gathered up the materials. He got a piece of 6-inch well casing from the irrigation well driller (a piece of scrap that he had leftover) and ordered two pieces of brass sand screen from Smith Moore Williams hardware (one coarse and one fine.)

I went to work, and before school was out in June I had the sand point finished. It was crude but looked like it would work.

As soon as school turned out Dad and me, with Delton's help, dug a hole in the Mulberry sand until we hit water, after which we drove the sand point down into the watery sand.

"Well, just look what we went and did. We went and made our own irrigation well," Dad said after we finished.

The centrifugal pump that Dad bought didn't have enough suction to lift water from 10 feet down in the ground. Dad always had a solution and this was no exception; we dug a big hole, lined it with boards and put the pump closer to the water.

Dad jerked on the starter rope and fired off the little pump.

Water came gushing ... a full 2-inch stream.

"It works!" Dad screamed.

Two whole acres went under irrigation.

"The system," as Dad called it, was a crudely constructed mess made out of garden hoses and lawn sprinklers. Dad was proud of "the system," and when the last set was finished watering, he was ready to start all over again.

He poured on the commercial fertilizer (10-20-10) and used lots of chicken manure. The combination of plenty of water and a lot of fertilizer kept him busy pulling weeds and hoeing. Dad's okra got taller than his head. The climbing butter beans formed a solid wall 10 feet tall, and he was going to need a ladder to gather the roasting ears from the sweet corn.

Records kept on my 10th acre of tomatoes, my FFA project, showed that I sold over $1,000 worth. Every time the subject about my irrigated patch of tomatoes came up, Dad would pitch his two bits' worth in: "And we sold them for 10 cents a pound."

To Dad irrigation had proven its worth.

The irrigation system kept us from losing the farm, kept us in something to eat and made the payments on the new truck we bought to haul our produce to market.

The drought continued to hold Mulberry in a death grip; it wasn't broken until the twin flood years of 1958 and 1959.

"Truck farmin' is just a get-by living. I'm gonna start fishing again to help make ends meet," Dad announced.

Red River fishing had captured Dad's heart again, and he was forever lost to nature's ways. He placed his trust in Red River to give us more than just a get-by living.

Dad came down the lane from Red River with the biggest grin I can ever remember seeing on his face.

He stopped at the water hydrant, rolled down his overall legs and washed the river sand out of the creases before he came up onto the back porch.

"I have found an opportunity to make me a fortune from Red River," he announced.

Mother was leery. She knew, though, if she didn't ask, she was going to hear anyway.

"What opportunity have you found ... now?"

"Well, this much I can tell you ... it's legal. Just as sure as you and I are standing here, though, as soon as the government finds out I'm making a fortune, they'll illegalize it or regulate it to death."

12
RED RIVER TO THE RESCUE

"I'll tell you all about how Red River is gonna make us rich while we eat supper. I'm so hungry, my stomach thinks my throat's been cut," Dad told Mother as we settled around the table.

"Well, you're always thinking Red River is gonna rescue us from the poor house, and I'm always willing to listen to you ... tell me all about it." If Mother was excited, she wasn't showing it.

"When I went to run my trotlines this morning, I got to noticing how many minnows there were in the water along the sandbar. They were there by the millions. They were so many of 'em that as I walked along they would scare each other out onto dry land. They were big, nice, river chubs, the kind any fisherman would be proud to put on a hook. All I gotta do is figure out a way to build a net small enough to catch 'em. I think I figured that part out on the way home."

"Catching 'em sounds easy enough to me ... I guess. What are you gonna do with them after you catch 'em?" Mother said as she passed Dad his third helping of beans.

"Well, that's not gonna be a problem. The gettin' rid of 'em is what's gonna make us rich. Lake Texoma is in its prime right now as a fishing lake. I've heard stories of people catching two and three sand bass on one minnow. Those rich city fishermen ain't gonna seine their own minnows; they're buying them from somewhere. The way I have it figured out, wherever the fishermen are buying their minnows ... that place will buy them from me."

Mother wasn't convinced. Dad's get-rich schemes came and went like bad storms. "Well ... I just pray you aren't on another one of your wild goose chases, Joe ... or should I say, wild minnow chases."

After all the talk about minnows ended, Dad took a couple of empty quart mason jars off the cabinet and went to the smokehouse. He left Mother scratching her head.

Over in the corner of the smokehouse by Dad's workbench lay one of our window screens that Dad had promised Mother he would repair as soon as he got enough money to buy some new screen wire.

Dad knew how to cut material for a teepee, so he measured around the jar with a piece of net twine, then cut out a round piece of screen wire that was the same diameter as the length of the string. Then he cut the circle exactly in half. Presto, he had two screen wire tepees for his mason jars. When he put them into the jars they weren't exactly the shape he wanted, but with a little trimming they soon fit the jars. He cut the tips off the tepees and put them in the jars and bent the excess wire down around the outside. Lastly he screwed the rings onto the jars over the screen wire and tied short strings around their necks.

Dad held his completed minnow trap up to the light and admired it for a long time. The screen wire throats looked pretty good. *They have gotta work; they can't help it,* he thought.

Dad put the minnow traps in a metal bucket and set it in the doorway of the smokehouse. He went to the house whistling his usual, happy tune.

The next morning – before daylight and without breakfast – Dad made a sashay through the kitchen and filled his overall pockets full of cornmeal. He went to the smokehouse and picked up his bucket full of minnow traps and left to go to Red River.

Sometime after noon Mother heard Dad. Lee Price was with him, and they were both whistling. They hopped up on the back porch, grinning from ear to ear.

Mother met them at the kitchen door. "Well, how'd your minnow trapping experiment go?" She was anxious, and before Dad could answer she continued. "Well, tell me all about it. Could you get them little minnows to go into your fruit jars, after that cornmeal?"

"Don't you know it," Dad said. "Why, they would fill those fruit jars full so fast, they would commence dying from lack of oxygen. It wasn't any time until we had so many that they were dying in the bucket. We spread them out real nice on the dry hot sand and made jerky minnows for my trotlines."

"We are gonna have to do some figuring, though, about how to keep 'em alive until we can sell 'em. Lee here is gonna be my partner."

Lee was Uncle Frank's and Aunt Edna's oldest son, Dad's nephew. He and his wife Jeannine had moved back from Dallas and had settled in Mulberry on the Warren place. Jobs were scarce as hen's teeth, and Lee felt honored to go into the minnow trapping business with Dad.

The rest of the afternoon they schemed together about how they could find a market for their Red River minnows. They decided to go to Lake Texoma the next morning and see if they could find a bait shop that would buy them. Before daylight Lee cranked his old car and came to pick Dad up. They headed out to Lake Texoma with intentions of checking to see if any of the bait stands around the dam were in the market to buy minnows.

"We ain't gonna take the first offer that comes our way," Dad told Lee.

They made all the bait shops around the Lake Texoma dam and didn't have much luck.

They took their egg sandwiches and went below the dam and sat on the bank of Red River and ate dinner. Several fishermen had gathered there, so Dad and Lee started to question them as to where the best place to buy minnows was. One fisherman told them just what they wanted to know.

"The best place on Texoma to buy your minnows is Dub's bait shop at Gordonville ... that is if he's got 'em. He's out a lot of the time. When he can get 'em, he has Red River chubs, and they're the best there is for sand bass."

Dad and Lee left in high gear.

"Did you hear that?" Dad asked. "That fisherman said, 'When Dub's got 'em'; thanks to you and me, Lee ... that is anytime he wants 'em."

"Yep ... if the price is right," Lee added.

When they arrived at Dub's Bait Shop, they were greeted by a women behind the counter. She said Dub was out back in the bait shed with a customer and for them to go on back. She pointed toward a door in the back of the shop. The sign over the door read "Bait Shed" and had an arrow pointing straight up.

Dad laughed. *I guess the bait shed's in heaven.*

A tall, heavyset man greeted them when they walked under the shed.

"Look around ... I'll be with you shortly."

His voice was mellow and friendly, but to the point. He was standing over a concrete vat marked TROTLINE CARP, with a dipnet full of flouncing little fish. He never looked up from his counting.

Dad found the sign over one of the empty concrete vats encouraging. The sign read RED RIVER CHUBS. Dub had marked through the letters and under them scribbled OUT.

Dub finished counting out the fisherman's carp, put them in a plastic bag, shot some oxygen in on them and then sent the man to pay for them.

"What can I do for you salesmen?" he asked.

"First off, we ain't salesmen ... we're fishermen," Dad countered.

Dub chuckled with a jolly laugh. "Funny, I ain't ever seen me a fisherman in a khaki suit."

"Well we come off of Red River and cleaned ourselves up, so we could come sell you our Red River Chubs." Dad had Dub's full attention.

"Red River Chubs, you say! What might your names be?"

"I'm Joe, and he's Lee."

"Well, Joe ... I'll give you boys five dollars a thousand and guarantee you I'll take all you can catch if you'll grade 'em for me."

"Five dollars a thousand, hunh ... I guess that sounds fair enough," Dad thought for a moment then added, "if you don't 'spect us to count 'em."

"What do you mean by grade 'em?" Lee asked.

"Come on, follow me, boys." While they walked to a rickety shop down by Dub's house they made small talk about sand bass fishing.

When they got to Dub's shop, he reached up overhead and retrieved a number three washtub from the rafters. It had a truck inner tube stretched around its top so it would float. Dub had cut slots in the side of the tub and he started explaining minnow grading to Lee.

"When you dump your minnows in this tub, the ones that are too little can go back to Red River, through these slots, and grow up. What's left will be fish bait. The silver sides or ghost minnows – that don't get out – we won't worry about them unless they get to be too many. Here put this grading tub in the back of your car," Dub instructed as he handed it to Lee.

"Now, Joe, as far as counting them: When I come to get them, I'll weigh out a pound of minnows and then count them. That way we'll know how many minnows there are in a pound. From then on, we'll know how many thousand minnows you have by how many pounds you have."

By then Dad and Dub were getting pretty well acquainted, enough so that Dad joked about who was going to furnish air for the inner tube.

They shook hands on the deal, and Dub promised, "I'll come every Friday morning and buy ever Red River chub you can catch."

Dad and Lee didn't waste any more time; they had lots of work to do before the next Friday rolled around. They were both whistling a tune as they climbed into Lee's car and "lit a shuck" for Mulberry. "Lit a shuck" was an expression Dad used a lot to indicate that he was going someplace in a hurry.

When Dad and Lee got home, they began in earnest to build screen wire throats and put them in wide-mouth, quart mason jars. Neither Dad nor Lee called them minnow traps anymore, after they heard Dub call them minnow jugs. When anyone asked either of them what they did for a living they would answer, "We're Minnow Juggers."

Joe and Lee had only jugged minnows two days, Wednesday and Thursday, when that first Friday came. They had a considerable amount of minnows in the tub, they thought maybe five thousand. Lee couldn't resist stirring his hand around in the tub and feeling the minnows to see how many they had.

They made one more run of the jugs after dinner and then took them up. They wanted to be at the minnow tub when Dub came.

Unbeknownst to Dad and Lee, a water snake had been eyeballing the minnows in the tub. He had decided that it was dinnertime, too, and crawled over into the tub. The snake ate more at his dinner than Dad and Lee had at theirs, and when he finished eating his sides bulged so much that he couldn't wriggle over the side of the tub.

Who cares anyway? the snake thought.

Dub showed up at our house pretty soon after dinner anxious to know about Dad's and Lee's minnow catching. "Did they have any luck? Do they have many? Did they catch some?"

"Tolerable," Mother said. She was shy when it came to talking to strangers, and her one word answer left him knowing very little more than before he asked.

Dub didn't ask any more questions.

Mother and Jeannine went with Dub to the river to show him where Dad and Lee were.

As they drove down the pasture lane that led to Red River, Dub thought, *What kind of answer is tolerable?*

Dub drove a brand spanking new Chevy pickup; he had put big water tanks in the bed of it with 12-volt agitators on them to keep the minnows alive. He parked his minnow truck at the edge of the high sand bar, and they walked the rest of the way to the river. When they arrived, the usual greetings were exchanged. Then Dub spied the minnow tub. "I see y'all keep the minnow tub tied to a snag out in swift water so the minnows will have plenty of good fresh water; that's good."

"Had to," Dad answered "They kept trying to die."

"That many ... huh?" Dub sounded surprised.

Lee wadded out, untied the tub and waded back toward the bank with it. Dad stood in the edge of the water ready to hold the minnow tub when Lee handed it to him.

Mother, Dub and Jeannine walked up to the edge of the water and were peering over into the tub. The water was black there were so many minnows in the tub.

Lee bent over and rammed his hand down in the washtub.

He swirled his hand around and around and then lifted it up to the top in order to bring up some minnows for Dub to see.

The snake came to the top, his white belly shining in the sunlight.

Jeannine screamed – Mother froze – Dub's teeth rattled.

Lee flung the snake in their direction.

It plopped down on the sand where Dub's feet had been.

When Dub finally came down, the snake was gone, and everyone laughed until their sides ached. The laughing died down somewhat, and Dub made a suggestion.

"Joe, you're gonna have to make a lid for that tub to keep the snakes from eating up your profit."

"And to keep you from having a heart attack," Jeannine added.

The best surprise was yet to come.

Everyone carried five-gallon buckets filled with water and minnows across the hot sandbar to Dub's minnow truck. Dub climbed up in the bed and weighed out a pound of minnows, then poured them into a dipnet and started picking them out and counting. As he counted he dropped them into the vat with the whizzing agitators. When he finished he told Dad and Lee what their count was; to their surprise they had caught 10 thousand and that in two days.

Dub climbed down out of the pickup and counted out 10 crisp $5 bills.

Dad winked at Dub and told him, "Hand the money to Sybil. She's our bookkeeper."

That much money took Mother's breath away and when she handed Jeannine Lee's share of the money Jeannine lost her breath, too. Mother peeled a $5 bill off and stuck it in her apron pocket and handed Dad the other four. "Don't look at me that way; the Lord's gotta get his part first."

"We really oughta pay the light bill and the grocery bill ... kinda get caught up first ... and then we can start giving the Lord his part."

"Joe Price! They can wait. The Lord can't."

Farm workers were earning 50 cents an hour. Dad had been earning $27.50 a week if he worked sunup till sundown and until noon on Saturday. So the $50 for only two days work came as a gigantic surprise.

Mother's faith grew. Dad had never earned that much money in such a short time in all his life.

And just think ... I get to work on Red River, Dad thought.

Dad and Lee spent Saturday building more minnow jugs and going to Doggett's Grocery in Ravenna. Dad paid some on the grocery bill and bought a bag of Purina Dog Chow for minnow bait. They were all fired up; minnow jugging was all either of them could talk about. They were apprehensive about Monday; they knew the river would be very low, and they wondered how that would affect the minnows.

Were they in for a surprise.

Every morning, Monday through Friday, the U.S. Army Corps of Engineers opened the gates and let water flow through the generators at the power plant on Lake Texoma. The power plant generated electricity all day and then closed the plant come 5 o'clock. They followed that schedule all week, and on Sunday the power plant shut down. The on and off schedule of the power plant caused a great fluctuation in the water level in Red River. When the plant shut down for a whole day, the water level in Red River fell like a rock. The Red River sandbar where they jugged minnows was around a 100 miles, as the river ran, from the Lake Texoma Dam, and that meant it was Monday before low water reached their sandbar.

When they arrived at Red River on Monday morning, their empty minnow tub was setting on dry sand.

"It looks like the bottom has dropped out of the river. She is running low and slow," Dad observed.

Lee dragged the minnow tub farther out in the river and tied it to another snag; then they both left to go set their minnow jugs.

Dad started at the head of the sandbar, just down river from the minnow tub, with four buckets full of minnow jugs. He waded out until the water was just below his knees then turned and waded downstream. When he came to the first little ripple in the sand, he took a jug and put a pinch of dog food inside and unwound the string from the jug's neck. He wiggled the jug down in the dark sand below the ripple so the minnows would have a level run through the throat. He stepped back and watched the string with the stick-bobber float slowly downstream. He waded about 25 yards and repeated the process.

Lee took four buckets full of jugs and went to the tail end of the sandbar and set jugs back upstream toward Dad.

When they met in the middle, they took their time walking to the tail end of the sandbar. As they walked along, Dad noticed he kept seeing silver flashes in the jugs as they passed them.

By the time they got to the end, where Lee had started setting his jugs, the minnow jugs were cram-packed full. They didn't even take time to roll a cigarette. They started emptying and resetting the jugs. When Dad picked up the one by the minnow tub it was so full of minnows, they were beginning to get sick from lack of oxygen.

Lee raised the lid up on the minnow tub and emptied their buckets of minnows into the tub. As they walked back to the tail end of the bar they rolled cigarettes. They had only gotten a few puffs by the time they got to the jug at the other end of the sandbar. The minnows had packed themselves into the jug so tight they were starting to die. Dad and Lee threw down their smokes and ran the jugs again.

There was no time to eat dinner, and that was the last chance they had to smoke.

Finally late in the evening the river began to rise and the minnows quit running. Dad and Lee took up their minnow jugs and went to the house.

Mother and Jeannine met them as they dragged themselves up on the back porch.

"We can tell y'all didn't do any good from the washed-out look on your faces," Mother said.

After the kind of day that they had had, that kinda rubbed Dad the wrong way.

The excitement returned to Dad's face. "All day long, those minnows kept stuffing themselves in the jugs like there was a tornado after 'em."

"Yeah," Lee agreed. "We didn't get time to smoke but one cigarette all day long – our 'drenaline kept us going."

"We ain't had dinner either," Dad added.

"Well, your 'drenaline might have kept you going, but you're dragging now. Y'all come on in. Jeannine and I've got your supper ready for you."

"Too tired," they both said as they blew air and slumped down on the porch steps. It didn't take them long to get un-tired when the smell of fried taters come wafting through the screen door.

After supper they got in Lee's car and went up to Alley Hall's house and borrowed his phone to call Dub.

"You're gonna have to come pick up our minnows. We can't keep anymore in that tub without 'em dying. And bring us another tub," Dad instructed.

Early the next morning Dub showed up, and after he weighed and counted all the minnows, the tally came to 25 thousand.

Dub changed the day he would pick up their minnows from Friday to Tuesday and he brought them another grading tub so they would have two for Monday's big run.

Dad could never figure out exactly why Mondays were better than any other day. He thought the low water put the minnows on a feeding frenzy. Lee thought it had something to do with the minnows not having as much water to hide in; they went into the jugs to get away from the falling water.

~

Dad had taken control of the situation. Red River had come to his rescue once more. He became the "Minnow Man" to Mulberry folks and to Dub. For the next four years, armed with over 100 minnow jugs, Dad followed his dream of being able to make a living from Red River. Making a living from Red River fast became Lee's dream, too.

For the next four years, too, Delton and I followed the "Minnow Men."

We spent our summers on the river with Dad and Lee and developed a passion for fighting black wasps. We had a trail cut through the dogwood and willow thickets that wound around and passed every black wasp nest in the area. A daily regimen for us was to take off running down the trail and shake the bushes that the wasps' nests were in. We ran like the devil was after us. We had the black wasps so aggravated that they couldn't even stand each other. It got to the point where the slightest movement along the trail brought a horde of angry wasps to attack whatever happened along.

Dad and Lee got aggravated, having to put up with angry wasps every time they needed to go to the bushes.

We made a shield out of a piece of corrugated sheet iron that had blown off some farmer's barn and landed on the sandbar. We hid behind the shield and approached a wasps' nest with our fighting paddles ready. A horde of angry wasps flew from the nest in a beeline and popped the tin shield. The tat, tat, tat was letting up, and I made the mistake of peeking around our shield.

I spent the rest of the day lying around camp, nursing two swollen eyes and a swollen forehead. The next day was Tuesday, the day Dub came to pick up the minnows, and my head looked like I'd been kicked by a mule.

"What happened to you, Dean?" Dub asked as he cringed.

"Oh, I stuck my head out from behind my shield, and a big black wasp popped me twix the eyes."

"Those boys are aggravatin' us to death fightin' black wasps ... can't even go to the bushes without getting stung."

"You ought to put 'em to work ... I could use some more minnows. Dean's big enough to operate a boat motor. I've got one I'll give you, and you can rig your boat up and send them down the river to that next sandbar. You'd get 'em outta your hair and they could make some money."

"Sounds like a winner to me," Dad said.

Dad put sideboards on the boat, mounted the Johnson motor Dub gave him and sent us down the river to find our own sandbar. We did make some money, but mostly it just got us out of their hair.

After four years, Dad and Lee were about ready to give up the minnow business. They were only catching a fraction of what they used to catch, and they couldn't supply the market any more. They thought the reason they weren't catching as many was there were bone fragments in the Purina dog meal that killed off the minnows.

One thing Dad and Lee would never adhere to was Dub's idea: "Boys, you have just caught 'em all out."

Whatever the reason, farmers were always looking for a new crop, and some of them started to raise minnows in ponds made especially for raising minnows.

When Dad and Lee couldn't supply Dub all the minnows he needed anymore, he turned to them.

"Well, its bust again ... but it was fun while it lasted," Dad said.

13
FISHING WITH BURLEY

Burley kept me intrigued for hours telling me how Granddad had lived back in the "good ol' days."

"When your dad and I were just kids, your granddad gathered switch cane from Caney Creek and made his own fishing poles. Back then there were bears, panthers and wompus cats all over Caney Creek bottom. There weren't that many deer, but your granddad was the best deer hunter that ever lived. Any time someone found a deer track, they would come get your granddad and he would track him down."

"Was Granddad a bear hunter?" I asked.

"Nah ... he was a deer hunter and a fisherman. He would sneak through the woods like a shadow and then after a while he would step off to the side of the trail and watch his backtrack. He said that a big ol' buck deer always wanted to know where you were and if he ever struck your trail that he would follow it right to you. He killed a lot of deer that way."

"Tell me 'bout his fishing." I said.

"When he went fishing he would set so many fishing poles that when he caught a fish they would tangle his lines into a mess, almost beyond undoing. That way he never lost a fish. After he got too old to go fishing anymore, he gave his switch cane fishing poles to us, and that is them under the house."

"Did Granddad ever catch a big flathead?" I asked.

"Nah, he never fished anywhere but Caney Creek. Little mud cats are all he ever caught, but no matter how little they were he always kept them ... claimed if they were big enough to bite, they were big enough to eat."

Burley got his fishing pole out from under the house and showed it to me. "As long as I can go fishing, I'm going to use this special fishing pole. See how your granddad notched the end so it wouldn't slip out of his hands?" he bragged. He let me hold it and while I relived the history behind his special fishing pole~handmade by my own granddad~Burley boasted, "Now, your granddad was a real fisherman."

~

The years passed and so did John Price's handmade switch cane fishing poles. The one Burley owned was the last one left.

Delton and I really enjoyed the visit at Grandma's and Granddad's and weren't ready to go home. We usually set in on Burley to go home with us, but this time it was different. Burley told Dad that he was gonna go home with us and do some fishing.

Dad bragging about good fishing lately, about the big flatheads we caught, must've had something to do with Burley's decision.

Burley made it clear, though, there would be no checker playing this time. "Come rain or shine, I'm gonna go fishing."

"Well, you better start gathering your stuff up then; we're gonna go in a couple of hours," Dad told him.

It took Burley about that long to gather up his fishing gear and load it into the pickup truck. It was plain to see speed wasn't his long suit.

Burley was very particular when it came to taking care of the things he owned. He rolled his pocket knives up in little pieces of flour sack that he had oiled with 3 in 1 machine oil. Then he put them in little paper bags, one knife to the bag and rolled each paper bag up tight. "A person can't be too careful ... I don't want them to get rusty" was his reasoning.

After Burley packed away his knives, he took time out to smoke before he packed his smoking things. When he finished smoking his pipes, he took them apart and cleaned them with a pipe cleaner that he made from broom-weed stems. He kept store-bought pipe cleaners crammed down in the pipe's bowls to absorb the excess moisture. He had paper bags for his pipes, tobacco, cigars and pipe cleaning tools, too.

Burley's fishing tackle got extra special care, more so than anything else he owned. He kept his fishhooks in the little white bags that Fishy Frair at the Ravenna grocery store put them in. "That way the sizes don't get mixed up," he claimed. All the little bags of fishhooks went into a larger brown paper bag that he marked "Fishhook bag." The laundry bluing stoppers, which he used for bobbers, went into another bag. He used snuff cans to store his lead weights in, and he kept them in his "Lead weight bag." He laid all of his small bags out on his bed and sorted through them for hours, it seemed. Finally he stuffed them into a big paper bag that had brown corded handles.

"I'm ready now," Burley announced.

Burley's fishing tackle box was nothing more than a sack full of sacks.

Dad drove and Mother rode in the front of the pickup with him; Burley, Delton and I climbed up in the bed of the truck. We sat flat down on the floor and leaned back against the pickup cab for the ride home.

I got tired of sitting flat and decided to sit on the side of the pickup bed. Burley didn't say a word; he just pecked on the rear glass.

I moved back to my place between Burley and Delton before Mother could turn around. I didn't say a word either; I knew I wasn't supposed to sit on the bed railing.

The topic of the conversation all the way home was fish bait.

"What do you boys reckon we should use for fish bait?" Burley asked.

All three of us had a different idea as to what the catfish might be feeding on.

Delton answered first. "Up there in Baker's pasture where the bank is caving, the yellow grasshoppers are jumping off of the bull nettles into the water. That is where I'm gonna go, and that's what I'm gonna use for bait. You can't beat yellow grasshoppers in a place like that."

"Dean, are you gonna go with Delton and use them hoppers, too?"

"Nope ... minnows are always better for catching catfish than yellow grasshoppers. I'll take me some of Dad's minnow jugs and a pocket full of dog food and go to the sandbar. I'll catch me some Red River chubs. I bet I out fish all of you," I said.

Burley made an educated guess as to what Dad's choice for bait would be.

"Bullfrogs are what Joe is gonna want to use. He doesn't think you can beat 'em this time of the year. He's gonna go to the swamp and catch him some leopard frogs." Burley added, "It won't hurt to have a variety of bait, though."

"I'll tell you what let's do; we'll get up real early anyway, probably before daylight. Let's shine grasshoppers on the way to the river. That's the easy way to get them," Delton said.

"Shine grasshoppers ... I ain't ever heard of such. What is that?" Burley scratched his head.

"Dean and I do it all the time. Early in the morning before they get off of their roost, you can shine a flashlight in their eyes and get 'em by the zillions. A lot of the time they'll be stacked up on top of each other, and you can get 'em two at a time."

Burley's face flushed, and he busted out laughing.

"Well uh ... uh, I reckon so; anyway Joe says, 'You can't ever depend on what catfish want for supper.' That's his theory."

"Burley, you haven't told us what your favorite bait is. Let's hear from you," Delton pried.

Burley pulled a Prince Albert can from his hip pocket and held it up for Delton to see. "This here is full of fat red worms from your granddad's barnyard. I've got some little perch hooks in my bag, and I'm gonna catch me some perch. There ain't anything that a flathead catfish loves more than a sun perch."

The old pickup truck went bouncing and rattling down Mulberry hill. As soon as the road gets to the foot of the hill, there's a big sand bed, then an old wooden rickety bridge. When you cross that bridge, you're in Mulberry bottom.

We crossed the bridge just as dark overtook us, and the talk about fishing and fish bait ceased.

Mulberry is rabbit country, and it's always a lot of fun to count rabbits. We got up on our knees and faced the cab in anticipation of seeing some. By the time we arrived in our yard, Delton got tired of counting rabbits and fell asleep in the bed of the truck.

When we drove up in the yard, Dad honked the raspy sounding horn. The reason he did that was to wake Delton up. He knew Delton always went to sleep riding in the back of the truck after dark. The honking horn brought the 'coon dogs out from under the house and sent the yard rabbits scampering.

Delton roused up, rubbed his eyes and reached for Dad to gather him up in his arms and carry him in the house and put him to bed.

"I wish we hadn't even gone," Delton grumbled.

~

"It's 5 o'clock ... are y'all gonna go fishin', or are you gonna sleep all day?" Mother hollered.

Before she could get the word fishing out of her mouth, my feet hit the floor; Delton was a little slower. He dragged out rubbing his eyes.

We went and paid the wash basin a visit, then ran and grabbed our chairs at the table. Dad, Burley and Mother were already there, busy eating.

Dad looked up from his biscuit sopping. "We're waitin' on y'all fast as we can," he said as he dragged another biscuit through his egg juice and jelly.

Laid out in front of us on the table was a scrumptious breakfast.

Mother had fried her special fried chocolate pies, enough to fill a big platter, but they were half gone. She had fried a platter full of our smokehouse cured bacon, but they had really made a dent in that too. The big platter of buttered biscuits was missing the top layer.

"There ain't enough plum jelly left to feed a jaybird," Delton complained.

"You want me to over-easy you some eggs? Mother asked

"Not with all those chocolate pies we don't," I spoke up.

"Blessings already been said ... y'all dive in," Mother said as she opened another quart jar of her sandbar plum jelly and set it on the table.

It didn't take long for us to catch up; then we all scooted our chairs away from the table, stuffed to the gills.

Mother issued her instructions: "I put some sausage and biscuits and the makings for coffee in your syrup bucket, Joe. I put beans and taters, a skillet and some lard and salt in your grub box. Don't forget your bedrolls ... I put them in the Army duffel." As an afterthought she asked, "How long do you reckon to be gone?"

"I reckon three or four days at the out most. If someone comes looking to buy fish, send 'em on down," Dad told her.

"We better take the tractor boys, considerin' the rain we've been havin' lately ... and it still looks like it may rain some more. I don't wanna get the pickup stuck crossin' the slough." Dad had what he called "a severe distaste for digging trucks out of mud holes."

In a little while Dad had the trailer hooked to Ol' Johnny, and we had everything loaded.

We arrived at our Red River fishing camp about midmorning and found that Red River was on the rise. The boat had swamped, and the river was getting swifter by the minute.

"We had better get the water bailed out of the boat and get her tied high, or Red River will take her away from us," Dad said.

Delton and me rescued the boat while Dad and Burley pitched camp; all the while Dad was making small talk.

"With the river muddy like she is, we're gonna have good trotline fishing. I don't know 'bout cane pole fishin' though ... it might be a bit slow," Dad said for Burley's benefit.

"It matters not to me ... I'm a slow fisherman anyway," Burley said.

I don't know how slow he fishes, but he's sure slow getting ready to go fishing.

Striking camp kept us busy until the middle of the afternoon. By then the sun was getting low enough that it was blinding as it reflected off the river.

"Watching a fishing pole and looking into the sun ain't all that much fun," Burley said.

We whiled away the rest of the evening waiting for the sun to go down behind the trees that lined the western bank of Red River. Once the sun went behind the trees, we cast out our rod and reels and sat with them awhile. We decided to get supper over with before dark, so we tied our fishing poles securely and cooked supper.

Dark closed in pretty soon, and the temperature dropped ... in a hurry. Nights are always cool and damp on Red River, even during the dog days of summer.

Just as we finished supper, a whippoorwill cut loose with his nightly serenade. Pretty soon the hoot owls and then the coyotes joined in, and the nightly chorus – nature's song to the rising moon – was underway.

We went over to the bank of the river, sat dangling our feet off, and watched our rods and reels until bedtime.

The night was crisp and clear, and the stars looked as if they were just barley out of reach. The ambiance was awesome – no one wanted to break the silence by speaking. We just sat and soaked up the wonders of nature.

The Milky Way makes the heavens look as if God took white satin ribbon and wrapped the beautiful evening ... as his gift to us. I thought, as I lay in bed waiting for sleep to come.

The next morning, way before daylight, Burley and Dad crawled out of their dew-dampened covers and were eager to start fishing.

Just downstream from camp, Burley found a big rift of logs. One of the logs jutted straight out into the river and made a perfect place for Burley to sit and fish just as slow as he wanted to. Burley climbed out on the raft and unwound the line from his cane pole. It would be awhile before he got around to wetting a hook, though.

Dad headed to the sloughy area behind camp to chase bullfrogs.

He cut himself a good dogwood switch and set out to catch as many leopard frogs as he could before the sun's heat sent them hiding. He had been gone over an hour and caught several when he decided to return to camp and check on Delton and me. He rousted us out of our covers, and the three of us went to check on Burley.

When we walked up to the bank Burley hollered, "Boy's have y'all caught anything yet?"

"Nope, we ain't wet a hook yet. We just got up." Delton spoke for me, too.

"What about you, Burley? Have you had any luck?" Dad asked.

"Well, as a matter of fact, I have." Burley said as he lifted a stringer with a nice 10-pound flathead on it.

Seeing the big catfish prodded Delton and me into action, and we parted ways, headed for our own fishing hole. We went up the river to where the bank was caving on the Baker's pasture. Red River's current had cut across the sandbar from the Oklahoma side and headed straight into the high bank on the Texas side. The swift current was causing big hunks of dirt and grass to sluff off into the river. Along with the grass went grasshoppers, and catfish would be feeding on them.

We caught enough grasshoppers to bait out two throw lines, one for Delton and one for me. Then we went to a sandbar and set some minnow jugs, hoping to catch minnows for rod and reel bait.

It didn't take long. Two runs of the jugs and we had enough minnows to fish with for a while.

We went back and ran our throw lines and staked our catch, six nice channel cats, out on a stringer. We baited up our rods and reels and fished for a few minutes. "Fishing there in that drift, Burley's liable to get a big flathead on that cane pole and as little as he is, the sucker might pull him in and drown him." I was serious.

"Nope," Delton tried to reassure me, "he'd let him have that pole before that."

"No ... not that pole he wouldn't." I reminded Delton about *that* pole.

Our talking caused our patience to wear thin, and we decided we better go check on Burley.

Dad took the boat down the river to the slate shoals, where he stretched a long trotline across the rapids and baited it with bullfrogs. He paddled to the bank and rigged his rod and reel with two hooks and baited one with a frog and the other one with a hellgrammite that he found under a rock and cast out into the current. *Hellgrammites are my secret ammunition ... I'll show 'em,* Dad thought.

When we got to Burley's drift, his full attention was on his bobber, his mind riveted on the next big catfish that might come along. Nothing else in the world mattered.

"Hey, Burley...."

Delton was going to ask him a question, but Burley jumped like Lucifer goosed him. Delton held his question ... Burley teetered on the log.

Finally he regained his composure and Delton finished asking, "Have you caught anything else?"

Burley grabbed for his stringer and almost fell in the river again. He grinned as he lifted his stringer and sent two big flathead catfish flouncing into action. Burley shocked the catfish more than Delton had shocked him. They drenched him.

"I hung another big one a while ago. I saw that I couldn't handle him, so I wrapped my line round that root there." He pointed to a big root sticking up from the log he was sitting on. "He dove down to the bottom and snapped my line like it was kite twine, and it's 100 pound test."

Dad showed up about that time and we went to camp, to wait until it was time to run our lines again.

We left Burley fishing ... waiting on the next big one to come along.

Dad sent me to the river to get a bucket of water while he stoked up the fire. He hollered down the river bank, "Be sure you rake the foam back before you dip the bucket in ... we don't want foamy coffee."

Dad poured the fresh water in, loaded up the pot with some more grounds and set it on the grate where it would catch the full brunt of the smoky fire. He set his tin cup on the grate to warm and leaned back against his tree.

"Someone ... when you hear the pot start to boil, pull the pot over to the side of the fire. Don't let me doze long, just till the coffee boils," he said.

When the coffee started boiling, I put Dad's hot tin cup of boiling coffee in his lap and let the rising steam rouse him up. The coffee continued to boil in his cup as he turned it up to take a swig. That is the way Dad liked to drink coffee ... boiling hot. He always allowed that girls sip coffee ... men swig it.

"Have you boys ever watched Burley fish?" he asked.

"Nope, fishing is fishing, ain't it?" I said and winked at Delton.

"Y'all ought to go watch him; you might learn something about being a patient fisherman," Dad encouraged.

We left, and Dad settled down for a real nap.

Burley's switch cane fishing pole was extra long, a little thick on the butt end and tapered to a rather thin tip. He had wrapped about 2 feet of the tip with twine to give it some extra strength. The pole had become a little crooked from the way Burley kept it stored under the house in a cramped-up spot. Burley handled the long slender pole with the finesse of a man skating on thin ice.

The only thing he would use for bobbers was the cork stoppers that came in laundry bluing bottles. "You gotta buy laundry bluing, and there ain't much of anything else that the stoppers are good for anyway," he said.

We watched Burley as he slowly guided his bobber upstream. He stopped it at an eddy caused by fast water detouring itself around a large bois d'arc snag, and he put the tip of his long pole on the snag. He let his elbows rest while the current swirled his cork around for several minutes.

Slowly ... ever so slowly Burley lifted his cane pole, until his cork was about three inches above the surface of the water; then he let it back down. He repeated the process several times; with each lift he raised the pole a little higher from the water. Finally his very aggravated sun perch surfaced, and Burley held him right on top of the water, teasing him into wanting to swim back to the bottom.

Burley held the cane pole perfectly still.

The perch's head rested in the water, but his tail flounced around on top of the water.

Burley looked up from his fishing and saw us watching him aggravate the perch. "Those big flathead catfish can't stand this kind of teasin', boys," Burley said.

When Burley turned around to look at us, the perch came completely out of the water and flopped furiously trying to get himself back into the water.

"I bet there's a big catfish down there, eyeballin' my perch and makin' him scared," Burley excitedly told us.

"Well, if there is, he ain't gonna come out on dry land ... for goodness sakes, put the perch back in the water," Delton begged.

It was too late.

The water exploded.

A flathead with a mouth big enough that he could have swallowed a water bucket came up from the deep. Silver beads of water trailed from his splotched, golden body as he twisted skyward in an attempt to retrieve the frightened sun perch.

One gulp and the perch met his maker.

In Burley's excitement his foot slipped off the log he was standing on. The log saved him from going all the way to the bottom ... he straddled it. Burley's scream of desperation and his flouncing legs only added speed to the fleeing flathead.

The giant flathead dragged Burley's fishing pole off to wherever it is that giant catfish go when they steal a fishing pole. Burley called it his bailiwick.

Burley, Delton and I climbed the bank and went to camp.

"Burley, you been noodling with your clothes on?" Before Burley could answer, Dad asked, "Did you boys learn anything?"

"Yep," Delton replied, "I learned that there ain't anybody on God's green earth that has got as much fishing patience as Burley."

I said, "If you're gonna tease 'em, then you've gotta be able to handle 'em ... that is what Burley taught me."

After hearing the big fish story from Delton, we all had a big laugh ... except Burley.

"I don't know what hurts the most. That big catfish sure bruised my feelings, stealing my fishing pole like that ... but then I got other bruises that hurt, too."

Burley and us boys headed to the swamp after we ate dinner, to find Burley a fishing pole. It turned out that Burley was just as particular about his fishing poles as he was everything else. He spent most of the afternoon finding one, one that suited him perfectly that is, and Delton and I were right in his tracks.

By the time Burley found the right pole and we got back to camp, the sun was in the blinding position over the river again, so we lay around camp and drank coffee.

After supper we all went back to the riverbank above "Burley's drift." We just sat there and dangled our feet off the steep bank. We baited up our dogwood rods and reels with minnows and threw them out. You didn't cast a dogwood fishing rod; you threw it. Dad baited up his store-bought rod and reel and cast it out beside ours. He laid it down on the ground beside him and rolled a Bull Durham cigarette.

I wondered, *What do rich people have to look at?*

We all sat and watched the sun set behind the trees, in distant Oklahoma, and swigged hot coffee for a long time before anyone said anything.

I finally broke the silence. "Boy, it just doesn't get any better than this."

"How did it get this good?" Delton asked.

One at a time we all got up and went to bed. We had had a trying, tiring day.

Dad, Burley and Delton were already snoring, dreaming about the big ones that got away and the fishing tales that a new day would bring.

I was the last one to go to sleep. Finally I made it a quartet. Burley snored lead, Dad snored bass, Delton just snored and I snored tenor.

14
FAMILY SECRETS NEVER DIE

A mockingbird doing his constant trilling chitchat from a treetop right above my head startled me awake. I rolled over in hopes of finding ground with no lumps and discovered that Burley's bedroll was empty.

Burley has shucked back his covers and disappeared into the night or into the river.

"Dad ... Dad ... wake up. Burly is gone!" I screamed.

Dad was gone, too.

"Delton ... Delton ... wake up! Ever one's gone and left us!"

Delton roused up enough to say that they were probably diving in Red River, trying to find a big catfish with a fishing pole.

"No, Delton, I mean it ... they're gone." I ran toward the riverbank. Delton was right behind me dragging his bed covers between his legs and rubbing the sleep out of his eyes with a clenched fist.

There setting on a cottonwood log in the middle of "Burley's Drift" were Dad and Burly. They each had a number two tin can of coffee, swigging and fishing in leisure.

"They think we're still asleep. Why don't we go get us some coffee and come back? We can hide and watch 'em," Delton suggested.

We hit camp on the run. I poured coffee, and Delton raised the lid on the Dutch oven to get biscuits for us. When Delton bit into his biscuit, he let out a squeal of delight. "Hey, guess what? There's sausage hiding in here."

We headed back to the river to spy on Dad and Burley. We plopped down behind a cedar tree that was growing right on the edge of the bank, and I parted the branches and peeped through. They were talking about a secret they had kept ever since their childhood days.

"Burley, do you remember the barn owl stunt that we pulled?"

"Yeah, Joe ... it all started when we caught that barn owl up in our hay loft. Do you remember the vow of secrecy us boys all took?"

"I sure do," Dad said. "That was the most scared I've ever been in my life, and I ain't ever told a soul. Have you?"

"Nope ... why, if Pappy had ever found out what really happened, he would have run us off from home."

There was a lull in the talk, and Delton got anxious. He nudged me and whispered, "This is gonna get good. Do you think they'll ever say what happened?"

"If they don't find out we're here, they might. Just shush it for now," I told him.

Burley opened a can of Prince Albert and took all kind of pains to pack his pipe bowl. After a long while of adding a pinch of tobacco and tamping, he struck a kitchen match and drew the flame down through the tobacco. He billowed clouds of smoke and kept drawing on the pipe stem until the flames flared up out of his pipe.

Reckon he's gonna set the drift on fire? Smoke boiled from Burley's pipe and hung heavy around his head.

Dad faked coughs and fanned his arms. Burley let out a sound that sounded somewhere between a laugh and a dying cough.

Dad frowned. "What happened wasn't funny."

"Didn't mean to laugh," Burley said. "It wasn't what the owl did; it was how stupid we were. Do you remember what in tarnation us boys were thinking about when we dreamed up that bit of stupidity? I can still see that barn owl level off and fly straight as an arrow for Dowel's barn."

Dad didn't say anything. Smelling pipe smoke made him want a cigarette. He got his papers and Bull Durham out of his breast pocket, rolled a cigarette, then whizzed a match up his britches leg and lit it.

Delton could hardly stand the suspense.

"Quit your fidgeting; they're going to see us. They're fixing to talk about it ... when they get their smokes going," I whispered.

Delton started to sneeze.

"Put a lid on it; they're gonna hear us."

Delton squelched the outburst in mid-sneeze and whispered, "You nearly caused me to blow the top of my head off."

I giggled.

Dad and Burley had become so engrossed in childhood memories, neither of them suspected they had eavesdroppers. They never heard Delton sneeze or me giggle; they never suspected a thing.

Will they ever say anything else?

Finally Dad quit blowing smoke rings and started talking. "You know how it is with a bunch of boys, Burley. One of 'em will get a spark of imagination, and then all the rest of 'em will keep fannin' the flames. The first thing you know everything gets out of control."

"Yeah, that's what happened, all right ... things got out of control," Burley agreed. "One of us boys – I ain't gonna name names – got the idea to tie Mother's braided rug material to his leg and let him fly around in the barn loft with a streamer."

"That Owl was so perty flyin' with that streamer on his leg. I wish we could have let well enough alone," Dad said.

Dad and Burley lowered their heads in shame. Silence prevailed again.

"Did you hear that, Delton? Dad said that he wished they had left well enough alone. I bet they did something awful."

"Wonder what in the world it was that they didn't leave alone? Do you reckon that they didn't leave that owl alone ... until they killed him?" Delton asked.

"Nope, Delton ... they wouldn't do that. Dad wouldn't kill an owl unless they were fit to eat, and he ain't ever told us owls were good to eat."

Delton and I knew how much all the Prices respected wildlife. We couldn't bring ourselves to believe Dad or Burley would have ever been in on such a thing.

Dad and Burley still hadn't started talking again. Their heads remained lowered, as if to pay tribute to the owl.

Delton could hardly stand the wait and asked, "What are they doing, Dean? Are they praying for that owl?"

Finally Burley started to talk again, but when he did, his conversation took on a different tone, a dead serious one.

"After that owl flew around with the streamer for a while, one of us boys – I ain't gonna say which one – suggested that we could soak it with coal oil and he could fly with fire."

"Yeah, Burley ... we just kept getting in deeper. We were convinced – by you know who – the owl would fly straight up, maybe a hundred feet, and then the fire would burn the string in two, and he would have his much-deserved freedom. After we saw him fly the streamer around, why couldn't we have let the poor thing go? Why in tarnation did we have to see him fly with fire?" Dad shamefully said.

They hung their heads again.

Dad looked around, then leaned over and whispered in Burley's ear.

Burley answered: "I had forgotten whose idea it was until you reminded me." He shook his head. "How in the Sam Hill were we to know that owl would fly straight into the loft of Dowel's barn and burn it to the ground?"

Dad shuddered then reminded Burley, "You know till this day no one knows, but us, why Dowel's barn burnt to the ground or that the idea was ...."

A giant splash ended Dad's sentence.

The owl incident was forgotten for the moment.

The biggest flathead catfish caught so far was on Dad's line. The fight was on.

"Did you hear that, Delton? They tried to make that owl fly with fire."

"Yeah ... and they burnt the barn down, Dean."

We bailed off the riverbank to watch Dad fight the big catfish. It was a battle to the end, but Dad finally landed the big flathead.

"I wish I could talk flathead," Burley said. "I would ask him if he has seen my fishing pole."

The fishing trip ended with Burley having caught the most pounds of fish, Dad caught the biggest fish, and Delton and I caught the most fish. Everyone was a winner, and the argument still raged about what was the best bait for catfish.

The owl subject never came up again. Delton and I knew that if Dad ever found out we knew about the owl thing, he would know we had been eavesdropping. The whole thing remained a dark family secret. Dad and Burley and their brothers were sworn to secrecy; Delton and I couldn't afford to spill the beans.

15
OUT BEHIND THE BARN

Dean is at an awkward stage, Dad thought. He remembered that once there was a time in his own life when he was just like that. *Give me a gun, or a rod and reel, or a dozen steel traps and turn me loose on Red River, and I was happy.*

Mother and Dad didn't worry about me.

"Dean can take care of himself," Dad told Mother. Mother believed Dad had taught me well. However, she didn't like the feeling she had in the pit of her stomach.

"Dean hardly ever comes 'round any more ... other than mealtime. I don't like the way he's outgrowing my apron strings so fast," Mother complained.

"Yeah, he's outgrowing the nest all right ... he'll be flying out of here soon. He's getting interested in girls. I saw him peeking in the women's underwear section of the Sears Roebuck catalogue last night when he thought that I wasn't watching."

"Joe, you don't mean it." *It is true ... he is growing up ... he's finding Red River more alluring than playing around the house ... girls can't be far behind,* Mother thought.

~

I am growing up. On July 11th, I'll turn 10. I'm almost a teenager. Playing with my little brother wasn't that much fun anymore, and I had never enjoyed being with a bunch of kids. I liked being by myself.

Girls were a distant concept in my mind, but I was beginning to acknowledge there was such a thing. When I wasn't at school and Dad didn't have something for me to do, I was gone. Sometimes I would stay gone a day or two at a time, down on Red River. Sometimes I would just camp out down on the bluff behind our house. A lot of the time I would hole up in the barn.

~

My birthday finally arrived, and I wasn't about to get too far from the house. I hoped Dad would decide to take me fishing for my birthday, and I wanted to be ready. I sat on the back porch steps, rigging my saltcedar fishing pole and listening for Dad to call me.

I had found a perfect saltcedar sapling growing on the sandbar where Dad and Lee were jugging minnows. Only a few weeks earlier it had been a green sapling and not very straight of character. I'd spent hours drying and straightening it. Now it was as straight as an arrow and as light as a feather.

My saltcedar fishing pole was fixing to get its test run.

Dad opened up his voice, loud enough so I could hear him even if I was out behind the barn.

"I wonder where Dean is. I thought he might want me to take him fishing for his birthday. I guess he don't want to go fishing," Dad hollered again.

I ran into the house, hollering, "Fishing ... did I hear you say let's go fishing for my birthday?"

"You're dreamin'. I ain't even mentioned the word ... *yet.* Come to think of it, though, do you wanna go fishing?"

Dad took Delton and me to the slate shoals. They were downstream from the sandbar where he and Lee jugged minnows. The shelf of slate was covered with about 6 inches of water and then at the edge of the slate the water dropped off to 10 feet deep or more. Dad poled the boat along the edge of the slate shelf until we got to the lower end where the water was deepest.

When we got there the needlenose gar were as thick as thieves and twice as sneaky. As soon as we dropped our hook in the water, a gar would pick it clean. Pretty soon we were running out of minnows. Dad ran his hand around the minnow bucket and made the announcement that the only minnow left was tiny. He gave him to me seeing how it was my birthday.

Dad and Delton watched as I let the baby minnow down into Red River.

My bobber never stopped.

The tip of my saltcedar pole chased after the cork. My arms stretched to stay with the pole.

"I can't handle him Dad." I begged for help.

Dad refused. "You have got a catfish on that's gonna show you that 10 years old ain't so all fired big."

That was true; the flathead at the end of my line weighed 10 pounds, and I started thinking I wasn't big enough to land him. I finally wore him down, though, and after a few minutes rest I felt big enough to land anything in Red River.

"I'm ready to go home now," I said.

"Well, you might as well be; you fed our baby minnow to your baby catfish." That did it – Dad had to pull me off Delton.

When we got home I decided I had better not use that fishing rig anymore. The big flathead cracked the brittle saltcedar pole and frayed the string in several places. I hung the whole rig, pole and all, on the wall in our bedroom.

I bragged to all my buddies that I saved the rig so I would have it to remember my big flathead by. I reminded them how Dad always retired the fish hook after he caught a big fish, partly in honor of the fish but mostly because he was afraid that the fight had weakened the hook.

~

After my 10th birthday I felt different. Mother and Dad treated me differently and so did Delton. Delton had always been my shadow, but now, sometimes I didn't want a shadow, especially when I got with friends my own age.

It must have something to do with me being in the double digits, or maybe because I will be a teenager soon.

Delton and I were playmates and best friends all through grade school, but now that I had graduated from the lower grades into junior high I started to make new friends. Kenneth Baker (KB) and I started to chum together a lot; he was my best friend. He had a little brother (Johnny) who had been his shadow, too. Delton and Johnny became pals. KB and I stayed "out behind the barn" a lot in an attempt to get away from Delton and Johnny.

Delton and Johnny spent a lot of time eavesdropping on us. When KB and I confronted them, their defense was, "We're trying to get the goods on y'all. That way, if y'all don't include us in your fun, we can go tell on you," Delton explained.

My first venture into the world of commerce began "out behind the barn."

I had watched Dad cut dead grapevines and smoke them one time when we were down in the river bottom squirrel hunting. Dad had run out of Bull Durham, and he cut himself a grapevine, lit it and puffed away. He coughed and spit so much that it discouraged me from trying grapevine smokes right then, but the idea stuck in my mind as something I wanted to do.

After we killed enough squirrels for supper, we went to the house. I helped Dad clean and dress them then I went to the barn. The fence row behind the barn had a lot of wild mustang grapes growing on it, and I gathered enough, just the right length to go into a Prince Albert can. I set my can of grapevine cigarettes on a two-by-four behind a barn pole and left them there to dry and cure.

Several weeks went by and then one day I carried them to school to smoke when I got with the bigger boys. I only lit one up, when I had to, in order to convince someone they were okay to smoke. I found out, to my surprise that the big boys wanted to buy them. Instead of selling them, though, most often I traded them for marbles. Delton blackmailed me into sharing the marbles with him, payoff money for him keeping his mouth shut.

I had only taken an occasional puff until one rainy day when I spent the whole day in the barn. I smoked a couple of them during the day. The next morning it felt like my lips had turned wrong side out. I skipped the breakfast table and didn't come home for dinner either. By supper I starved out and timidly took my chair at the table.

"What's wrong with your lips? Kissing the girls ... huh?" Dad asked.

"Uh ... I don't know about my lips ... *NO* to kissing the girls."

"I know," Mother said through clenched teeth. "You've been smokin' grapevines, Dean Price."

My face flushed.

Is he flushing from his thoughts of kissing girls or from getting caught smoking grapevines, Mother wondered. She must have figured that by the time my raw, cracked lips healed I would have been punished enough. Mother dropped the subject, and I never developed grapevine lips again.

~

Everyone who grew up in the country shares a fondness for barn meeting places. Remembering events that took place "out behind the barn" conjures up warm feelings from deep within. Kids felt like they were safe from the eyes of their parents there. All boys, upon entering junior high school, begin to say and do things they don't want their parents to hear or see.

I thought our barn was the perfect hideout. I argued that it was the best place to hold meetings because we weren't using it for anything. Dad had long given up on raising cattle, and the barnyard had grown up with an abundant crop of blood weeds. The 8-foot-tall blood weeds, interwoven with morning glory vines, hid the barn's front door from view of the house. Behind the barn, on the side away from the house, was the old cow lot, and nothing would grow there. Cow manure had rendered the ground too rich, and trampling cattle had packed the ground down too hard.

KB argued that his barn was the best hideout for holding slingshot fights because it had a loft. The Baker barn's loft was vacant except for a few bales of peanut hay that the rats had tunneled through looking for peanuts. Carl wasn't putting up hay much anymore; he had switched to corn silage for his dairy cows.

"From *our* barn loft, you can see the house and see what's going on," KB said, and he had a point.

~

I started to improve our out-behind-the-barn hideout. The first thing I wanted was for the hideout to be a comfortable place where us boys could meet and while away the time.

I carried several elm stumps, remains of fence row elm trees we were unable to split, from the woodpile and put them behind the barn.

The best chairs in the house I proclaimed, as I arranged the stumps where the stump sitters could lean against the barn.

A good hideout must be safe from intruders, like our little brothers.

We went to all kinds of trouble to keep Delton and Johnny out of the hideout when we weren't there. We wanted to be sure we knew if Delton and Johnny went there in our absence. Around the back barn door I built a moat, not with water but with sand burs, goat heads and the stems from bull nettles, to ward off barefooted little brothers. We also took pains to rake the sand smooth every time before we left.

What I didn't realize was that our little brothers could care less about sneaking into our hideout if we weren't there. Eavesdropping was what they wanted to do.

A hideout with just plain barn walls ain't much fun.

That is where I decided I could impress my friends most of all. I slipped the new Sears Roebuck catalogue out of the outhouse and took it to the barn. I didn't think Mother or Dad would miss it. I hurriedly tore out the pictures of the prettiest girls, the ones wearing nothing but undergarments, and hung them on the barn wall.

I stepped back and admired the wall. Mixed in with the girlie pictures I had steel traps, fur stretchers and some skunk and 'possum hides.

Wow ... I wish I could decorate my bedroom like that.

I rushed the catalogue back to the outhouse in hopes of replacing it before anyone needed any of its pages.

I opened the outhouse door and glanced toward the house. Mother was coming.

I pitched the catalogue in the door and ran back to the barn. I ducked in and sneaked a peak back.

Mother stepped into the outhouse.

Whew ... She almost caught me.

Within the confines of the outhouse was the only place that Mother dared look at the women's undergarment pictures, so as soon as she settled down she reached for the new catalogue.

"It is gone!" W*hy is it crumpled up and over in the corner.*

Mother picked up the catalogue and fanned the pages across her thumb to skip to the women's wear section. The women's wear section was missing, torn out.

She remembered something that Joe had told her ... *Dean took it.*

I spent many an hour reading Fur Fish Game, a magazine about trapping. I daydreamed a lot and when Mother or Dad asked me what about, I would just shrug my shoulders and answer, "boy things."

16
"OUR CLUB"

When my junior high buddies and I graduated into high school talk about girls no longer played second fiddle to fishing, swimming and hunting. We talked about girls ... a lot. It was all talk, though; none of us wanted girls meeting with us in the barn, tagging along to the river or joining in our barn fights ... or going hunting with us.

KB and I decided to form a club and invite the rest of the Mulberry boys to join us. The first meeting was to take place in our barn. Dad agreed that we could use the barn for our clubhouse with one stipulation: "y'all are gonna let Delton and Johnny in on your fun."

When I told KB, he said: "Well they can attend, but that don't mean that we have to let them join or get a vote."

The first meeting didn't accomplish much, except to let Jerry Don Overton (JD) join and to establish that when we had walnut fights or horse-apple fights we would use the Baker barn. Corncob fights would take place at JD's barn; their loft overlooked the pigpen which held an abundance of mire-soaked corncobs.

Not much thought was given to naming our club. As far as we were concerned, "Our Club" was sufficient. What we were concerned with was how to keep the city dudes, the girls and our little brothers out of the club. A few simple rules would keep the girls and the city dudes out, but keeping our little brothers out would be a different matter. A meeting was called for the coming Saturday, so we could set rules "to keep out the undesirables," and we left to go to Red River and go swimming.

It was common during the 1950s for teenagers to want to call each other by their initials, but they had to have a certain ring to them. No one could explain what the certain ring was; however, every boy recognized it.

Some how my initials, DP, and those of Delton's, DP, didn't have that ring to them; as a result, we never got tagged. I was envious of a person whose initials had that special ring.

When Saturday came and after everyone got their chores done up, we gathered in our barn. Several new members were present: There was Teddy Crumby (TC) who lived up on Mulberry hill and Kenneth Caplinger (KC). KC was the only club member who didn't live in Mulberry bottom. He lived out south of Bonham somewhere. KC's daddy (JW) loved to fish in Red River and they came to Mulberry nearly every weekend to go fishing. All of us liked KC and considered him a Mulberry boy because he was country just like us. Delton and Johnny were the only little brothers present.

I called the meeting to order.

"If you're here ... say present. Not here ... say nothing.

Delton and Johnny said present, too.

"Dad said you and Johnny could be here, but you can't say *present*," I said. "And you can't vote either," KB added.

"I'm writing the rules," KB said, "and we have our first rule. Little brothers can be here, but they can't vote or say present."

"I'd like to put in a rule." JD dangled his hand in the air and continued. "It is a simple fact, girls don't like to have things thrown at them. They wouldn't ever wanna get into our club if our meetings were mostly about corncob fights."

"Yeah," KC said, "especially if we used mire-soaked corncobs from your pigpen."

"Whoa ... I agree. Pencil that one in," TC said.

"Not till we vote," KB said. "Everyone that is against having corncob fights raise your hand." Not a hand went up. "Corncob fighting wins, *hands down,*" he announced.

"I got one that'll keep the city dudes out," KC announced. "City dudes won't want to join our club if we use our slingshots and have fights with green walnuts."

"Bring it on!" TC hollered. "If walnuts are out of season, we'll throw bois d'arc apples."

KB called for a vote – not a hand went up – "Slingshots and green walnuts or bois d'arc apples wins hands down."

I hadn't said a word, and I stood up with my rule: "Country boys, like us, have grown up knowing that girls, city dudes, school teachers and our mothers don't like the smell of skunks."

Everyone, except KB, looked at me in wonderment, like where in the world is this going? KB and I had decided beforehand there was gonna be a skunk rule. I continued: "If you are going to be a full-fledged member of Our Club, you gotta kill a skunk with a stick." Before anyone could stick up their hand, I told KB, "Pencil it in ... it wins hands down."

KB penciled it in. However, the battle over the skunk rule was fixing to be the next fight – not throwing corncobs or horse-apples.

KC and TC felt like KB and I had slipped a rule in on the rest of them that we didn't need. JD rode the fence rail; he didn't like that he didn't get to vote, but he liked the skunk idea.

"This is getting serious," I said. KB said it was time for us to go into executive session, and we dismissed Delton and Johnny. They went home bawling.

After they had time to get to the house, I continued. "By the time we get through filling them full of tales about skunks with rabies, they will all be afraid to get close enough to a skunk to kill it with a stick. Can any of you think of a better way of keeping them out of our club?"

That convinced KC and TC. They wouldn't hold up their hands.

JD came up with a proposition that if I agreed to, he wouldn't hold up his hand either. "Dean, you're gonna have to do it first and at our very next meeting."

"I'll go first, but it ain't fair. We oughta draw straws," I complained.

"Talk about a lack of parliamentary procedure ... we ain't got any," KB said as he called for a vote.

Not a hand went up.

The taunting started, and they all joined in. "We can't wait to see you kill a skunk with a stick. We don't believe you can ... try it, man ... see if you can."

"I'll tell you boys this much: If I'm gonna have to be the first one, I'm gonna pick the place. I'll do the skunk the honor up on Mulberry Hill by all of them springs. There are skunks there by the zillions."

"We'll camp under that big pecan tree by the bridge where the one-armed ghost lives. There is plenty firewood there, and it's not far from the county road in case any of the city boys show up."

"You're gonna do it this Friday night, Dean ... no backing out." JD ended the meeting.

~

I had a week to get ready for my skunk killing feat. I was determined to learn all I could find out about skunks, and I knew just the person to ask.

Dad trapped skunks every winter and somehow he killed and skinned the critters without them ever throwing their scent. I wasn't about to let Dad know what was up, so I knew I would have to ask questions carefully.

After supper we retired to the front porch, as usual, but this time Dad wasn't going to get to set a topic for our discussion.

"Dad, I got a question."

"Fire away, Dean."

"We – me and the boys in our club – we want to know how you kill the skunks that you catch in your traps without them ever throwing their scent."

I knew Dad delighted in being the authority on anything, and that he would go all out to explain how he did it.

"Well, let me just give you boys a lesson in Skunkology."

"First off, skunks are very timid. They don't want you looking them in the eye. They like everything to be slow and calm; fast moves scare 'em. You have gotta go slow and easy with 'em; you can't be pushy. You can lead a skunk to water, but you can't push him anywhere. I make my skunk sets in a special way. I set my trap at their den holes and use an extra long chain. That way when the trap springs shut – POW," Dad clapped his hands together

– "they can go down in their hole."

In Dad's talking, he did that hand clapping thing every time he got a chance, just to scare the wits out of Delton and me.

"When I come up to one of my traps and it has a skunk in it, I slowly untie the chain and tie it to the end of a long pole and then get around behind his den hole. He's down in there grinning 'cause he knows I can't see him. I just put a little pressure on the pole, and pretty soon Mr. Polecat will start to follow the pole out. I just finesse him outta there ... finesse is the opposite of pushy. As soon as I get him out of his den – don't look him in the eye – I ease him off of the ground and put the pole over my shoulder. Remember never look him in the eye and don't be pushy. When you get your skunk off of the ground, he's your polecat. You can carry him to water and drown him. That's the way I kill 'em, and they never throw their scent." *Dean ain't listening to what I'm telling 'im. His mind is way off in left field,* Dad thought.

I analyzed Dad's lesson in Skunkology. The key factors were: Don't scare them by looking them in the eye; don't push them; lift them up on a pole because they can't throw their scent if their feet are off the ground. I misread Dad's sound advice ... my mind wandered way off into left field.

I've got it figured out ... I'll show 'em how to kill a skunk with a stick, and he wont even throw his scent.

We invited some of our classmates from Bonham to join our campout. Delton and Johnny, Delton's friend Gary, and Gary's cousin Jerry would be there, too. It was our hopes that after the city boys and the little boys saw me kill a skunk with a stick and found out they had to do it, they wouldn't want to join Our Club.

Friday finally came around. I wasn't worried ... I had a plan.

We got off school, did up our night chores, then headed to Mulberry Hill. Delton and I rode our bicycles and carried our camping gear in Army duffels on our backs. KB and Johnny rode old Grady, their big gray mare, and carried their bedrolls behind Johnny. TC walked from his house; he only lived a mile east on Mulberry Hill. One of the city dudes owned a car and he brought his friends from Bonham. JW Caplinger dropped KC off on his way to Red River to go fishing.

Gary and Jerry were already under the pecan tree where the campout was to take place when everyone else arrived.

The air was thick with tension; the little boys were scared to camp that close to the Mulberry Bridge.

The road into Mulberry came off Mulberry Hill and went through a long sand bed, then crossed a slough over a rickety old bridge. All the young men in the community had their own version of a ghost story about a one-armed ghost that lived under the bridge. The person telling the story would always end his story by saying something like: "It's a known fact, because I saw him." After hearing the ghost stories, the younger boys were convinced that a one-armed man lived there and they weren't gonna camp anywhere near that bridge. Delton, Johnny, Gary and Jerry refused to camp there and threatened to go home.

We moved our campsite.

"We want as far as a long way will get us from that bridge," Delton said.

A giant pecan tree that grew alongside one of the many springs that seeped out of the bluff was our next choice. After we struck camp there, we built a pecan wood fire and let it burn down to coals, to cook supper over. The little boys were sent out to bring some green hickory saplings back to camp to cook supper on.

"Y'all don't settle for anything but green hickory; they make the best," KC told them. "And be sure you get everyone his own stick."

While the little ones went looking for cooking sticks, KC, JD and I took our .22 rifles, our book satchels and one of the city boys that had a .22, and spread out in search of supper.

Blue Jays and field larks were plentiful, and our book satchels were soon bulging.

When we got back, there was a plentiful supply of roasting sticks propped up around the fire.

KC, JD and I spread our birds out on the ground in order to divide them up. The city boy reached in his satchel and pulled out the only bird he killed and threw it on the pile.

"Whoa ... we have got a problem," TC said. "I ain't eating that mockingbird there on top of the pile."

"They don't have much breast meat on them and besides they are the State Bird of Texas. Whoever killed him is likely to go to jail," KC said.

"Well, he's dead now ... we've gotta eat him to save his honor. We'll draw straws," I proclaimed.

It was decided the little ones would draw straws for the mockingbird.

"Whoever draws the short straw has to eat him, but then whoever gets him will have an extra bird to eat," Delton said.

Delton, Johnny, Gary and Jerry drew; Delton got the short straw.

He shoved his stick into the fire with both birds on it and rubbed his belly and licked his lips while they roasted. He ate the blue jay as soon as it browned and kept turning his stick. He'd take the mockingbird out of the fire and look him over, then put him back in the fire for some more cooking, then take him out and study him again. He couldn't quite make up his mind to eat him. Finally after everyone was through eating their birds, Delton lit in on the mockingbird.

"He tastes better than blue jay. Only thing is he's a little skinny so he cooked up tough. I think if he had some salt on 'em he'd be delicious, though."

All of us sat on the ground around the fire and smoked grapevines and munched on raisins.

I carved my name on a bois d'arc club I had made for the occasion ... and waited. I was preoccupied with my plan.

Dark was slow in coming.

We swapped stories about rabid skunks biting people and making them go stark raving mad. One story about an old man whose hair and eyeballs fell out and his teeth grew into fangs and caused him to run around every night biting little boys in the neck and giving them rabies even made me shiver. The little boys sat and listened, their mouths agape, and absorbed every detail.

"It is dark enough for the skunks to start roaming. Dean, your time has come," JD announced.

I clutched my skunk killing club and shivered. It was time to put up or shut up. I started to brag. "I have figured out a way to keep from getting sprayed. Dad told me that a skunk must first raise his tail over his head, then push his feet against the ground before he can throw his scent."

The giggling and the "yeah, I bet" that everyone expressed got under my skin. I didn't want to push the subject too far, though. That wasn't exactly what Dad had said, and I knew it. "Here's my plan: I'll run up behind the biggest skunk we can find, grab him by the tail with my left hand and at the same time lift him off the ground. Just as soon as I have his feet clear of the ground, I will reach into my overalls pocket, take my club in my right hand and do him the honor with one blow to the head. There is no way Mr. Skunk is going to be able to spray me because Dad said skunks can't throw their scent unless they have their feet on the ground," I bragged.

TC bought into my explanation. "If Joe Price said that I'll buy it. It's dark enough; let's go watch Dean do it."

The confidence TC expressed in what Dad said made me feel a little better about the predicament I had gotten myself into.

Well, as plans go, mine sounded foolproof. Everyone was convinced my plan would work. As the events unfolded, however, the skunk refused to be the *fool,* and that was the rub.

We hadn't gone far before KC spotted a monster big skunk. "There by the spring-fed cow-watering trough ... see him, he is huge and black." KC pointed him out to me.

I could see that he *was* gigantic. His white stripe went all the way down to his fluffy tail. The cat waved its tail, and my eyes focused on the white.

I barked, "KC, hold the lantern higher. I have gotta see him better. Yep, he's a skunk all right." My heart raced and a lump came in my throat.

Everyone busted out laughing ... "It is a known fact that the critter is a skunk," one of the city boys prodded me.

The laughter frightened the skunk. He bristled and then broke for the open pasture, bobbing along in a skunk trot, carrying his dancing tail proudly over his back.

"Catch him, Dean," JD hollered.

I stalled for a second then took off.

KC was right behind me carrying the lantern. The rest of the gang was right behind us.

I hollered: "Hey ... y'all run around and get in front of him. When he sees you, he'll stop, and I'll grab his tail."

Some did – some straggled farther behind – someone fell in a gopher hole.

I kept my eyes focused on white ... and ran. I pulled my club out of my pocket when I saw JD, TC and KB making a move to get in front of the skunk.

I was right on the skunk's tail. Suddenly the skunk saw a line of boys in front of him and threw on his brakes.

I lunged for the white fluffy tail.

To my surprise the skunk jumped ... my hands closed around thin air. The skunk planted both hind feet firmly on the ground, cocked his tail and went to work. His aim was perfect.

Yellow venom filled both of my eyeballs.

The skunk disappeared and left everyone to deal with the cloud of yellow mist as best they could.

"I'm blind ... I'm blind!" I screamed. "I can't see ... I can't see!"

I fell to the ground and started kicking myself around in circles. KC held the lantern while KB and JD rushed to my side. They held their noses pinched between thumb and forefinger and helped me stand up. I ground at my eyeballs with tightly clenched fists. My hands, stained yellow by putrid skunk scent, only added pain and tears to my red-hot eyes. TC screamed, "Laudy, Laudy Miss Claudie."

I jerked away from my well-intentioned rescuers and went to my knees in the yellow, stench-soaked grass, wallowing and pulling my hair.

About that time the rest of the gang arrived on the scene. Delton leaned down and put his arm around me. "What's the matter, Dean ... you got rabies?"

"What's the matter ... I can't see ... I got the blind scares."

Saying it made it real; I jumped up and took off running, completely blind to everything around me. I didn't run far though before I stepped in a gopher hole and tumbled head over heels.

I felt groping hands on either side of me, getting me up, and heard KB's comforting voice. "We are gonna take you to the cow trough and wash your eyes out."

Someone led the way and someone pushed me from behind; the whole gang made its way to the cow watering trough.

KC raked the scum off the water. I felt a hand on the back of my head shoving my head down and heard the command, "Open your eyes." Someone grabbed me by the hair of the head and jerked my head violently, up and down.

First the skunk made a fool of me ... now I'm blind ... and now this panicky mob's gonna drown me.

The blind scares possessed me again.

I became a gyrating mad man, scattered boys in all directions and fought my way to the top of the water. I stood there, eyeballs flaming yellow fire, spewing sour tasting water out of my mouth, sucking air. *Air, I need air ... y'all almost drowned me.*

It might have all been funny if I could have seen the looks on their faces.

Getting fresh air brought me back to a sense of reasoning. "Take me to the spring. I need *fresh* water," I demanded.

KB led me to the edge of the spring and helped me kneel down. KC cupped his hands and dipped them full of sweet, cold spring water and splashed it into my face and eyes. The cold spring water cooled the embers in my eyes, but my world was still pitch black.

I'll be blind the rest of my life?

JD and TC shoved me down in the cold spring, grabbed hands full of wet sand and scrubbed my overalls with me in them. I wasn't in any shape to avoid the roughhouse scrubbing; besides, I wanted to rid myself of the stench that burned at the hair in my nose. Finally the bath givers gave up. They decided they weren't doing much good anyway.

I wanted nothing more than to somehow get back to the campfire. I was blind, stinky and wet, as cold as a drowned rat and coughing up water. Getting warm and dry, that's all I wanted.

With the help of everyone I made it back to the warm campfire, all except the city dudes, that is. All of a sudden they had to go back to town.

We taunted the city dudes as they left to go get their car. "If you leave now, you can't belong to Our Club."

"Fine by us," they hollered. "Fighting skunks with sticks ain't our thing. We'd rather play with girls."

The little boys wanted to jump ship, too. Gary and Jerry held to the idea that going to all that trouble to get rabies wasn't worth it. Delton and Johnny were afraid to walk home in the dark by themselves.

Discussions broke out as to what we should do about the skunk rule. I leaned over and whispered in JD's ear. "Things are working out just the way I thought they would; our little brothers don't wanna pay the price."

JD leaned over and whispered back in my ear: "Blind is an awful big price to pay!"

We discussed going home so Mother and Dad could get a doctor for me, but everyone knew the trouble we would be in when our parents found out what we had done. It was decided the best thing to do was to stay put until daylight. We'd had enough trouble for one night.

Several hours passed. No one was sleepy ... everyone was too worried to be sleepy.

Sometime after midnight the blackboard in front of my eyes got a hole in it. Fuzzy light became visible through the hole. It was the moon setting; that's how I knew it was sometime after midnight.

"I can see ... I'm gonna see again ... whoopee!"

"How much can you see, Dean?" Delton anxiously asked.

"The moon looks like a cantaloupe on the bottom of Red River, and the campfire looks like a flickering candle." *Hallelujah!*

Now everyone got sleepy.

The next morning my eyesight was normal, but my nose told a different story. "Boy that sand bath y'all give me last night did the trick. I just smell a faint whiff of skunk odor," I said.

"Man, I don't know what your definition of faint whiff is. You are down right odorous," KC observed.

The Friday night campout ended and so did the fun; if you could call skunk fighting fun.

I coined a phrase that night, "the blind scares," that became a common saying with the members of Our Club. It was years before doctors came up with a real name though (Severe Panic Disorder).

~

By the time the next Friday night came, it was too cold for a campout on Red River.

Mother and Dad and KB's parents put their foot down. The weekly campout took place in KB's barn.

KB called the meeting to order and busted everyone up in the process. "The *odor* of business is skunk business. Raise your hands, and we will vote out the 'kill a skunk with a stick' rule ... raise 'em now."

"Whoa ... now wait a minute ... listen to me," I protested.

"Whoa, why ... After last Friday night you couldn't possibly want to make it a rule for killing skunks with a club. Could you, Dean?" KC and TC asked.

"This is Our Club. We don't have to prove anything to join; we're already joined. I think girls, sissies, little brothers and city dudes should have to prove themselves if they wanna join Our Club. They gotta kill a skunk with a stick. Don't raise your hands." I pled.

Not a hand went up.

KB wrote the rule into the Big Chief tablet: *New members* will have to kill a skunk with a stick before they can join Our Club. KB shivered when he underlined new members.

17
THE BIG BOYS AUXILIARY

KB and I were faced with little brother problems.

I presented the facts for consideration; quoting exactly what Delton had told me, the next morning after the skunk incident. "Delton said, 'If y'all don't include Johnny and me, we're going to be constant thorns in your sides. We'll run and tell on you for ever thing you do, for ever thing you say and for having girly pictures.' We gotta do something."

"Not we ... we don't have any little brothers. Y'all have to come up with a plan." TC spoke for JD and KC too.

We did, and it was a brilliant idea.

"How about if we help them form their own club? After all, we need enemies to fight against in our barn fights," KB suggested.

"We'll have to think up a good name. Anything with *little* in it, and they will hit the ceiling," I said.

"I got it," KB said. "How about ... Big Boys Auxiliary?"

"That'll do it! They will eat that up," we both agreed.

The meeting adjourned so KB and I could go tell Delton and Johnny.

It turned out that they loved having their own club and they loved the name. They were a little suspicious, though. "Y'all are buttering us up to something by calling us *Big* Boys Auxiliary." Hands were shook and the deal sealed.

Delton and Johnny immediately held a meeting and asked Gary and Jerry to join them.

The Big Boys Auxiliary came up with a couple of demands at their first meeting which Our Club gladly met. First off, they wanted to take Our Club on when we had our barn fights.

"The only thing is there are five of y'all and only four of us, and we're littler than y'all. One of you big boys will have to come over to our side and help us even things out," Delton suggested.

Oh boy, this is gonna be fun.

~

The big Saturday barn fight had been brewing all week.

School's out was approaching fast, and the walnuts were about half grown on the walnut trees in Bakers' front yard. Those two milestones in a country boy's year called for a special celebration.

Our Club and the Big Boys Auxiliary had planned to have a slingshot fight to celebrate the occasion. The ammunition would be green walnuts, and the fight would take place in Baker's hay barn ... come rain or shine.

Saturday finally came, a bleak, rainy, drizzling day. A perfect day for a slingshot fight between two rival boys clubs in an old hay barn. Everyone felt the excitement in the air.

As soon as Delton and I completed our morning chores, we went in and told Mother we were going to the Bakers' and we wouldn't be home for dinner.

Everyone showed up at Baker's barn and everything was set and ready.

Our little brothers were convinced into thinking that the upcoming slingshot fight was going to be the most fun thing they had ever done. The proof of their convictions lay in the fact that every member of the Big Boys Auxiliary was present and accounted for.

Every boy had a bucket to collect his ammunition in. KB timed the rush to the walnut trees in their front yard: "On your mark ... get set ... go!"

Every boy for himself, the mad dash toward the walnut trees was underway; buckets dangled from our arms as we ran to gather up ammunition for the slingshot battle.

The black walnuts were about half grown and had thick green outer husks on them. It didn't take long before we had our buckets full and brimming over. While we gathered walnuts, I refreshed the only two rules the fight had for everyone.

"The side that runs out of walnuts first loses, or if anyone gets themselves kilt, their side loses."

Anyone who found a walnut leftover from last year was lucky and put it in his pocket. They were walnuts that had evaded the eyes of the squirrels by lying hidden in the grass and were dry, hard and wrinkled and were the perfect weight to fly with great speed. They fit the slingshot pouch perfectly and where always on target. If one of them hit you, it was a guarantee; you were the proud owner of a bleeding, very nasty pockmark.

Johnny wasn't strutting; his pockets were so full of last year's walnuts that he waddled when he walked. He was the smallest boy in the Big Boys Auxiliary, but he was muscular and quick on his feet, and his mind was quick as a steel trap. More than those things, he now owned more hard dry walnuts than anyone else. Our Club knew that he was the one to fear.

Delton screamed, "Last one to the barn is chick duke," and like greased lightning all of us sped toward the hay barn.

The rain was coming down hard and fast now, and we were all drenched by the time we dashed into the barn. The members of Our Club outran the Big Boys Auxiliary and got up in the hayloft. The Big Boys Auxiliary got in the corner of the barn by the corncrib and built them a hay bale fort.

"Who are y'all gonna send down here to help us?" Johnny hollered.

We hurriedly drew straws. JD drew the short one and announced, "Here I come; don't shoot," as he baled out of the loft.

"Y'all ain't playing fair. We're pinned down, and our only way out is to jump out of the loft window," I taunted.

"Y'all chose the loft" was just part of their answer. The rest of it came in the form of a black walnut whizzing through the air. Ping ... it dented the sheet iron roof, right over my head. The fight was on.

The object of the fight was not to shoot one of the little boys of the Big Boys Auxiliary. The plan was to shoot as close to them as possible and keep the walnuts flying furiously. Sooner or later they would get scared, and we could rush them and flush them out. When the Big Boys Auxiliary went hightailing out of the barn, then Our Club could declare we won.

The plan had its flaws. Neither KB, KC, TC nor I took into account: The Big Boys Auxiliary was going to be trying their dead-level best to shoot us in the head; they weren't about to waste their walnuts, and they weren't about to get scared. They had it figured that sooner or later one of their walnuts would connect with one of our heads. They remembered what I said: 'If somebody gets kilt ... his side loses.'

As the fight wore on, KB and I noticed a pattern in the methods of the Big Boys Auxiliary. They were trying to conserve their ammunition. One of them shot at a time, and they all ducked down and waited for us to send our barrages of walnuts.

The rain ended, the sun popped out and the heat of the battle caused the barn to become a sweatbox. KB opened the loft window. The fresh air felt good.

It sure is a long fall to the ground.

The Big Boys Auxiliary recognized a pattern in the way we were fighting, as well.

"They have figured out that we're only shooting one time apiece. When they hear our fifth walnut ping the sheet iron, someone shoots; then TC pops up and shoots; then everyone else cuts loose," Delton noted.

"Yeah, it's always TC ... they got a rhythm," JD observed.

Our walnuts were raining down on the Big Boys Auxiliary in the most furious attack thus far. They stayed ducked down while Delton and Johnny discussed how they could take advantage of our pattern.

Delton came up with the perfect battle strategy. "Johnny, when they finish this gosh-awful onslaught, you shoot and then reload with one of your old dried walnuts. Gary, you go next, and then Jerry, and then I'll shoot. When I shoot, you draw back; when you hear it ping the tin above their heads, raise up and fire. They will be counting 1, 2, 3, 4 ... 5. They ain't gonna expect 6 ... TC's head is gonna pop at the same time your walnut gets there ... bingo!"

"They are through," Johnny whispered as he fired. He reloaded and got ready.

Delton's turn came, he rose up and shot.

Johnny drew his red inner tube rubbers to the breaking point and held his shot.

Ping ... Johnny turned his dried walnut loose – Johnny's walnut was on the way – TC's head popped up.

Johnny's timing was brilliant. His aim was perfect.

The knurly walnut smashed into TC's head right where his nose grew in.

"I ... eeeeee ... waugh ... whoa! I'm kilt ... we give up," TC screamed.

TC stood up and clutched his bloody head with both hands. He knew how to cuss better than any of the rest of us and he did – a blue streak.

BLEEP ... "I'm bleeding, BLEEP ... I'm dying, BLEEP ... BLEEP ... BLEEP!" He squalled and flounced around. The hay on the loft floor was slick, and the loft window was open. He flounced one time too many. Out the loft window he went.

We rushed to the window. There in the muddy cow lot TC laid, in the fetal position, not moving, not groaning – just bleeding.

No time to do a normal exit.

I bailed out the loft window. KB and KC followed.

By the time we hit the ground Johnny was there standing over TC, wringing his hands sobbing, "He's dead ... I've killed him!"

Hearing the word dead shocked KB into action, and he ran to the house. We all threw our slingshots into the tall blood weeds. In moments KB and his dad came running. By the time they got there, TC was up on his knees, digging his elbows in the mire. He had his fingers intertwined behind his neck and his eyeballs were rolling out of control.

"He definitely ain't dead," Carl said. "What happened?"

"A wasp popped him." Someone, I ain't gonna say who, spoke up.

"I ain't ever seen a wasp do that kinda damage. You boys have got some explaining to do."

"He'll wear the imprint of my walnut for a few days; at least I didn't kill him, though." Johnny's voice quivered as he tried to tell his dad what happened.

We all declared we would never have another slingshot fight with walnuts ... we might throw them, though. Next Saturday we would go over to JD's barn and gather up all the wet soaked corncobs from the pigpen and have us a good, old-fashioned corncob fight.

The week went by very slowly at school. The talk was how the Big Boys Auxiliary had beaten the Our Club boys at their own game. The city boys taunted and called us the "no name gang."

Every time I heard someone call us "the no name gang," it stuck in my craw.

TC missed school Monday and Tuesday with a headache, a swollen bloody pump knot and black eyes. He spent the rest of the week bragging and shaking his fist at Johnny and telling him, "Y'all just wait till Saturday. We have it figured out how we're going to get even."

When it came time for the Saturday corncob fight, TC made an announcement. "Y'all think were gonna be throwing corncobs at you, but the way I got it figured out, what we oughta do is gather up a bunch of muddy, mire-soaked cobs and scrub your heads with 'em."

18
RIVER RATS

The need for a real name became a constant nagging. The name of Our Club had served us well, but we wanted a name that we could hold up to the public. We didn't like the city boys calling us "the no name gang."

One of the things we were taking a lot of pride in was that we were going to Red River for a monthly campout and a swim, and our plans were to continue the practice right on through the winter. It was the wintertime Red River campout and swim that caused everyone to start calling us River Rats. We all liked that name and adopted it as the official name for our club.

"We're in for a hard, cold winter ... everything points to it," Dad predicted. "Here it is only early November and the geese are already winging their way south and the fur on that 'possum y'all brought in last night is already prime. Another thing is every barn rat, pack rat and mouse around here is trying to gnaw into our house."

Dad's long range weather predictions were better than the Farmer's Almanac or the weatherman's. "The weatherman on the radio is pretty good at predicting what's coming tomorrow because they talk to somebody out west or back north and find out what kinda weather they just had. They ain't worth a plug nickel at predicting into the future, though. That's why we got blindsided by this cold snap," Dad told Mother.

The cold snap which we were recovering from was a real humdinger; even a jar of Mother's sauerkraut froze solid sitting on the kitchen table in the house.

KB and I called a special meeting of Our Club. The special meeting was on Saturday, the weekend before Christmas in our barn. The temperature was in the zero range, and it was spitting sleet from a new Norther. We discussed going swimming in Red River, in depth. It was decided what we needed was a rule on paper.

"Swimming in Red River in January and February is risky business," KC said.

"I bet it is gonna take a rule – one in writing – to make sure everyone does it," TC figured.

"It's gonna take a rule to make me do it," JD offered.

KB already had the rule in the Big Chief tablet and read it so we could take a vote. 'The swimmer will stand on the bank and shuck his clothes, all of them, and then dive in head first. There won't be any pussyfooting around, like wading in, or prancing around complaining about how cold it is. A fire if it is snowing or sleeting, to melt the goosebumps after you get out, is okay. At least one other club member must witness the event."

"What's meant by shuck all your clothes? Even your shorts?" JD asked.

"All ... means you can't even leave your necktie on." KB cleared that up.

"Hey, what if you don't come out of the river?" TC asked.

KC said, "TC, if you don't come out, we'll make up another rule."

After the discussion, KB continued reading the rule. "Swimming every month makes you a River Rat. If you miss a month, you won't be a River Rat anymore. Now let's take a vote."

Not a hand went up. The River Rat swimming rule won hands down.

One problem KB and I anticipated was that Delton and Johnny would spill the beans to our parents. There wasn't any way around that happening, unless the River Rats included the Big Brothers Auxiliary in the fun. Having a little River Rat brother couldn't be all that bad anyway, KB and I decided. The other River Rats decided that would be the price we would have to pay to keep our parents from finding out.

~

An extremely harsh Norther had blown in every few days during the whole month of January. Thank God January was coming to a close and would soon be history. The River Rats and the Big Boys Auxiliary were glad to see the first month of 1955 go ... except Delton and me. There had only been one decent Saturday in which to take the required swim. We had had to miss it, and time was running out for us. It was Thursday, January the 27th, and the last weekend of the month was coming up fast.

The coldest Norther of the season was due to arrive on Friday, the 28th. Saturday, the 29th, was the last day we could get our swim in because Sunday was church day and Monday, the 31st, was a school day.

We were in a pickle. We couldn't miss the swim; we would be outcast.

I'll exile myself to a Red River island.

Friday the blizzard blew in, and there was no way any of the parents were going to let the regular Friday night campout happen in the snow flurries, pelting sleet and awful gale winds.

When Saturday morning got there, the mercury was in the thermometer's bulb and it didn't get out all day. Drizzling rain froze as it hit, snowflakes swirled and the winds were so horrendous that Mother couldn't keep her washing on the clothesline. She had to dry our Sunday-go-to-meeting clothes in the house behind the stove.

Delton and I knew the rule about Sunday: no fishing, no swimming, no anything ... but church. The ice storm continued to worsen through Sunday, so Mother, Dad, Delton and I had church at home.

The last day of January, which was Monday, didn't promise to improve; and then there was Dad's rule. No skipping school.

There was nothing Delton and I could do but plan a hooky day from school and go to Red River on Monday. Either that or I would never be a River Rat again.

I can't face it ... banned from my own club.

Delton needed some convincing, though. "I ain't a real River Rat anyway. That's just something y'all come up with to keep us from telling on y'all. The club I belong to is just a put up; for y'all to have someone to fight with. I ain't skipping school."

"Okay, be that way, but you're gonna be a castaway. Everyone is gonna be saying, 'Don't have anything to do with that baby Delton ... he's just a baby ... he's a chicken ... cluck, cluck, cluck.' Skipping school will be easy; when we walk to the mailbox to catch the school bus, we can hide in the bar ditch, and after the school bus runs off and leaves us, we'll head to Red River," I pleaded.

He finally agreed, but it was all for naught anyway. Sunday night, about midnight, it started drizzling rain in earnest and freezing as it hit. When we woke up Monday morning a sheet of ice covered everything. The pigpen fence was a solid sheet of ice. We were out of electricity. The school bus couldn't run if it wanted to, and it didn't matter anyway ... school turned out.

That was our first break, but somehow Delton and me had to get out of the house long enough to go to Red River and go swimming.

By noon the drizzling rain had turned to snow and I was getting desperate. Delton and I sat around the dinner table with long faces. It was obvious to Mother something was wrong. Her concern caused her to question what our problem was.

"We're tired of being cooped up in the house," I blurted out.

"For goodness sakes, why don't y'all go out to George's hay barn and play?" Mother glanced at Dad as if to get his approval.

"Yeah, that last cuttin' of hay filled his barn, and it'll be cozy in amongst all the bales of hay," he agreed.

That was our second break, the out I was looking for; we grabbed our coats and headed for George's hay barn. We ran in the front door, climbed over the hay and ran out the back door on our way to Red River.

Once there, it didn't take but a few seconds to shuck our clothes and dive in. It took even less time for us to swim.

"Where's the fire?" Delton asked as he crawled out of the water dragging his blue body.

I shivered – the goosebumps popped out. "Didn't think we'd need one what with the hurry we're in," I managed to spit out between chattering teeth.

We climbed the bank to get our clothes as fast as our blue-cold legs would allow. When we popped up over the river bank, my heart sank.

Where's our britches?

"Look, Dean, the wind blew our britches up in that saltcedar bush," Delton observed.

Within the hour we were back in the hay barn, acting as though nothing had ever happened.

~

Most people were of the opinion that January's weather was an indication of what Februarys' would be. If that were true, February was gonna be a bugbear.

Everyone dreaded February except Dad; he was looking forward to it. *It gets warm enough to start fishing sometime in February, and I can hardly wait,* he thought.

Dad's old saying proved true. If January goes out like a lion, February will come in like a lamb. February first, Tuesday, offered promise; the sun was shining and the mercury came out of the bulb for the first time in days.

If every day is getting a little warmer ... Red River will be bearable by Saturday ... I ain't missing my chance this time.

The River Rats hopes were running high for a fun camping trip. Delton and I had learned the hard way not to put off till tomorrow what you can get done today. Not a single one of us was going to miss Saturday's swim.

There was not a hint of the approaching Norther. Dad didn't depend on the radio for weather forecasts much in the '50s. "All they can tell you is what someone else tells them, which has already happened up-wind. I can look out there and see what's fixin' to happen," he maintained.

Our Friday night campout was sanctioned by all the parents concerned. The plan was for the River Rats and the Big Boys Auxiliary to meet at our barn, then go on to Kavanaugh's Point on Red River.

Friday was still three days away, though.

School turned out on Friday afternoon, but by the time we all arrived home from school and finished our chores, there was a special feeling in the air. Dad referred to it as a bad omen. When he had that feeling, he would say, "D'rectly a Norther's gonna hit," and he was always right.

After quite a bit of pleading by me, Dad finally gave in to the camping trip, with some stipulations, though. "You can't take Delton; he doesn't need to learn how to survive winter storms yet." Dad put his foot down, and nothing Delton said could change him.

I jumped on my bike and rode as fast as I could over to KB's house with the news that Delton wasn't gonna get to go.

"It's not a problem; Dad has already said Johnny can't go either," KB said.

Dad and Carl always got squeamish about Delton and Johnny camping in a Norther, and Carl had as much country wisdom about the weather as Dad.

The River Rats started arriving at our barn. The excitement mounted as each one arrived and the wait began for the next one to show up. It wasn't sure if everyone would get to go. The last one on the scene was KB, and he finally showed up riding Ol' Grady. Blackie, their snaggletooth bulldog, trailed along close on Grady's heels.

We made a last minute check to make sure we had everything we needed. When we arrived at Kavanaugh Point we chose a little depression, a small swag with several big cedar trees growing in it, for our campsite. Around the little swag's rim was an outgrowth of small cedar trees, dogwood, grapevines and rattan vines that offered the camp good protection from the north wind, just in case a Norther did blow in.

The steady warm wind had blown from the south all morning, but during the afternoon it had become gusty and wishy-washy. It couldn't make up its mind from whence to blow: from a southwesterly direction one moment to northeasterly the next. Nor could it make up its mind how hard to blow: gale force one moment, a gentle breeze the next. None of us placed much confidence in our parents' weather predictions ... it was just too pretty and warm. We halfheartedly gathered what little firewood we thought we would need.

Sometime after midnight, the south wind that previously couldn't decide from which direction to blow made up its mind and changed itself into a straight-forward, full-fledged Norther. The last wisp of smoke, from the last stick of firewood, was gone ... on its way to the South Pole.

The mercury in the thermometer plunged. TC shivered himself awake and woke up the rest of the River Rats with his chattering mumbles. "That north wind is cold."

"Dad must've been right about a Norther being on its way," I said.

"My toes are like lollypops. I think I've kicked the bottom out of my quilt," JD complained.

KC convinced us we'd better get up and gather in a supply of firewood before we all turned into icicles.

We jerked on our brogans and stumbled around gathering up driftwood to feed the fire. After we got the fire stoked up with a huge offering of wood, we dove back into our blankets. Our shivering soon gave way to snoring. Sleep was fast coming but not long-lasting.

With a razor edge, the gale force winds cut at my previously warm bedroll. I woke up to frigid winds and goosebumps that I couldn't shiver away. I crawled from icy-cold covers and threw more wood on the fire. The rest of the River Rats soon followed. The night had spent itself freezing its hostages, but the sun was fixing to rise.

If it has any warmth to it, it'll be welcome.

"Camping out on Red River during a winter storm like this one has taught us a good lesson ... to get set for the worst," KB reminded us.

"We won't ever let the warm south winds' blowing all day lull us into being unprepared again," KC said.

"I bet the mercury is hiding in the bulb," JD said, and everyone agreed.

"That's probably the only way it could get out of the north wind," TC cracked.

We spent the rest of the night hovered around the campfire ... anxious for daylight but dreading the swim.

The sun came up on a blue-gray day that wasn't going to do anything but get colder. The heavy buttermilk clouds made it look as though it could start snowing any minute.

"Let's build a huge bonfire, put on the coffee boiler and get the job done, in that order," I suggested.

KB and JD protested. "Don't you think it's gonna get warmer when the sun gets a little higher?"

"I reckon it could," KC said, "but if we wait for sun, we could get snow."

"I'm ready," TC shivered out. "I'm ready to go home and get behind the wood stove."

No one wanted to go first. The custom was to draw straws and whoever got the shortest straw went first. KB held five straws in his hand – the straw not drawn would be his.

I made the first draw and knew by the short little straw I drew.

As luck would have it ... but I'll be the first one back to the fire.

The other four River Rats assured me that they would be right behind me.

After we shucked all our clothes, we stood in a ring around the blazing fire, as close as our bare skins could tolerate.

TC shoved me out of the ring and hollered ... "GO!"

My birthday suit changed colors; from the pink our fire put on me to a cold-blue from the falling snow that had started to flutter down.

I looked toward the high river bank and hesitated ... *dad gum their giggling* ... I backed up to get up a lot of speed.

"Yee-haw," I screamed, as I left the safety of the river bank.

I hope no logs are floating by.

I reached the height of my jump. Just before I tucked my head under my outstretched arms, I caught a glimpse of a campfire down the river.

Red River had my full attention now, and its icy water was approaching fast.

"Yippee," I screamed and lost my breath. *Ice water in my face.* I went out of sight but only for a second and popped to the top like an empty jug released underwater.

Where are the other River Rats?

I looked toward the bank – to see where – just as they splashed into the river all around me.

I swam furiously toward the bank. The down-river camp was in plain view from the river but hidden from our camp. Blue-gray smoke billowed from a roaring fire, and three men were hugging it. One of the men was pointing out to the other men what he had just seen: five white butts punching holes in Red River.

The icy water and thoughts of our own campfire caused me to put the other camp in the back of my mind.

Long, powerful, overhand strokes propelled me toward the bank. I reached the sandy, 20-foot-high riverbank and started climbing. I kicked and clawed at the sand bank in an attempt to climb. All I could think about was the driftwood fire waiting for me at the top of the bank.

KB, KC and TC were right behind me.

JD was laughing so hard he couldn't climb. The sight of three shiny hineys shinning up the bank in the sandstorm busted him up.

I reached the fire and jerked on my warm dry britches. I was dragging warm socks on over my wet, sandy, frozen feet when KB, KC and TC scrambled over the rim of the bank.

"Where's JD? Did he drown?" I asked.

"Nope ... we left him at the edge of the water laughing," TC answered.

I rushed to the edge of the bank. JD had reached the top of the bank by then and was clinging to a salt cedar. He was so hysterical he was unable to pull hisself over the edge. I lent him a hand and dragged him to the fire.

KB, KC and TC clawed at their eyes and complained about having grit in their teeth. They didn't let it interfere with them getting their warm dry clothes on, though.

"Did y'all see that camp down yonder?" I asked, pointing in its direction.

"No," KB answered, "but someone better sneak over there and see if there are any girls in the camp."

"Man, that would be embarrassing if girls saw us. Since you're the only one that saw the camp, you should be the one to go," KC figured.

"Okay ... I'll do it, but I gotta warm a little first." I shuffled my hands in the edge of the crackling fire until I got the blue-cold out of them and headed down the river.

I kept in the dry slough bed that ran parallel to the river toward the strangers' camp. At its narrowest point I would be within 50 yards of it. I reached the point and climbed up on the root ball of a giant uprooted cottonwood tree. What I saw gave me a growling, gut-empty feeling in the pit of my stomach.

There was a giant steel skillet filled with sizzling bacon. A gallon coffee boiler sat cock-eyed on two mismatched logs. Steam gingerly floated from the spout.

I can almost smell the coffee.

Half a dozen sticks, propped over one of the logs, held big rolls of dough, browning into loafs of bread.

The men look so familiar.

I could hear the men talking plainly. One of them announced that he was going to invite the Red River Rats to breakfast. I recognized him ... he was Weldon Underwood. We all called him Dad ... he was KC's uncle. One of the two men left standing by the fire was JW ... KC's daddy. The other man spied me and motioned for me to come on in to the fire. I didn't know who he was.

I filled JW full of questions. "Did you see us dive into the river? You got any girls? Where is KC's sister, Linda? What are y'all doing here?"

"Before I start shelling out answers, Dean, this here is my brother, JD Caplinger. I don't think you have ever met him. He lives at Munster, Texas."

"Pleased to make your acquaintance, Dean," JD said.

"Me, too," I answered.

"Okay, here goes," JW said. "No to seeing you ... no to having girls here; Linda's at home. As far as what we're doing here, we're doing some fishing; but right now I'm cookin' you boys some breakfast. Now does that answer your questions?"

"We've got plenty of extra coffee cups; grab you one of those blue granite ones," JD Caplinger said as he shoved a tin cup into my hands.

Why extra cups?

JW moved the coffee boiler over to the edge of the fire and at the same time braced me with a warning. "JD Caplinger made this here coffee, and if your hair weren't so wet, it would stand it on its ends. He'p yerself."

The coffee inside was hissing, after calming down from a rolling boil. I swirled the pot around a few times in order to get it pouring then tipped the sooty black pot toward my cup and oozed out a cupful.

I swigged a little through my lips so as not to burn the hairs off my tongue.

Mother would like Mr. JD's coffee.

My mouth puckered and the wrinkles in my forehead deepened as the hot bitter brew caressed my taste buds.

"Wow ... that's good. How do you keep it in the cup? It's strong enough to climb out," I said.

JD Caplinger took my words as a compliment. He had been watching my actions ... and reactions, and he felt it necessary to comment on the strength of his camp coffee. "Most people don't know just how little water it takes to make a good pot of coffee," he said.

Soon the rest of the River Rats came walking up, following Dad Underwood. He was feeding them some cock-and-bull story about how I had already eat everything up from them ... but they could have some coffee.

The smell of fried bacon and boiled coffee wafted through the air to meet them, and they bolted. KC was leading the pack. They had all passed Dad Underwood, and he was bringing up the rear.

As soon as KC saw JD Caplinger, he threw up his hands.

"Well, of all things, if it ain't my Uncle JD! What in the world are you doing here?" he asked.

"Fishing," is all KC's Uncle said. Short answers were the norm for him. We all suspected there was more to the answer than fishing. *Extra things, food include.*

After a pause that seemed like forever, JD Caplinger continued.

"You boys call yerselves River Rats, huh? I guess y'all and me are of a kind. I'm a river rat, too. I love to fish, hunt, and trap and hang out on Red River."

We hovered around the fire drinking coffee and swapping stories for the better part of the day. KC's uncle JD really had a way of building suspense into his stories. They seemed right on the edge of being true, right up to the point where they turned into outright fabrications. When anyone sighed or gave JD any indication of disbelief, he would say, "I'm dying if I'm lying." Of course everyone could see that lightning didn't strike him off his stump.

Every story had gotten bigger and bigger as the day wore on. Everyone had tried their hand at telling a tale so tall that JD couldn't top it, but every time he had. One of us River Rats, after finishing a fine tale, looked over toward KC's Uncle and proudly spurted, "I bet you can't top that one, Mr. JD Caplinger."

JD Caplinger got up and stretched and then walked over to a big elm tree and pulled off a small twig. He chewed on it as he returned to the warmth of the driftwood fire.

We anxiously waited for JD Caplinger's tale – we knew it was coming.

JD Caplinger sat down and shuffled his feet around closer to the edge of the fire and chewed on the green twig. We thought he was making himself a toothbrush, but actually what he was doing was sucking us in ... to another JD Caplinger story. He spat a few shrivels and started to tell it.

"Boys ... JW and me...," he paused and pointed a finger in KC's direction, "your daddy, KC. Anyway we were back 'hind Lake Fannin last week fishing." He ended his sentence there and stretched his legs while he chewed on his elm twig a moment and then repeated himself to build suspense. It wasn't as though he needed to build suspense; just the fact that it was JD Caplinger telling the story added enough suspense.

"Anywho ... we was back 'hind lake Fannin, and I hung into a great big fish." He spat some shrivels into the fire and added, "or something." He interlocked his fingers, turned his hands wrong side out and popped his knuckles.

We sat enthralled by JD Caplinger's story.

He knew he had all us sucked into his tale when I asked, "What do you mean 'Or something?' Was it an eel?"

"Well ... I've asked around, and I ain't found anybody that has every seen anything like what I hung into. Now, take you boys ... y'all are on this here river, most all the time – I know you boys can tell me what that thing was." He spat elm shrivels into the fire and let his thoughts hang there for us to mull over.

I withstood JD Caplinger's pause just as long as I could. "Well, I tell you what ... if we can't tell you what that thing was, Dad will know what it was. He knows ever fish in this here river," I said.

"Yep," TC chimed in, "Mr. Price knows ever fish in there."

"Well now, boys ... I ain't sure the thing was a fish."

"Maybe it was a sturgeon. Those are the strangest-looking critters ... that I know anything about," I offered.

"Nope, not a sturgeon and it definitely wasn't an eel," he said. "Do you boys know where that giant cottonwood tree is that grows right on the edge on the river bank, up above Lake Fannin? It's there where the river makes a turn from running east and heads north. Right there ... right there's where it happened." He really got excited and raised his finger as if to point up in the tree.

By the long pause that followed I guessed that JD Caplinger wanted one of us to ask what happened. However, we all held our ground and didn't say a word.

He finally gave in to his long pause of silence and continued. "It happened just at the crack of dawn; the sun was just breaking through that big ol' tree and a light breeze was fluttering her papery leaves." He pointed toward JW. "Your daddy. KC ...."

KC exploded, "I know who my daddy is. Will you please just get on with your tale?"

"Hey, man, this ain't a tale. I'm dyin' if I'm lying. Anyway, your daddy and me, we had just finished a pot of my boiled coffee. KC, you know that big heavy catfish pole that I made; well, I commenced to get a bite on it. It was a funny kinda bite." He made sure he had added enough facts to his story to keep our attention. He let that phrase, "funny kinda bite," dangle in front of us. He mouthed his toothbrush and spit some more shrivels into the fire. "Do y'all know how a big, old softshell turtle will hold down your line with his front foot and chew on your bait? Well, that funny kinda bite was somethin' similar to that. I've been told how much your daddy likes turtle soup, Dean. Whenever I catch another one, I'm gonna give it to him."

JD Caplinger read the contempt in our eyes, for his wandering away from the story and his stalling, and he realized he'd better get to his story and stick with it or he was fixing to lose us. He threw his masticated twig into the fire and quickly returned to his story. "Dreckly, as in after a while, that thing got tired of messing around with my hook and grabbed aholt of it. I reared into my rod and set the hook. The fight was on. I figured out pretty quick that whatever I had hooked into was a fighter. He dove to the bottom of the river and then took off downstream like a greased BB shot out of a Red Ryder."

JD shuffled his feet back away from the fire a little. The story was heating up. "The thing took a turn – he swam straight toward me. Boils of water was coming up behind 'em. Just then he surfaced and commenced swimming like a floundering goose with a broke wing. The thing made it all the way to the bank with me reeling as fast as I could to keep the slack out of the line. He climbed out on the bank dragging my sinker, waggled over to that cottonwood tree and then spat my hook out."

One of them walking catfish I've been hearing about on the radio.

Y'all ain't gonna believe what happened next."

"What happened?" Our eyes were wide.

"He clumb plumb to the top of that cottonwood tree and flew off."

Silence set in. We knew JD Caplinger wanted us to start laughing.

We refused.

He looked around and saw our mouths agape in disbelief. He got a dead serious look on his face and looked into each one of our eyes. Then as if to add insult to injury, he asked, "Do you River Rats have any idea what that thing was?"

"You're lying!" TC jumped up shaking his finger.

"I'm a dying ... if I'm a lying." JD Caplinger held his ground.

We didn't say much as we walked home on that cold clear pre-dusk evening. We didn't want to go home. When we reached Baker's Pond, we sat down to rest and reflect on the day's events before we separated and went our own ways.

"You reckon that thing JD Caplinger caught could've been one of those water turkeys?" TC asked out of the clear blue.

"Augh, man ... Uncle JD relishes in making up stuff. He probably just caught a sturgeon or a shovelbill catfish and then let his imagination run wild; or, on second thought, his super duper coffee probably had his brain in a headlock."

"Yeah," I agreed, "did y'all hear him say that he and JW had drunk a whole pot?"

19
THE LEGEND OF BAKER'S POND

Delton and I sat flat down on the porch and leaned back against the wall. Mother and Dad sat in the brand new porch swing he had just finished building. Dad opened the Bible to the newspaper clipping he had cut out of the *Bonham Daily Favorite* and started reading it to himself. The headline read: RED RIVER FLOODS, PAST AND PRESENT. Lake Texoma had everyone worried; it looked as if she might go over the spillway. We watched it rain. It had rained for days on end.

Dad glanced up from his reading long enough to give us the weather forecast. "According to the paper it doesn't look like an end is in sight to the rain, and the weather reports on the radio are full of reports from people out west telling about the rain storms they're getting. As long as they get it, we're gonna get it," Dad said.

"Pretty soon the TV weather man will have a thing called RADAR, and then we can see for ourselves what we're gonna get," Delton said.

"Yeah, I'll believe it when I see it ... that seems pretty far fetched to me," Dad said.

"Yeah ... it does to me, too," Mother added. "I wouldn't put much faith in them ever being able to take pictures of what's fixing to happen."

Dad went back to his newspaper. "They say here the biggest flood back in olden times was in 1892."

Dad looked and pointed to the old river bluff about a hundred yards north of the house. "That liked to have been Red River right there boys. That '92 flood is the one that took Pope's Point away from Oklahoma and left it in Texas. When the water went down from that flood is when it left the big deep, natural pond down yonder on the Baker place. He buried his head back in the paper and continued reading.

The old pond held some kind of special attraction for all us Mulberry boys. The way the pond came about "way back in '92 by the great Red River flood" and the yarns that Dad spun about the pond – always with great mystique in his voice – had grown into something he called "the legend of Baker's Pond."

There were two sides to the legend of Baker's Pond. One side captured the imagination of everyone who heard it, and then there was the dark side designed to scare little kids away from slipping off and going there.

Finally he glanced up and said, "It says here ... back when they built Lake Texoma in the early 1940s, the engineers said it probably would never go over the spillway – maybe once ever hundred years. Boy, those engineers might have to eat crow because if it keeps this rainin', it's fixin' to do it."

"Tell us some more about Baker's Pond," I insisted. "You said one time that a big ol' catfish lived in Bakers Pond."

Here we go again; this will keep us from having to go to bed for a long time.

"That old pond used to be a mighty popular place. After the Great Red River flood, way back in '92, someone put a ferry in at the slate shoals on Red River and built a wagon road to it. The road went right by the pond, and people passing by would stop and water their teams and their horses on the way to and from the ferry. Some people on their way to foreign places, like Oklahoma City, would camp several days before moving on. Some Gypsies camped there and built willow furniture. That is where your grandma and granddad bought theirs."

"Pretty soon people started taking their kids there for picnics and swimming, and the old pool got tagged the community swimmin' hole. Sunday evenings on the pond got to be a regular event. All of the old folks, as you boys call 'em, learned how to swim there. People from all around would come and spread their pallets down under the walnut and cottonwood trees and then lay their babies and picnic baskets on 'em. After the kids swam and played in the crystal clear water for a while, they would come running to the pallets, all starved out. Picnic basket lids would start flying open, and then someone would turn thanks. The Amen was the invitation to dive in, and everyone knew that meant the food.

"After the fried chicken, scrambled egg sandwiches, and peanut butter and jelly sandwiches were all gone, the grownups played Rover while the kids let their food digest. After the hour was up – that kids have to wait before they can swim or they'll get the cramps – the swimming would resume. The men folk would start playing baseball and leave the women to watch the kids swim. Mothers clapped their hands as one kid or another learned how to dogpaddle around.

"Young women and their beaus come to the pond in horse-drawn buggies to spark under the moonlight. Then when they got ready to get hitched, they did it under the graceful walnut trees."

"Did you and Mother ever spark on the pond?" Delton asked

Mother's blushing.

Dad saw Mother's face flush, too, and used the opportunity. "Ask your mother."

"Never," she answered, "because we didn't live here and that's all you need to know."

After the distraction, Dad got back to his reminiscing about Baker's pond. "One time I slipped up on the pond and took a pot-shot at a flock of mallards that had taken refuge there from a bad Norther. I crawled on my belly for more than an hour, and when I got up on 'em they was all wadded up in a knot; they knew something was up. I couldn't stand to see myself make a potshot into the whole helpless flock, so I scared 'em up to give 'em a fair chance to escape. When I lowered the boom on 'em, they fell out of the air like rain. I killed 10 with that one shot."

After the duck story we got up, went inside and went to bed.

Mother didn't like Dad pumping Delton and me full of stories that made Baker's Pond sound so exciting, and she lit in on him.

"Why, you'll have all the boys in Mulberry slipping off and going to that old stagnant pond. You're gonna get 'em in trouble. You better pump 'em full of scary stuff before you get everyone of 'em drowned in that stagnant old stock tank."

"Well, I can do that. I love conjuring up scary stuff," Dad told her.

The next time I asked to hear more about Baker's Pond, Dad was ready for me.

"One time there was a feud going on between two brewing families, and there was a boy from one of the families that wanted to marry a girl from the other family. The girl's family caught them sparking up on the bluff overlooking the pond. They claimed that the boy was sparkin' their daughter illegally because the feud was going on, and they up and shot him ... stone cold dead. The distraught girl waded out in Barker's Pond, went under and never came up again. Her ghost lives in the pond until this day, and when boys like y'all try to swim in the pond, she drowns them to keep them from getting shot by their parents."

Boy, he's really spreading it thick. Mother couldn't help but snigger.

"You told us one time that a big ol' catfish once lived in Baker's Pond. That's what I wanta hear about," I said.

"Well ... yeah, there was a giant catfish that got trapped in there when the flood of '92 went down. He has broken everyone's fishing line that ever tried to catch 'im. When anyone in the community had baby chickens, little pigs or 'coon dog puppies that died, they would take 'em to Baker's Pond and throw 'em in, just to watch him come and get 'em. He got nicknamed Old Whiskers.

"Old Whiskers ... how'd he get that name?" Delton asked.

Dad had an answer ready.

"One Sunday evening while all the little kids were swimming, one little boy got too far out. Suddenly a pair of giant whiskers, they were as big around as your wrist, came to the top and headed toward the little boy. A giant swirl engulfed the little boy, and he disappeared. No one ever saw hide or hair of him again. The little boy's mother named the catfish Old Whiskers. That ended the swimming in Baker's Pond once and for all. I suppose that Old Whiskers has grown big enough by now to eat a boy as big as you, Delton, if you were unlucky enough to fall into the pool – supposing me or your mother one weren't there to save you.

If we ever have anything die, I'm gonna go try to get Old Whiskers to come eat it.

Those stories, kept alive by the need to keep the little kids away from Baker's Pond, are the kinds of stories Delton and I grew up hearing.

~

During my teen years, memories of the blue swimming hole were all that remained. Swimming ... not anymore; the pool had became a stagnant pigsty. Baker's Pond was now only about 3 feet deep; a foot and half water and a foot and a half of mud. In the summer a thick green scum engulfed the water, giving the frogs, tadpoles and cottonmouth water moccasins cool refuge from the sun.

The "in" place to go on Sunday evenings had become Lake Fannin.

The Rural Resettlement Administration purchased land in Fannin County near Red River from farmers whose land had eroded away after the dust bowl days. The WPA built a beautiful lake complete with a swimming beach, bathhouse and boat slips. They built some beautiful little cabins and a big kitchen-dining hall combination overlooking Red River.

Every kid in the country wanted to go to Lake Fannin on Sunday evening, so the place was always crowded. A boy who lived in Bonham and had a car and a girlfriend, too, would on occasion bring another girl and they would pick KB up, then the four of them would go there. At that point I didn't have much interest in girls, but I wasn't going to let them have all the fun; I would strike out on my bicycle. It was about 30 miles round trip, and I would have never worked that hard hoeing peanuts.

~

The monthly swims in Red River were getting easier to enjoy. Warm, sun-filled days in March and April were easy to come by. Red River's water didn't feel any warmer, though, than it had in the dead of winter; it was just that the outside air was warmer. If anything, the goosebumps that the cold water and the windy days of March brought were even harder to shake off than wintertime goosebumps were.

May and June swims were a pleasure, and we spent more and more time camping, fishing and swimming in Red River. School turned out the first part of June, and after that there would be even more time for fun.

After school turned out, Dad hired us out to Audry Cain to hoe out his peanut crop. His peanuts had completely grown up with Johnson grass, and the only way for him to salvage them was to dig the grass out with a hoe and pull it out by hand. The rows were so long and the grass was so bad that hoeing from one end of the field and back used up all of half a day. By the end of the day a person could jump to the row where he had started hoeing that morning.

One particularly hot, sultry day we lay down on the cool linoleum after dinner and took a nap. It didn't do anything but make us lazy, and after we went back to hoeing, we couldn't get it in gear.

"It's so humid, the snakes are sweating ... on top of that my breadbasket's overstuffed," Dad complained. We all got tickled and started laughing. "Now my tickle box is turned upside down, too," he said.

Things went from bad to worse. We couldn't hoe; there wasn't any use trying. We stopped, leaned on our hoe handles and laughed at every wisecrack. In an attempt to get serious, Dad turned the talk to the giant catfish in Baker's Pond. The more we talked, the more we leaned on our hoes and daydreamed. Before that evening was finished, before the sun went down, I made up my mind I was going to catch Old Whiskers.

It had been several years since I helped Dad tie and hoop a fishing net, but I remembered how and knew I could make one without his help.

As soon as Delton and I got our night chores done up, we told Mother we were going to Red River and go swimming, and we headed straight to Baker's Pond.

We sat on the bank discussing the legend of the giant catfish until moonrise before we went home. The next morning the talk around the breakfast table was about Old Whiskers.

"Just don't y'all ever dare go swimmin' in Baker's Pond," Mother commanded. "It's sure to give you yellow fever if you do.

"What's yellow fever ... why that water is so muddy, it can't even give the moon a reflection. We ain't about to swim in it," Delton assured Mother.

Delton and I wanted to swim in Baker's Pond like all the old folks had. The looks of the water, though, plus what Mother told us about it turning your skin yellow with the fever, or making you shed your skin like a snake before you died, convinced us it wasn't worth the risk.

~

Noon Saturday came, and with it came the trip to town, to Ravenna. As usual Dad kept all the money that the three of us made from the week's hoeing. We knew that the family needed all the money for groceries, the light bill, chicken feed and the collection plate at church, so we didn't mind.

Dad usually bought Delton and me a few .22 shells to pay us for our work; that is, if he had any money left over after Mother bought groceries. Weldon, at Doggett Grocery in Ravenna, always had a soft spot in his heart for the kids. He didn't make them buy a whole box of .22 shells; he would open a box and count out however many a kid could afford at a penny a piece.

On the way to Ravenna, I finally picked up enough courage to tell Dad my problem. "Dad, I have still got three .22 shells left over from last week. What I sure would like to have is some net twine."

Delton realized it was his chance to voice his wants, and he asked for a Holloway all-day sucker ... instead of .22 shells.

"Well, we'll see if we can take care of that," Dad offered. "Y'all have been so good to work and not complain."

~

By the middle of June the peanut vines had gotten so big that digging the Johnson grass out of them did more damage than good. Audry laid his peanuts by, and we found ourselves out of work. Dad took a job at the Iron Foundry in Bonham and worked until farm work opened back up at harvest time.

Audry came by and hired me to work in the hay. He needed someone to ride the sled that he pulled behind the hay baler. My job was to stack the bales of hay on the sled as they came out of the baler chute. When I filled the sled full of hay, I would cram a big iron bar into the ground at the front of the sled. Audry would keep pulling the hay baler down the windrow until the haystack came off the sled. When we finished baling hay, the neat haystacks made it much easier for the hay haulers; they didn't have to run around all over the meadow to pick up individual bales.

Other than baling hay, there wasn't much farm work to do until harvest. Between hay cuttings, I tied on my net with big ideas of catching Old Whiskers.

~

It was nearing the end of July when I finished tying my hoop net. Putting the hoops in and rigging it was all I lacked. Rigging the net was what Dad called needling the throats down and making it ready to fish.

I tied the hoop that held the first throat to the big cottonwood tree in the backyard, stretched the net out and drove a dogwood stake in the ground to hold the tail end of the net. I tied the string from my net needle to the center mesh on the left side of the throat, took it around the dogwood stake and back to the throat, and tied it to the mesh above, back around the stake and to the mesh below, back around the stake and to the mesh above. I repeated the process until I finished the left half of the throat, then did the same thing on the right side. I needled the front and back throats down in the same manner.

Needling the throats down is where I found out I had troubles. I had tied my net with an uneven amount of meshes around it, and the throat had no middle mesh.

So what if the throat sets wonky-jawed. Old Whiskers ain't gonna notice.

I stretched the net out and admired it. It was no longer than 10 foot and too big around, which gave it a fat, dumpy look. Dad's nets were at least 20 feet long and no bigger around than my net.

I thought it looked pretty good for my first attempt at tying without any help from Dad. Dad said it looked fair to middling, which kinda hurt my feelings.

"We will go set it in the morning, Delton, and catch Old Whiskers," I bragged.

The next morning as soon as we finished eating breakfast we ran out the back door, jumped off the porch and gathered up the net.

Mother hollered, "Y'all watch out for them cottonmouth moccasins ... and the yellow fever, you hear."

Dad hardly ever gave us warnings, so when he said, "If that water is stagnant, you boys stay out of it," we knew it was worth paying heed to.

When we arrived at Baker's Pond, it was still early morning cool, but the turtles were already out in force. Loggerhead turtles, alarmed by our approach, bailed off their logs into the pea-green bloom that hid the water. There was more than one reason why the water was pea green. The "dog days of summer" was the thing that caused algae to bloom. Cows wading out for a drink of water and "excusing themselves" had provided plenty of nitrogen, and that was the reason the algae was thriving in the first place.

We sat down on a cottonwood log and took off our cutoff overalls.

I cautiously tiptoed around the edge of the pool looking for a likely place to set my net.

Every cow track could hold a cottonmouth.

As I slinked along, bullfrogs leaped to take cover with the turtles. With the leap of every frog – my muscles tensed – expecting the strike of a cottonmouth. The croaking of frogs and the shrill ringing tweet of locusts mixed with the cooing of mourning doves was anything but soothing.

"Does pea green mean ...?"

I jumped like Delton shot me with his BB gun. "Mean what?" I asked.

"Mean that the water is stagnant?" Delton asked. "Dad said if it was to stay out of it."

"Nope. Pea green algae won't grow in stagnant water. Don't you know that?"

"If you're thinking you're gonna talk me into getting in that water, you got another think coming. A loggerhead turtle or a cottonmouth might bite my toe off. You ain't gonna get me to even wade in it," Delton said.

I waded out by an old rusty fence that crossed the pool. I was sinking up to my waist in mud, and the algae bloom on the warm soupy water tickled my belly button. The algae shielded the muddy bottom from the sun, and it felt ice cold on my legs. I stepped off a ledge and suddenly found myself up to my armpits.

I ain't going any farther ... deep enough.

I placed the net beside a fencepost and tied the lead line to it. I finally got my feet unstuck from the mud, waded back to the bank and sat down on the cottonwood log with Delton. As I wiped the slimy algae off my body with cocklebur leaves, I told Delton what a good set I had made. I pulled on my cutoff overalls over muddy feet and started to clean the stinky ooze from between my toes with a stick. I didn't have any socks ... or brogans.

Not a cottonmouth moccasin had we seen.

I formed the opinion on the way back to the house that there weren't any in Baker's Pond. There were too many loggerhead turtles. "Loggerhead turtles eat baby cottonmouth moccasins. I saw one do it one time," I told Delton.

I could hardly wait until the next morning to go run the net. Delton wasn't all that enthused, though.

During the night, the net received plenty of action.

First a mud cat went into the net for the biscuit I used for bait. He nibbled on the biscuit, and soon two overgrown sun perch joined him in the fun. The three of them did fine until the mud cat decided he had rather eat perch. They were too fast for the mud cat to catch, but he chased them until they ran out of breath and died. A big loggerhead turtle who had been watching all the action swam in for dinner. After the mud cat finished eating the perch, the loggerhead turtle decided to eat the mud cat. Pretty soon his brothers and sisters and his mommy and daddy joined him; they wanted a bite, too. The feeding frenzy attracted more mud cats. In the cool of the early morning hours, some cottonmouth moccasins that had been watching the whole affair from the bank decided it was time to join the feast. They had flicked their forked tongues and whetted their appetites until they couldn't stand it anymore. They writhed across the soupy water and dove down and slithered into the net. They soon filled their stomachs so full of fish they couldn't swim out through the meshes like they went in. The net was jam-packed. Several of the gorged turtles died; there wasn't enough oxygen to go around.

That is when Delton and I showed up.

We sat down on the cottonwood log, and I shucked my cutoff overalls and slowly waded out toward the fencepost that my net was tied to. I felt in my bones that Old Whiskers was in my net.

Delton leaned back against a snag and watched. He refused to help.

I untied the string and lifted up on the net.

It is so heavy ... I think it's stuck in the mud ... It's all I can do to lift it.

I hollered to Delton, "I think I got Old Whiskers. This thing is so heavy."

Delton got up off his log and moseyed over to the edge of the water mumbling, "It's probably a snapping turtle."

The net was about to break through the pea soup when something busted against the side of the net like it was trying to get out.

The water turned frothing green. I got excited.

I dropped the net.

"I got him ... Delton, come help me quick. I got Old Whiskers ... come help ... hurry!"

Before Delton knew it, he was at my side.

We grabbed the net and lifted ... all of a sudden the net came to the top of the water. The turtles and the snakes inside went mad dog crazy.

Loggerheads snapped at thin air. They stuck their gnashing beaks, suspended on slender necks, through the meshes. Their red eyes glared. Snakes dangled through the meshes, their bulging bellies keeping them from escaping; their fangs gnashing in every direction.

Then, things got serious.

It was all too much for the net. The razor sharp edge of a turtle's shell cut a hole in the side of the net, and everything spilled out.

For a moment we stood knee deep in mud and belly deep in snapping turtles and mad cottonmouth water moccasins.

We tried to run.

The mud sucked at our legs. Delton's legs came free; he fell and then disappeared under the pea-green scum.

I panicked, flounced about and went headfirst under to find Delton.

Suddenly we were standing on the bank spitting green algae; how we got there, a mystery.

Pea green soup covered us head to toe.

We made our way to the log where our cutoffs were and sat there painting. After we got over the blind scares, I bragged, "Well, now we can say we have swam in Baker's Pond."

"Yeah," Delton agreed, "now all we got left is waiting for the yellow fever to kill us. Do you believe what Mother said, about yellow fever making us look like a banana in our casket?"

"Oh, man ... she was just trying to scare us to keep us from swimming in that scummy pool. We are gonna die; but we ain't gonna turn yellow."

We went to the barn and hid out until our hair dried. We knew we would never be able to convince Mother and Dad that we hadn't gone swimming in Baker's Pond.

We never went back for the net.

The snakes and turtles can have it.

The fever was slow to catch up with Delton and me. It was a week later when I started running a high fever, and then a day later it hit Delton. Our fever went so high that our skin peeled off. Mother held us down in bed to keep the snapping turtles and snakes from eating us alive, and Dad rushed to Eldon Donaldson's and borrowed their phone to call Dr. Jack Saunders.

Dr. Jack came and gave us shots of penicillin. He pronounced what we had was malaria. When he left he gave Mother and Dad a bit of encouragement. "Malaria's easier to doctor than if a cottonmouth had bit 'em ... only thing, it takes longer. Keep 'em cool as you can by bathing 'em in ice water, and I'll be back next week."

Mother prayed constantly all week for the Lord to heal her babies. She would end her prayers with "If it be in accordance with your will, Lord," and then she would get up off her knees, sweaty and exhausted and crying.

We ran extremely high fevers all week; the dog days of summer weren't helping matters, either. Mother and Dad took turns sitting up with us ... day and night. Sometimes when Mother couldn't hold both of us on the bed at the same time, she would have to wake Dad up for help.

When Dr. Jack came back, he shot us full of penicillin but the only encouragement he could offer was, "Given a couple of more weeks, they should show some improvement. I'll be back next week."

Mother prayed, Dad kept wash rags soaked in ice water on us, and they took turns holding us in the bed when we went delirious.

Dr. Jack came back and gave us shots for the third week in a row, then he broke the news to Mother and Dad. "If they're gonna live, they are gonna do it this week. I have finished their penicillin. I won't be back unless you call me. By the way, do you have any idea where they could have contracted malaria?

"We suspect they went swimmin' in Baker's Pond. It ain't nothing but a stagnant stock tank anymore. But all we ask is for them to get well. If they do, we ain't gonna force 'em to tell us."

"Naugh ... it comes from mosquitoes; it doesn't come from stagnant stock tanks. Don't be too hard on 'em. Now let me give y'all a bit of advice: "When they sleep, y'all sleep, or else your systems will get run down and, *bingo* – a mosquito will give it to you."

It was toward the end of the week when our fevers broke. We begged for Mother and Dad to make a freezer of ice cream, and they knew we were out of the woods.

Our hiatus from field work and harvest put a crimp in the family income, but Mother and Dad never let Delton and me know that.

20
PUPPY DOG TALES

What young boy, growing up in the country in the 1950s, didn't want a good 'coon dog? Furthermore, what boy that grew up in the 1950s who had any kind of dog, didn't have a good 'coon dog? Wanting a good 'coon dog was especially true of Delton and me; we didn't have a dog, hadn't ever had a dog, and if we ever got our own dog, it would be a 'coon dog.

The way we had it figured, there wasn't any way a person could make easier money than selling 'coon hides.

I guessed that everyone, the whole world over, knew Uncle Earl Price because he was the man who owned Ol' Trailer, the world-renowned 'coon dog. World-renowned to Uncle Earl meant everyone in the world who hunted 'coons ... that he knew.

"Ol' Trailer is the best black-and-tan hound ever to strike a trail," Uncle Earl claimed.

The excitement mounted when Mother came in from the mailbox and plopped a letter from Uncle Earl down on the kitchen table. Our Aunt Dovie had written it for Uncle Earl to let us know that Queenie had her pups. Queenie was Joe Choice's bitch, and she was the next best 'coon dog in the country, Joe Choice claimed.

We knew the reason for the letter and jumped up and down, squealing with delight as Mother opened it.

With Queenie for a mother and Trailer for a daddy those puppies are gonna grow up to be the best 'coon dogs ever to strike a trail.

We couldn't wait to see Trailer's and Queenie's brand new pups, but one thing or another had kept us from getting to go see them.

We lay in bed and discussed the situation and tried to go to sleep. We decided that in the morning at the breakfast table we would press the issue.

"It's been three weeks, and we ain't got to see those pups yet," Delton said in a pleading voice as he reached across the breakfast table to get another fried chocolate pie.

"Come Saturday you'll get to see 'em. We have got to go buy groceries – we're out of everything – and then we'll go over to Joe's and Minnie's house so y'all can see the pups," Dad assured us.

The days seemed to drag by. Hoeing peanuts and waiting for Saturday seemed to cause time to drag. We were so exhausted by midmorning on Saturday that we could hardly hoe.

Dad knew the reason why.

We were about middle ways of our rows, headed toward the pickup, when Dad decided we would quit a little early and made his announcement. "Okay, boys, we've put in a good morning; let's quit and go to the house."

That was all it took; the exhaustion left us. We threw our hoes down and ran all the way to the pickup. Dad was right behind us.

~

When our pickup truck pulled into Joe's and Minnie's front yard, the first thing Delton and I saw was a porch full of black-and-tan pups. A little feisty runt bailed off the porch and came to meet the pickup. Five puppies had taken their place around a dried up 'coon hide and were growling in their efforts to take it away from each other. A big fat clumsy puppy followed underneath Queenie, getting his supper, as she waddled off the porch.

Delton grabbed the runt, and I took the roly-poly pup off its teat. We weren't about to interrupt the game of tag that the growling, fighting-mad pups were having. We petted and wagged the runt and the fat pup around while Dad, Uncle Earl and Joe Choice talked 'coon hunting and admired the next generation of 'coonhounds. Neither the runt nor the fat pup showed any interest in the game of tag their brothers and sisters had going.

Delton developed a soft spot for the little feisty runt; he thought he was so cute, he couldn't keep his hands off him. I fell in love with the big clumsy, lazy one. He was so fat he waddled along without a care in the world.

Our hearts dropped when we overheard Joe Choice and Uncle Earl talking about what kind of price they should be able to get for the pups. "Just having a daddy like Ol' Trailer automatically puts at least a ten dollar price tag on your head," Uncle Earl said.

"Well, having Queenie for a mother ain't a drawback either," Joe Choice added.

We knew that there was no way we would ever be able to own a ten dollar pup. Mother and Dad didn't have that kind of money.

~

The next couple of weeks Delton and I planned and schemed, trying to figure out how we could get hold of enough money to buy one of Trailer's and Queenie's pups.

We finally thought we had it all figured out. I decided to spring it on Mother and Dad at the supper table that night.

Mother called supper, and we didn't spend much time at the wash basin. Mother turned thanks, and we didn't dive in as we were accustomed to doing. Delton kept looking at me, and I kept trying to figure out how he was gonna break our plan to Dad.

Delton got tired of waiting on me.

"We want a loan," he blurted out.

I used some explaining to take the shock out of Delton's statement. "We figure we can catch a 'coon ever night and maybe two. In no time at all we can repay you.

In one breath Dad took the air out of our sails. "Okay ... but where are your mom and me gonna get the money to make you the loan in the first place? We just can't afford a puppy right now." Dad winked at Mother.

Mother put some air back in our sails, though. "Why don't y'all hit Uncle Earl up for a loan?"

If Uncle Earl will only let us pay for a pup later ... maybe?

Our family's total income at the time was extremely meager. Dad was making 50 cents an hour. Delton and I were making the same for both of us. We were hoeing peanuts for Audry Cain, and the wages of all three of us combined came to a dollar an hour. We were working from "dawn till can't," as Dad put it.

The rest of the week, Thursday and Friday, flew by at a snail's pace. Unless we could talk Joe Choice and Uncle Earl into letting us buy a puppy on credit, there just wasn't any way.

The pups were approaching six weeks old – weaning age. Delton and I were getting desperate because we knew that by the weekend the pups were likely to be gone.

It was Saturday, and although we hoed peanuts until noon, we weren't worth a hill of beans. Our minds weren't on hoeing; they were on petting pups, and Dad was just as anxious as we were.

We gobbled down our dinner as fast as we could and helped Mother wash dishes. Dad stretched out on the floor to catch a few winks, but a few was all he got before Mother hollered at him.

"Honey, you better come on ... or we'll run off and leave you. Dean's gonna have to learn how to drive sooner or later."

Dean drive ... the thought startled Dad from a sound asleep to underneath the steering wheel before you could blink an eye.

The old truck was puffing by the time it went across the sand bed and climbed the Mulberry hill. It was so happy to get to go to Ravenna that it wasn't about to die, though. We added water to the radiator and continued on; pretty soon we pulled to the curb in front of Doggett Grocery Store.

Ravenna had once been a bustling town. Now most of the commerce was gone, but Ravenna was still an exciting place for country boys to go to on Saturday afternoon.

On the west side of the street, as you came into town from Mulberry, were four businesses. The cotton gin was first, then you went about a quarter of a mile to the main part of town. Doggett's Grocery Store was on the right and then Fishy Frair Grocery. As you went out of town headed toward Bonham was Ice Man Pete's Ice House and Sye Frair's gas station all in the same building. Clyde Hodge's Garage was the only business on the east side of the street, and it was directly across the road from Doggett's and Fishy's. Those were all the businesses that had survived the depression years.

Dad aimed the pickup toward the embankment in front of the grocery stores, let off the foot feed and let the truck coast until its bumper rammed the concrete, his way of conserving the brakes on the old truck. Mother and Dad got out of the cab, and we bailed out of the back and sauntered toward Doggett's Grocery.

In front of Fishy's Grocery Store sat an old pine, wonky-legged bench. Over the years it had collected numerous initials and names, not only of people wanting other people to know they had sat there, but of young people wanting other people to know who they "claimed." Jerry laid his claim to Julia by carving Jerry + Julia. There was a Robert loves Judy and a lot of names with a year carved beside them going back to '33. Delton and I liked to check out the latest carvings, but Uncle Earl, Joe Choice and Audalee had the bench covered.

Mother exchanged a "howdy, how are y'all doing," for a "doing fine; how are y'all," as she walked past the bench and went into Doggett's.

Dad, Delton and I walked toward the bench. Seeing them sitting there sent cold chills down my spine; I wanted to go ask them if all the pups were gone, but I was afraid of hearing the worst.

We kept Dad between us and the bench. I held Dad's hand and stood my ground while Delton held onto Dad's britches leg and peeked around. Joe Choice motioned for us to come over to him. With shy grins painting our faces we left Dad and walked over to Joe Choice.

Joe Choice placed one of his big rough hands on my shoulder and the other one on Delton's shoulder, looked us in the eye and said in a man-to-man voice:

"Reckon you young men could get your daddy to bring you over to mine and Minnie's house when he's finished here? If you boys can talk your Dad into giving me and Minnie a ride home, I'm gonna give you boys a couple of 'coon dog pups. We need to get 'em off of their mammy." Almost under his breath he murmured, "All of the rest of the pups are gone ... except for the two that I'm giving y'all."

We looked at each other in dismay and jumped up and down with raw excitement. I ran my arm around Joe Choice's neck and almost pulled him off the bench. Joe Choice pushed me back, apparently embarrassed from all the making-over from me.

"It was your Uncle Earl's doings, too," Joe Choice said, not wanting to take all the credit.

I stepped back from Joe Choice and dashed toward Uncle Earl and flung my arm around his neck, and at the same time Delton replaced me on Joe Choice's neck. They had squelched our fears ... almost.

Are the fat one and the runt the ones left?

Aside from puppy business, the main thing I wanted to do while we were in Ravenna was see if I could find a red innertube. Black synthetic rubber was replacing the red rubber used to make innertubes, and it wouldn't stretch like real rubber; it wasn't worth a flip for slingshot rubbers. We took off running across the street to Clyde Hodge's garage. Right in the middle of the street Delton grabbed my arm and stopped me.

"Do you reckon the pups we wanted are gone? They were the best ones of the bunch."

"Now ain't the time to go worrying about it ... a car is coming!" I screamed and shoved Delton at the same time.

We busted through the door to Clyde's garage, full of vim and vinegar. "We're getting' two puppies and besides all that ... Trailer's their daddy," I told Clyde.

"Well, now ... what's with the vinegar?" Clyde asked.

"We're looking for a red innertube to make us some slingshot rubbers out of ... have you got one?" I asked. There was one lying across Clyde's anvil with about a dozen patches on it, and he was putting another patch on.

"Oh, I got this one, but it's still good. I'm patching some holes in it that was put there by goat heads." He looked up from his anvil and asked, "'Coonhounds, huh. What are their names?"

"They don't have names yet ... we just got 'em," Delton said.

"I think that Sye over at the gas station has a red tube laying round behind his water trough. He'll probably give it to you ... if you ask him for it."

I left to go ask Sye for the red innertube, and Delton headed back across the street to Doggett's.

Sye was proud to give me the red rubber innertube but asked for me to make him a slingshot in return. He claimed he wanted to give one to Ice Man Pete to shoot at dogs with when they didn't want their masters to get ice.

Mother's and Dad's business at Doggett's and Fishy's was finished and all that remained was to gas up the truck, and we would be ready to go get our puppies. Joe Choice and Dad loaded the groceries, chicken feed and dog food into the back of the pickup. Delton and I piled in, and we drove to Sye Frair's to gas up and get a block of ice from Ice Man Pete. Dad spent his last two dollars filling the truck up with gas, "The blame thing helt 10 gallons," he complained. Mother and Minnie walked up about that time, and we all loaded into the truck to go to Joe and Minnie Choice's. Dad, Mother and Minnie rode in the cab, and Joe Choice got in the back with Delton and me.

Joe Choice talked 'coon dog training with us all the way home. He never mentioned which two pups he still had left, and neither of us asked him. We were getting two of the finest 'coon dog puppies ever born, and we couldn't believe it. We kept our fingers crossed, though.

When Dad headed the truck down Joe's and Minnie's lane, we stood up behind the cab.

Not a puppy could we see. Our hearts raced.

When we pulled into the front yard, the feisty little runt clamored from a cardboard box, bailed off the porch and ran to meet the pickup. Our truck ground to a stop before the fat lazy pup waggled out of the box and stumbled down the porch steps to meet us. We bailed out of the truck and watched the beautiful black-and-tan pups, ears flopping, come straight to us whimpering and whining.

"They're begging y'all to take 'em," Joe Choice said.

The truth was every one of the brothers and sisters of the runt and the fat lazy pup was the pick of the litter. The two pups Joe Choice and Uncle Earl gave us were culls. As far as we were concerned, though, the feisty runt and the fat lazy pup were the pick of the litter.

Loading the pups into the back of the pickup wasn't a problem at all. You couldn't have pried those pups away if your life had depended on it. Everywhere we went, the puppies were right on our heels.

All four of us settled down against the cab of the pick truck for the ride back to Mulberry. As the truck rolled out of Joe and Minnie Choice's yard, Dad waved out the window and Mother craned her neck back to look at us. "Tell him thank you," she hollered.

We both did ... at the top of our lungs.

"You're much-a-bliged. You boys give 'em a good home now, you hear," Joe Choice's voice trailed after us.

When the pickup truck dropped off the Mulberry hill, steam started blowing out from under the hood. By the time we got across the sand bed, steam was coming out of the radiator like puffs coming from a tea kettle. Dad pulled over at the bridge that crossed the slough to water down the Old truck. We and both pups were sound asleep behind the cab.

"There ain't anything in the whole world that can make a boy happier than a puppy or a red innertube," Dad told Mother as he stepped out of the truck and went to the spring to fetch a bucket of water for the thirsty Chevy. The truck made it home fine without Dad having to give it another drink. Delton and I and our puppies were reveled awake by the squealing brakes as Dad brought the pickup to a halt in front of the smokehouse. We baled out of the pickup and went running to the barn with the pups hot on our heels.

"Come on, Andy," Delton cried out as he sped toward the barn.

"Come on, Amos, you lazy hounddog," I beckoned as Amos and I ran to catch up with Delton and Andy.

"Have you boys already tagged 'em?" Mother called.

"Yeah ... the skinny runt is Andy, and the roly-poly lazy one is Amos," I replied as all four of us disappeared into the barn.

~

Amos and Andy grew strong and fast; not only did they have plenty of table scraps to eat, Delton and I saw to it that they had plenty milk and a hen egg once in a while.

Mosey was Mother's Jersey cow's name, and she had only been fresh a few months. Once she calved and got her milk down, it wasn't like her to dry up so soon. Mother suspected that the problem wasn't with Mosey drying up but rather it was that Delton and I were slipping Amos and Andy some of her milk.

She talked the situation over with Dad. "The only explanation is Amos and Andy – or, should I say Dean and Delton," Mother told Dad.

"I think you oughta have a talk with the boys," Dad said.

We stopped giving them Mosey's milk, but what Mother hadn't suspected was that we were feeding Amos and Andy chicken eggs, too. Sort of their dessert, we reasoned.

The way we trained Amos and Andy to cold trail, like Trailer, was eventually going to lead to their demise if feeding them eggs didn't first. We should have known better than teach the pups to cold trail chickens to the roost and to feed them eggs. We had both heard Dad's expression many times. "I ain't gonna have a chicken eatin' or a egg-suckin' dog on this place."

~

It was the pups' birthday; they were one year old. Delton and I set in on Dad to let us take the pups hunting.

"We want to take them on a real 'coon hunt. They ain't gonna ever learn how to hunt 'coon ... hunting chickens," Delton pleaded.

"Whoa ... wait a minute. Did I hear you say you been hunting chickens? What do you mean ... how do you hunt chickens with a dog?" Dad was murder-judge serious.

I held my tongue and wished that Delton had, too.

"Did I say hunting chickens?" Delton stammered. "What I meant to say was that Amos and Andy were gonna grow up being too chicken to hunt."

Dad cut his eyes from Delton to me; he had deep wrinkles in his forehead. *Like Mother's washboard.*

"I want an answer now," Dad said.

"Tell 'em, Delton ... you got us into this mess."

"Well ... uh ... Dean said ...."

I held up my hand and pointed my finger at Delton. "Don't go saying, 'I said.' Trailing the chickens to roost was your idea, Delton."

"But you said it wouldn't hurt anything."

"Just stop the blame game. Tell me now, Delton," Dad ordered.

"What we did was after Mother shut the chickenhouse door at night, we would wait until the chicken trail got cold and then start Amos and Andy to trailing them to the chickenhouse."

Dad couldn't keep from sniggering; he turned his back and faked a cough. He finally regained his composure and turned back around.

"Well, since they never got the taste of chicken, it probably didn't do much harm. But I'm warning you two; if I ever see them trailing a chicken again ... day or night ... they're dead dogs. Many a good 'coon dog has been ruined by getting the taste of chickens, *or* tasting their eggs. Now that'll turn 'em into egg sucking, chicken killin' dogs every time."

Oops. I put my hand over Delton's mouth.

Joe Choice said what I had been waiting to hear. "You gotta get them off of chickens and start them on 'coon."

"I guess y'all better start taking Amos and Andy down on the river bluff tonight. I gotta warn y'all, though. Don't go off the bluff down into the river bottom. Things can happen to a man in the river bottom after dark. I don't want you boys going there until I say it's ok. I wanna know ahead of time that you're going, in case you show up killed ... understood."

From then on, almost every night after supper; we took Amos and Andy and headed to the river bluff to do some 'coon hunting. We would hunt down to the bluff, on the edge of the river bottom, but were too scared to follow the dogs off into the bottom. Dad had made going of into the river bottom sound so scary.

Amos and Andy seem to sense we aren't supposed to go into the river bottom either.

When Amos and Andy did venture into Red River bottom, we would hear them whining, and back up the bluff they would come with their tails curled up between their legs.

"They sense something's gonna get 'em," I told Delton.

Delton's idea was that they saw a shaggy river monster and it was fixing to eat 'em ... hair, hide, guts and all.

Dad told us that when a dog tucked his tail under his belly it was a sign that a grizzly bear or a black, yellow-eyed panther was after him.

Amos and Andy loved chasing rabbits, which went without saying, and they had plenty to chase. I would start them out trailing a 'coon, and before you could say Jack Sprout, they were barking in hot pursuit and running in a big circle, a dead giveaway that they were chasing after a cottontail.

The rabbit population for the last two years had run unchecked. Dad thought that it was because Pannell's pack of wolfhounds had forced the coyotes to change their home range.

"There ain't enough critters out there eatin' rabbits. Now days people can afford better grub than rabbit chili to keep their guts full. Now if it was back during the depression, it would be a different story. We would've kept them rabbits thinned out," he claimed.

Amos and Andy had stayed with the first trail I put them on, definitely a giant 'coon or a little 'coon with giant feet, until they jumped him and the race had gotten hot. The smart old 'coon immediately ran across a rabbit's trail and then went into a hollow log. Amos and Andy were sidetracked; they chose burr rabbit instead of grizzly 'coon. Suddenly the straight-forward race turned into a circular one, but the rabbit was smarter than them all; he circled back and ran into the log with the 'coon.

The pursuit ended with baying barks coming from Andy. When we arrived at the site of the catch, we found both dogs scratching and baying at the hollow log. They were groveling up to the log, slobbering and clawing like they could see what was inside it.

I sent Delton to get me a twisting stick, and he returned in a few minutes with a green dogwood stick about six feet long. I took out my jackknife and split the little end of the dogwood stick down about 4 or 5 inches. Then I broke the head off a kitchen match and wedged it down into the split end to hold the sticks slightly apart and handed it to Delton.

"Delton, you twist the rabbit out, and I'll hold the dogs off of you."

"Okay," Delton said. He was glad to get to twist out a rabbit.

I grabbed the dogs by their collars and instructed Delton in the fine art of twisting out a rabbit. "Ease the stick in so as not to scare the rabbit. When the stick touches him, you'll feel something that feels kinda squishy."

"I feel 'em ... now what?"

"Don't push ... he's apt to run. Just start twisting the stick around and around. When you get his fur wound up in the stick, it'll get his hide, too. When you feel old burr rabbit start squirming and kicking, pull him out."

"I got him; he's a kicking ... listen ... hear him hissing?"

"Yep, I hear him. I ain't ever heard a rabbit or a 'possum hiss, though."

To our surprise; what came out of the log wasn't a rabbit or a 'possum. It was a giant, grizzled, grey-bearded 'coon.

I couldn't hold the dogs, and Delton couldn't hold the skewered 'coon. It was a good thing Delton couldn't hold the 'coon, though; if he had, he would have been in the middle of the fight that broke out. The 'coon backed up against the log, stood on his hind legs and made his stand. Andy stood face to face with the 'coon, his teeth bared and shining, slobbering at the mouth. Amos dashed in and out and yipped. The 'coon squalled, and his fur flew as Andy snapped at his throat.

The 'coon's teeth gnashed at Amos's hind quarter. Amos went to the lantern and hunkered there in the light.

Andy saw his chance and dove into the 'coon; he grabbed his jugular vein between his jaws and seized up.

In a few seconds the fight was over.

The hunt was over, too. I threw the 'coon over my shoulder, Delton called the dogs in and we headed to the house.

After that we got serious about our hunting. We decided we wanted to break Amos and Andy from running rabbits. "Uncle Earl claims that rabbits are trash, that they're useless as teats on a boar hog," I told Delton.

"Well, he says 'possums and skunks are, too, but 'possums bring a buck and skunks three bucks, and that's not trash by me," Delton added.

We feared that we would never break Amos and Andy from running rabbits. Uncle Earl and Joe Choice – two of the best 'coon dog trainers in the world, they proclaimed of themselves – squelched our fears about Amos and Andy running rabbits.

"Young dogs and boys have gotta have a lot of action. Just don't ever show Amos and Andy any praise unless they hunt what you put 'em on, and they'll grow out of chasing rabbits," Uncle Earl said, and Joe Choice nodded his head in agreement.

We took their advice, and for a few months Amos and Andy didn't get much praise, but when they did deserve it, we piled it on.

It was working.

Occasionally Amos and Andy treed a 'coon, and they were running rabbits less and less. As the nights went by, the dogs got better, and soon they were getting a 'coon almost every night. And they always got two or three 'possums.

Mother warned us not to come home on school nights smelling like a skunk. On Friday nights we could take skunks; so unless it was Friday night when the dogs bayed at something in a hole in the ground, we always called the dogs off.

I thought we were ready to start hunting off the bluff down in Red River bottom. *Man, if Delton and I could only take the dogs there, we could make a fortune.*

We had finished eating supper, had helped Mother do the dishes and had finished doing our homework. We joined Mother and Dad on the front porch for a little relaxation before bedtime. During the nightly brainstorming session that cranked up, I set in on Dad to start letting us hunt down in Red River bottom.

"I'll think about it," Dad said. He looked Delton square in the eyes and asked, "How do you feel about going off the bluff into the bottom? It's likely to be foggy, and the hoot owls will be a hootin', and the moon will be pointing out hobgoblins."

"Why, that stuff don't bother me ... beside Dean said he would hold my hand if I got scared."

"Well, it's time to go to bed for now ... I'll think about letting y'all go to the river bottom and let you know something in the morning," Dad said. We went to sleep listening to Mother and Dad discuss the Red River bottom thing.

"I'm so tired of Dean's begging and hearing him talk in his sleep, night after night, about hunting 'coons down in Red River bottom," Dad said.

"Well, I'm tired of hearing the screen door open and finding him sound asleep, sitting on the porch steps. I'm sleeping so light. I never know when he's gonna walk off and go down in the bottom in his sleep," Mother added.

The next morning at the breakfast table Dad prepared me for their answer. "I think *maybe* the dogs are grown up enough now, so they can fight the grizzlies and panthers off of y'all. It's true what you said, Dean. There are a lot of 'coons in the river bottom; maybe those dogs can start earnin' their keep."

"We just want you boys to be extra careful," Mother added.

"Okay," Dad cleared his throat and forcefully said, "if both of you want to ... y'all can take Amos and Andy to the river bottom come Saturday night."

I jumped up and ran around the table to Dad and threw my arms around his neck. "Thank you, thank you, thank you ... you won't be sorry."

Man, we'll hunt Red River bottom until our heart's content.

Delton slowly walked over and halfheartedly hugged Dad's neck. He wasn't sure about Amos fighting grizzlies and panthers; he had witnessed Amos fight the big 'coon.

I was running around with my head held high, being cocky with Delton and smart talking Mother. It took Dad's words to put me in place.

"You're getting too big for your britches, Dean. Red River bottom will put you in your place. You're going down in the river bottom with the responsibility for two dogs and a little brother on your hands. That's a man's responsibility; you had better start acting like one," he said.

I thought about the responsibilities Dad spelled out to me, and by the time Saturday came I was as serious as a snakebite. Mother and Dad laughed at how the prospect of going into Red River bottom humbled me. I knew there were no grizzlies or panthers in Red River bottom. I also knew there was no place in the whole world that was darker on a moonless night.

Waiting on darkness to fall and listening to the hoot owl hooting from the cottonwood tree down by the barn was wearing on my nerves. Amos and Andy lay on the front porch and waited. Mother made us check our lantern and fill it with coal oil. Dark finally came, and the four of us made our way toward the Red River bluff.

Mother watched the light of our coal oil lantern out the kitchen window; we reached the bluff and turned down it toward Baker's Pond. Seeing the flicker of light disappear off the bluff into the eeriness of the river bottom and the hooting of the owl stirred her innards. She went to the living room, set in her rocker and read the Bible.

Dad went to bed.

I felt confident that if we could get Amos and Andy down in the river bottom, we wouldn't have any more trouble with them trying to run rabbits. The problem was getting them past the rabbits between the house and the river bottom bluff. I had a plan of how to accomplish just that. I tied a fishing line to Amos's and Andy's collars. We would lead them until we got deep down in the river bottom and then turn them loose.

We'll go home with enough 'coon hides to make Dad proud.

We led the dogs past Baker's Pond ... no problem yet. We approached the river bluff. When we went off that bluff, we would be in Red River bottom ... no problem yet.

"Amos and Andy must know we're taking them to the river bottom. They ain't even tried to break loose from us and run a rabbit," Delton noticed.

We dropped off the bluff into the river bottom, and the light from the lantern shined on a broken snag sticking up out of the edge of the slough. It was only a willow tree that high wind had broken off, but it looked like some sort of ghost.

"What is that?" Delton asked.

"Nothing ... just a broke off tree snag."

"Nope not that ... way out there." Delton pointed. "There ... something is going across the slough on that log."

I squinted and held the lantern up high. "It's a 'coon ... turn the dogs loose!" I hollered.

The unleashed dogs never saw what Delton and I saw. Instead they put their noses to the ground and started poking them at every clump of grass and 'coon track, and there were 'coon tracks everywhere. They soon picked up a cold trail. They sniffed, excitedly working the trail; Amos slow bawling and working his way south down the edge of the slough, Andy right on his tail.

We're home free if that 'coon track doesn't turn into a 'possum track.

"Why don't we set down and rest, while the dogs work the cold trail into something hotter?" Delton asked as Amos and Andy worked the trail farther and farther up the slough, away from us.

Suddenly it seemed like the dogs started to circle. Now they were out toward Red River in the big grass patch and coming back down the river bank.

'Coons never run in the big grass patches.

Suddenly dog yelps mingled with pain filled the dark night air. Caterwauling screams – like we had never heard before came from the grass patch.

"Sounds like Dad's 'wompus cat squalls' he makes," Delton said as he covered his eyes and got behind my back.

Then just as suddenly as the squalls started, they stopped.

"Listen, Delton, do you hear anything?" I asked.

Dead silence ....

I headed toward the dogs, at least where I last heard them.

Delton opened his eyes – *Dean is leaving* – the light from my lantern was disappearing out in the swamp.

Three giant steps caught Delton up with me, and he grabbed my overall suspender in a death grip.

I stopped to listen.

Amos and Andy's agonizing whines filled our ears. "They need us," I blurted out. I dragged Delton as I took off running again to rescue the dogs.

The dogs ran toward us and the lantern light. When they entered the light of our lantern, I got a glimpse of something riding the rear end of Amos, and then whatever it was turned and fled into the swamp.

"I saw it ... I saw it!" Delton shouted. "It was something big and awful."

Amos and Andy crawled under our feet whining and whimpering, carrying their tails tucked tight between their legs. Their ears were shredded and bleeding. I sat the lantern down by the dogs. The reflecting light made the blood sparkle in their deep bloody cuts. They had deep cuts in their flanks and on their backs. Delton got sick to his stomach but managed to say "Whatever that thing was, it was sure afraid of the lantern light, because it lit a shuck."

"One good sign," I told Delton, "they ain't squirting blood from their throats."

We grabbed Amos and Andy up in our arms. "They won't ever feel like walking again," Delton said.

"Yeah, they will, Delton, if we can get 'em home to Dad before they go dead."

We headed home. When we reached Baker's Pond, we put the dogs down and washed some of the blood off ourselves and off the dogs. We rested for a minute but were afraid to linger, the dogs were bleeding so bad. By the time we reached the house and climbed the steps to the front door, the dogs were moaning painful bloodcurdling whimpers.

We panicked.

Mother and Dad came to the door. I just stood there holding Amos, dancing up and down, unable to utter a word.

"'Coons zero ... booger won ... hunt's over," Delton blabbered out in a state of shock.

Mother saw the bloody mess – *A panther attacked my boys* – She started wringing her hands.

Dad kept his cool. "Is it the dogs, or is it y'all."

"It's the dogs ... they're dying." I finally got my tongue. "We're not hurt; we're just cut-dog bloody."

Mother settled down a little when she heard that we weren't hurt. "You boys don't dare come in this house, all bloody like that; you go to the well and wash up before you come in," she demanded.

Dad picked up where Mother left off. "Wash the dogs and then put 'em in the barn. We'll talk 'bout it in the mornin," he said, as he stumbled back toward bed.

Delton and I and Amos and Andy spent the rest of the night in the barn.

Early the next morning Dad went to the barn to milk old Mosey and found us all curled up asleep with Amos and Andy, in a straw bed we made for the dogs. Dad opened the corncrib door to get some nubbins for Mosey, and the squeaky door woke us up. We begged for Dad to look at the dogs' wounds.

"They're doing fine. If you boys will let me get the milking done, we'll give 'em some milk; that'll do 'em up right." After he finished milking, we gave some to Amos and Andy, then went to the house to check on breakfast. When we left, they were lying in the straw bed licking their wounds and slurping warm milk.

Mother heard us coming but rang the dinner bell anyway. "Come and get it while it's hot."

We all sat down to a platter of bacon, sausage and ham; scrumptious smelling steam oozed from the platter. A big cast iron skillet, brimming full of scrambled eggs, sat in the center of the table. There was a big bowl of rich white gravy full of sausage crumbles that gave it a come-and-get-me texture. A blue granite pan full of crusty biscuits, as big as a saucer, with a chunk of fresh churned butter hiding inside each one, made my mouth water. Mother's special wild plum butter, sorghum molasses from Venable's syrup mill, dark honey from a bee tree Dad and us robbed and chewy pear preserves that Mrs. Nixon made were arranged in quart jars on the back side of the table.

Mother turned thanks. Before I took a bite I cast an eye toward Dad and asked, "What do you think attacked ...?"

"Whoa." Mother threw up her hand with her palm flattened toward me. "This is my table ... you are not gonna ruin this beautiful breakfast I prepared for you with your bloody dog talk; either take your talk elsewhere or eat!"

I ate. For hours it seemed.

Finally Dad pushed back from the table, winked at Mother and asked her very politely, "May we be excused from *your* table? We have got some dog talk to take care of."

"Yeah ... I just don't wanna hear it. Y'all take it to the barn."

Delton and I sat down on a couple of bales of hay and watched Dad examine the dogs. He washed the dried crusty blood with cold well water until he got it all off, complaining all the while about the pesky green flies that continually tried to land on the nasty cuts.

"Amos and Andy are mighty stiff, and some of the cuts are deep. I think that they'll be all right, though, if we can keep the green flies off of 'em. We'll daub some Blue on the worst of the cuts and sew 'em up.

"Delton, you go to the house and tell your mom you want the Blue.

Bring me my needle that I sew peanut sacks up with and some heavy sewing thread. Dean, you go to the garden and dig some garlic bulbs and then take 'em to the smokehouse and crush 'em up real good and mix 'em into a little coal oil. Make a runny paste and bring that to me."

"What's Blue?" Delton asked.

"Blue's that cow and horse liniment we daub on y'all when you get cut ... you know." Dad wasn't sure what Blue was either.

"What do you think could've done it?" I asked.

"Well, there're reports of panther sightings along the river. It could've been a panther," Dad speculated.

"Could it have been one of them wild Russian hogs?" I asked.

"Nope ... hogs would've eaten 'em up, not clawed 'em to death." Dad got tired of the questions and demanded, "Now y'all go do what I told you."

We soon returned, me with my stinky concoction, and Delton with the Blue, needle and thread. Then he went into an explanation about what we saw. "We got a glimpse of the thing in the lantern light; the thing was huge ... bigger than the dogs. It seemed to be black. I think it was a bear," Delton said.

Dad removed the dauber from the Blue and went to working the medicine into Amos's deep ugly gashes, talking at the same time.

"Your Granddad Price use to see bears when he was a kid, down on Caney creek in the cane breaks, but there ain't been any sightings since then. My bet is that it was a housecat of some sort," Dad said with a laugh.

"Nope ... we know our dogs could whip a housecat of any sort." Dad riled me sometimes.

Dad saw my face drop at the thought of a housecat whipping Amos and Andy. "Maybe it was a wompus cat then," he quickly added. "Wompus cats are big but not as big as a panther, though. They have got tall pointed ears and short, bob tails." Dad finished daubing the Blue on Amos before he looked up again or said anything else. He doctored Andy next, then he smeared the garlic-coal oil concoction on their scratches and everyplace where their hair was missing. He sewed up the worst of the gashes and their shredded ears then stood up and admired his job before he commented.

"They're sure stinky, but the green flies won't be a blowing 'em. You boys are gonna have to give Amos and Andy a few days to heal their wounds and get their nerve back."

Dad sounded fairly sure that their wounds would heal. I didn't think he was so sure Amos and Andy would get their nerve back, though. Little did anyone know, before they could get their nerve back, another event would rob them completely ... of any nerve they would ever have.

Dad and us left the dogs to their healing and went to the well to freshen up before going into the house. On the way to the well, Dad told us, "We'll go to the river bottom in a little bit. If y'all can take me to where it happened and we can find any tracks or scat, that'll tell us what the thing was."

"I can take you to the place. The ground will still be wet where I was standing," Delton said.

The trip to the river bottom, to the scene of the crime, proved very fruitful. Delton found compelling evidence as to where we were standing when Amos and Andy met their undoing. It became apparent, though, that Delton didn't know what scat was, from the conversation that followed.

"Right about there," Delton pointed, "is where they came running into the light of the lantern. That's when the thing turned around and really scatted out of there."

Dad and I had a good laugh at Delton's expense.

Dad explained that scat was an animal's feces ... that it was dookie and not where something had kicked up the dirt taking off and running away.

Delton broke us up again when he said, "Dookie ... that's what Mother calls it. Why doesn't she just call it scat?"

Dad backtracked the dogs in the direction they had come from when they entered the lantern light. He soon found where the ruckus started and read the sign for us.

"Hey, y'all come here and see these claw marks Amos and Andy made when that thing jumped on 'em. Well, it was a bobcat all right," Dad said as he raked the leaves back and found cat tracks. "Look ... there are big and little dog tracks, 'Amos and Andy tracks.'"

Next he took a stick and carefully raked around in the leaves, grass and debris. He found plenty of scat, dog and cat, and one big spot on the ground that was soaking wet. He also found a few flecks of blood. Dad found more blood as he followed the scuffed-up ground in the direction the dogs left to get back to lantern light. The farther we followed the blood trail, the more blood we found.

We went back home satisfied that a bobcat was responsible for the attack on Amos's and Andy's lives.

~

After supper Dad popped a dishpan full of popcorn and we all went out on the front porch to eat it. Way in the distance, from the direction of our Red River pasture, a dog barked on the trail of a coyote. Every once in a while another dog with a higher-pitched voice joined in. As late evening approached, the trail became hotter. If things continued to develop, before dark, the dog pack would jump the coyote and the race would be on.

Mother didn't have any interest at all in hearing a dog chase a coyote. She finished eating her fill of popcorn and took the hoe to her zinnias and gave them a good weeding before she went inside to crochet.

Dad moved his straight chair back against the wall, cocked it back on its two back legs and listened. Sure enough just about the time it got good and dark, the pack of dogs jumped Mr. Coyote. The whole pack tuned up their voices and started singing their arrangement of "We're coming to get you."

Delton and I had been playing hopscotch, but when the race got hot, we stopped and sat down on the porch steps.

"The coyote is taking them down the river. If he takes them across the river, they'll go out of hearing; otherwise, they're gonna make a big loop and come back up the river, following our bluff," Dad said.

We listened as the coyote brought the big pack of dogs, just like Dad predicted they would, up the river following the bluff that ran just north of our house. They passed by the house and continued up the river bluff until they went out of hearing headed toward Caney Creek.

"The Pannell and the Caylor boys must've put their dog packs together; that's a passel of dogs," Dad calculated, then he announced it was time to go to bed.

During the wee hours of morning, we woke up to a tremendous ruckus under the house ... right under our bed. I had been dreaming about Amos having pointed ears and a bob tail. The noise jolted me straight up in bed.

A bobcat's got Amos.

Delton had been dreaming, too. When he heard the awful noise, he wrapped up in the bedsheet to keep the wompus cat that had attacked him from eating him alive. Before either of us knew it, we were standing at the foot of Mother's and Dad's bed, trembling all over. Delton had the sweat-soaked bedsheet draped around him. Mother and Dad were sitting up in the middle of the bed on their hunkers, stood there by the sudden outburst in the middle of the night.

We crawled in bed with Mother and Dad.

"What's the ruckus?" Delton cried out as big tears streamed down his cheeks.

"Goodness gracious, I don't know," Mother managed to say.

"From all the bumping, yelping and howlin', I'd bet that pack a wolf hounds we heard earlier have got a coyote under there," Dad said.

The raging fight rotated around and around under the house. Bloodthirsty dogs – the whole pack – kept moving, following the coyote. From the bedroom they moved to a spot under the kitchen. The coyote didn't find any cover there, either, and moved directly under Mother's and Dad's bed. The growling, barking and squalling intensified. They knocked a board off the house.

"Will they get in here with us?" Delton asked.

Then they went back under our bedroom. The battle raged on and on.

"That sounded like Andy," Delton said, as a higher pitched gurgling howl erupted from one of the hounds. They moved away from the bedroom area to somewhere around the back porch steps. Suddenly the sounds of battle stopped.

All we could hear was a dog howling that subsided into a gurgling whine. "Shoo ... listen," Dad said. He cupped his hand around his ear, up and went to the back door. He listened for a spell and came back to bed. "It ain't Andy ... It's one of those coyote hounds. The pinned-down coyote must have got a good lick in; I can hear the blood from his jugular vein painting the underside of the house red."

"*Joe Price* ... after that scare we don't need to hear about the gore."

Getting the good lick in was the break the coyote needed. He broke loose and headed toward the river bottom, carrying the pack of dogs hot trailing right on his heels.

No one could go back to sleep; we lay in bed and talked. We decided that chilling experience was one we would never forget. As was the case many times, Delton's dry sense of humor turned the horrid affair into a laughable situation.

"Do you reckon that coyote was giving them dogs rabies was what was making them so mad?" Delton asked.

After we all had a good laugh, Delton and I went back to our own bed.

We were trying to go back to sleep, but we kept hearing a low-throated, gurgling growl coming from a whimpering dog. He didn't like the pack leaving him behind, and he was trying to drag himself out from under the house so he could follow.

"Is that sound coming from Amos or Andy?" I called out. Dad was wondering about Amos and Andy, and he couldn't go back to sleep, either.

I heard him get up out of bed and make his way to the back porch. I crawled out of bed and was right behind Dad. Delton covered up his head.

The full moon shining through the fluttering leaves of the big cottonwood outside the window cast a wavering shadow of Dad on the wall as he made his way toward the back porch. His wavering shadow wasn't exactly welcome after the scare we had just experienced. Dad opened the kitchen door to go out on the back porch, and there Amos and Andy were. Somehow they had busted a hole in the screen door and were lying by the kitchen door, whining and shivering.

"The sound of the dying dog is coming from outside," Dad said as he opened the screen door.

I screamed.

Suddenly Mother and Delton were by our sides.

A dog with his throat cut had managed to crawl out from behind the porch steeps and was lying there door-nail dead. The whimpering low-throated growl was coming from another hound that had his throat slit ... but not quite as bad.

"Dean, go get me the .22."

Mother ran back, got in bed and covered up her head.

I took Dad the .22 rifle. I thought I just had to see Dad shoot, so I peeked around from my stance behind him. He took aim at the poor dog's head.

BANG ...!

I wished I hadn't watched. I felt sick and ran back into the house, jumped in bed and dragged a pillow up over my head.

The night had been long with many interruptions. I never heard Dad when he came back into the house, nor did I hear Mother calling.

"Breakfast is ready. Joe, Dean ... Delton, y'all come and get it."

The next morning Amos and Andy were still shaking violently from fear. The shaking and whining finally subsided, aided by petting and cooing from Delton and me.

"You boys might have petted and cooed the fear out of them, but they'll never have any nerve after their bobcat run in and the scare that coyote gave them last night," Dad said.

After breakfast we settled down with Amos and Andy with plans to talk some nerve into them, but it didn't work.

Every time a coyote howled after that, they would come lie down by the back door and commence shaking.

21
DON'T LET HIM BE DEAD

Uncle Earl and Joe Choice were saddened to hear about Amos and Andy running up against evils while they were still pups, and tried their best to console us.

"Don't give up on 'em, boys. I've seen pups get their nerve back," Joe Choice offered.

"We will never give up on Amos and Andy. They are going to get their nerve back; they just have to," Delton told them.

Nerve doesn't matter anyway; Amos and Andy will always be good rabbit dogs.

Every afternoon after we got in from school, we would take Amos and Andy hunting; they did fine as long as the sport was chasing rabbits, and it was daylight.

When dark settled in, Amos and Andy stayed inside the ring of light that the lantern gave off. When we got to the Red River bottom bluff, Amos and Andy left the lantern light – but it was only to go back to the house.

Six months lapsed before the dogs would hunt outside the lantern light, and then they started to tree a few 'possums.

They're gonna strike a 'coon, and they'll get their nerve back.

That never happened.

In the year that followed I learned a lot about training pups and what it took for a pup to become a real good 'coon dog. I learned there was never much hope for a fat, lazy pup nor was there much hope for the runt of the litter to become real good 'coon dogs.

What Uncle Earl and Joe Choice knew was that young boys and young dogs need to be together, and neither of them needs the other to be – or to ever become – real good.

~

We weren't making enough money working on the farm to keep our heads above water. First off we needed a vehicle. Dad had worn the ol' pickup truck completely to shambles and parked it out behind the barn in the weeds to do whatever it is that old worn-out trucks do. A payment on the farm was due, and school would start up come fall, and there would be the cost of school clothes and school supplies to deal with.

As usual Mother and Dad came up with a plan. The plan was – for every summer as long as it took – we would go to Modesto, California, and make the harvest. We would stay with Grandpa and Grandma Morgan, and

Mother could get a good visit with her folks. Dad, Delton and I would work in the orchards until the canneries opened up, and then Dad would get on at the cannery and work until time to come home and put us in school. After Dad got on at the cannery, Delton and I would have the rest of the summer off.

There was one hitch – for the plan to work, we needed a good vehicle.

Dad bought a 1949 Chevy car, which had seen six years of hard use, "but it runs good and should get good gas mileage," Dad rationalized.

It was 2,000 miles to Grandma and Grandpa's, and Dad worried about how we would save up enough money to make the trip. Gas prices had been on the rise, and although gas was 2 bits a gallon locally, rumor had it that out in the desert and out in California, you couldn't buy a gallon of gas for less than 6 bits.

The family had never owned a car; we were a pickup truck kind of family. In the past the trucks we owned Dad always called "my truck." Not the Chevy car; it became "the family car."

I was 14, a teen-ager, and I saw no reason why I shouldn't learn how to drive the family car. My continual begging to learn how to drive so I could help drive us to California finally got results. Dad took it upon himself to teach me. Mother and Dad were amazed by how fast I learned. So what if there were a few extra dents in the front fenders?

Delton and I looked forward to spending the summer in California. We hated hoeing peanuts, hauling hay and scooping corn, with a passion.

Working in the berry patches and orchards proved just as hard, but making good money made it easier to swallow.

What Delton and I enjoyed most was swimming in the irrigation canals.

The last week of August we packed up and headed back to Mulberry. I didn't care that much about getting started back to school on time, but I wanted to be home when dove season opened; that was the first of September.

~

Our financial situation improved by the next summer; so we didn't go to California to make the harvest. Another reason we didn't go was the school district decided to take up books right after July 4th and run for six weeks, then turn out and take up books six weeks later in the fall to accommodate farm families who needed their kids to work in the cotton patch. Summer school put a hitch in going to California.

By the time school started up in the fall, it was 'coon hunting time.

The summer we went to California I drove a lot of the way there and back, mostly across the deserts. Dad saw no problem with letting me have the car on Saturday nights to go to Uncle Earl and Aunt Dovie's so I could go 'coon hunting with Uncle Earl and Joe Choice. In return I agreed to keep my grades up and do my chores without complaining. I also agreed to stick to the back roads.

The prospect of having a new hunting buddy tickled Uncle Earl and Joe Choice. They gave me only one bit of advice. "We have got enough dogs; it'll be best if you don't bring Amos and Andy."

All of a sudden, KB, my best friend, developed an interest in 'coon hunting.

At the time, I thought KB's attraction was getting to 'coon hunt with 'coon dogs like Old Trailer and Queenie. The attraction, I soon learned, was the work of the birds and the bees.

My cousin Patsy, Uncle Earl and Aunt Dovie's daughter was the same age as KB and me. I was shocked to learn that Patsy didn't want to go 'coon hunting with us. That didn't compare to the shock I felt the first time KB announced that he wasn't gonna go 'coon hunting, either. I couldn't believe Patsy and KB were going to listen to records on her wind-up Victrola and miss a 'coon hunting trip. Pretty soon KB's talk turned from "Old Trailer and Queenie did this and that" to "Patsy did this and that."

The attraction wasn't mutual, however, and KB soon became my hunting buddy again. Uncle Earl, Joe Choice, KB and I went on many enjoyable Saturday night 'coon hunts together over the next several years although KB's 'coon hunts grew farther and farther apart as he learned to appreciate the girls more. I grew to appreciate Joe Choice and Uncle Earl as two of the best 'coon hunters who ever walked the night woods and the best dog trainers who ever started a 'coon dog.

~

Late one Saturday evening one of the most memorable 'coon hunts I ever remember going on got underway. The day was clear and cold but damp, the kind of dampness that a 'coon dog can really work a trail on.

KB and I were running a little late. We had stopped on the Caney Creek Bridge to put a bicycle innertube over the exhaust pipe, so the old Chevy would sound like a hotrod. I pulled into Uncle Earl and Aunt Dovie's yard a little too fast; squawking chickens scattered in every direction.

Uncle Earl and Joe Choice had unpinned the dogs and were getting ready to leave for a hunt on Caney Creek. If KB and I had arrived a few minutes later, Uncle Earl and Joe Choice would have already run off and left us.

Patsy's girlfriend was there spending the weekend with Patsy. For some reason KB decided to listen to records with Patsy and her girlfriend.

The usual discussion broke out between Uncle Earl and Joe Choice as to where we could get the best hunt.

Uncle Earl wanted to go to the mouth of Caney Creek, where it ran into Red River.

However, Joe Choice won the argument.

"We ain't been to the old rail road bridge that crosses Caney in a 'coon's age. Everyone is taking bets that I can't climb that giant cottonwood tree that grows there. I wanna prove to myself that I can climb Goliath; that's what everyone is calling that old tree. That's where I wanna go."

It was final; Uncle Earl wanted to see if Joe Choice could climb Goliath, too.

It was getting dark by the time we reached the branch that crossed the road where we intended to start the dogs. Joe Choice pulled his pickup over in the bar ditch. Trailer and old Queenie and the rest of the dogs were rattling their chains. When the truck stopped, two of Joe Choice's dogs, Jake and Lady, jumped out and their chains got tangled; they were choking themselves. Joe Choice rushed to untangle them and in the excitement he forgot to turn the pickup's lights off.

Uncle Earl snapped Trailer to his leash. Joe Choice led his dogs on a chain to which they were snapped individually. That way he could release them as he saw fit. We led the dogs off into the woods and down into a branch before Uncle Earl unsnapped Trailer's chain and told him, "We're after 'coons," and then sent him on his way. It was slap-dab-dark when Trailer hit a cold trail and bawled for the first time. As soon as Trailer struck that cold trail, Joe Choice unsnapped Queenie.

The rest of the dogs would have to wait their turn.

When Queenie and Trailer worked the cold trail into something hotter Joe Choice would release the rest of his dogs and they wouldn't scatter in all directions; they would go straight to Trailer and Queenie.

Trailer's slow, drawling bawl echoed through the creek bottom, and then Queenie joined him with her clear bell-like voice. Pretty soon the trail warmed up, and first one dog then the other sounded their voices in anticipation of seeing the 'coon. Joe Choice released the rest of his dogs except Jude; he remained on the leash, his punishment for treeing a 'coon when a 'coon wasn't in the tree.

We sat down on a log and waited. After dark had set in, it got downright cold.

I built a small fire.

We had been listening for what seemed like hours to Trailer and Queenie cold trailing, and now that the other dogs joined in, Trailer hushed his bawling. My mind wandered.

Trailer is the smartest 'coon dog anyone ever hunted with ... he knows what Uncle Earl wants him to hunt ... why would anyone want to play with the girls? ... I bet KB ain't havin' as much fun.

Trailer had gained himself a reputation for his voice. There was none more resonate, none louder nor sweeter than Trailer's. Uncle Earl claimed that on a cold clear night you could hear him treed five miles away.

The pack of dogs pushed the 'coon faster and faster; we finally had a race on our hands. Trailer saved his voice for the time the 'coon would go up a tree.

"It's a hot race to the finish now. They're hot on his tail ... they're pushin' him 'cross Caney," Uncle Earl said.

"Yep ... I hope to that giant cottonwood on the other side of the creek," Joe Choice said.

Suddenly the tone of Queenie's voice changed, and Trailer joined her.

"They're treed!" Uncle Earl announced.

It was a duplicate of the way it always was: When Joe Choice heard Uncle Earl announce, "They're treed," he took off. He never needed a light because he had what he called night eyes. Uncle Earl was right on his heels with the lantern, and I was keeping up the best way I could. I was used to following crashing sounds and the ever-dimming lantern light.

I heard Uncle Earl holler from somewhere up ahead, "They're on the other side of the creek in Goliath ... the giant Cottonwood tree."

For my benefit ... Uncle Earl knows if I lose sight of the light that I know where Goliath, the giant Cottonwood, is.

I arrived on the scene to see Uncle Earl and Joe Choice standing on the creek bank urging the dogs into a tizzy. Sure enough, the dogs had treed in Goliath.

"Get him, Trailer," Uncle Earl hollered.

"Get him, Queenie," Joe Choice echoed.

They hollered "Get him" alternately; Uncle Earl, then Joe Choice, Uncle Earl again, then Joe Choice. Uncle Earl encouraged Trailer, and Joe Choice encouraged each dog in his pack by name – Queenie, Jake, Lady and Bow. They ended the chant with a flurry of "Get him, get-em, get-em." With every "Get him," the dogs jumped higher and higher. Jude whined on the leash.

The dogs clawed and bit chunks of bark from the tree. Growls and barks filled the air.

There was a silent oath between Joe Choice and Uncle Earl – made to their dogs. They would never drag them away from their tree without first whipping their prey out for them to fight. That was an understood oath between most 'coon hunters and their hounds. 'Coon hunters have chopped at a hollow tree all night to fell it and deliver a 'coon to their pack of dogs. No obstacle was too big to keep the greatest bunch of 'coon hunters in the world from honoring their oath to their dogs. As far as Uncle Earl was concerned, the obstacle facing them was not Goliath, the giant cottonwood tree; it was the long deep hole of water between them and Goliath.

Long ago, there had been a railroad bridge at this point on Caney creek. The train hadn't operated along those tracks in years, and the abandoned bridge had caved into the creek. The caved-in bridge partially dammed the creek and created the longest deepest hole of water anywhere on Caney Creek. All the crossties from the railroad track had wound up in the water and created ideal dens for cottonmouth moccasins. Over the years they had raised their young there, and the place had become infested with big moccasins. Some people called the place "water moccasin hole."

"Neither Goliath nor cottonmouth moccasins are gonna stop me," Joe Choice bragged, "if I can get some help from Uncle Earl and you, Dean.

Goliath was not just any tree; all the old-timers claimed that Goliath was the biggest cottonwood tree in all of Caney Creek bottom and maybe even Texas. The old-timers all laughed about Goliath being so big that any varmint in its right mind was too afraid to climb it. "Any varmint, that is, except Joe Choice," they claimed.

Joe Choice had very long, very thick and very hard toenails, made for climbing, he claimed. Anyone who had seen Joe Choice climb a big cottonwood tree, believed him. He would walk up to a tree, look up to see how far it was to the first limb, and then bear-hug it, hook his toenails into the bark and shinny plum to the top without stopping.

"Joe Choice can climb so fast, you can't keep your light on him," I bragged.

Joe Choice would tuck his head, embarrassed-like, and say, "I'm fast ... but I ain't that fast."

Joe Choice barked orders.

"Earl, us you and me shuck our overalls and swim over there. I'll shinny up Goliath while you hold the dogs, and then I'll whoop that 'coon out. Dean, you start us a warmin' fire."

"Hey, wait a minute," Uncle Earl protested. "I ain't 'bout to swim that creek with all of them cottonmouth moccasins in there. Frost hasn't hibernated 'em yet. I'll walk down the creek bank, find a crossing and come back up the creek to the tree. But I ain't takin' my britches off," he added.

"Nope ... that'll take too long," Joe Choice said as he clicked his overall's suspenders open. "That 'coon ain't gonna wait that long. He'll climb across the treetops and be gone."

Joe Choice stripped down to his pure white boxer shorts and scolded, "You and Dean get a move-on."

Caney Creek heads in the black land region of southern Fannin County. The rains through the centuries displaced the black dirt from Caney Creek's watershed and deposited it in a thick black coating along Caney Creek's banks.

We heard a big splash, and the next thing we knew Joe Choice was scaling the creek bank on the other side.

Joe Choice's body, being about the same color as the creek bank, left nothing to see except the white blur of his bleached boxer shorts as he climbed up the muddy creek bank.

"Look," Uncle Earl laughed, "there goes a pair of boxer shorts with no one in 'em."

"Get a move on, Earl," Joe Choice hollered from across the creek where he stood bear-hugging the tree in preparation for the climb. "The 'coon's on the move, and if he goes in a hollow, I'm gonna see to it that you saw Goliath down by yourself.

Uncle Earl ran down the creek about 50 yards and found himself a place to cross and then ran back up the creek.

I built us a warming fire.

Finally Uncle Earl got to the tree where Joe Choice was and got all the dogs under control. He held Trailer and Queenie with one hand and Jake, Lady and Bow with his other hand. The moon was full and silhouetted Joe Choice as he passed through its beam on his way to the top of Goliath. The big legs on his white boxer shorts flapped like wings. Joe Choice was at least 50 feet up the tree when all silence broke out.

"Why are you so quiet, up there, Joe?" Uncle Earl hollered.

"Do you hear that buzzin' that's coming from up here in this tree with me?"

Uncle Earl cupped his hands and placed them around his ears. "Yeah ... I hear a buzzing. What's causin' it?" Uncle Earl asked.

"I can't hear anything," I hollered from across the creek.

"Honeybees," Joe Choice screamed. "They are down below me ... I've clumb up past 'em."

"Climb back down ... fast as you can," Uncle Earl advised.

"I can't ... I can't stand to go down through 'em."

"Give it up, Joe; you have got to climb back down through 'em," Uncle Earl pleaded.

"Too many of 'em ... sounds like a cream separator whirrin' down there. What am I gonna do?"

"Turn loose. Jump out," I advised from across the creek.

"I can't do it, Dean. Uncle Earl can't hold five dogs off of me."

Uncle Earl got sarcastic. "You gotta choose, Joe. Stick it out ... bail out, or climb down. You can't fly."

"Augh ... they're swarmin' inside my shorts ... Lordeeeee!"

Joe Choice's voice, for the first time ever showed fear; his voice trembled. If you've ever seen a critter whooped out of a tree and seen him hit the ground among a pack of frenzied dogs, you will appreciate Joe Choice's concern. That split second before the dogs recognized him had the potential – in his mind – of being more dangerous than a 50-foot freefall.

"I can't stay up here with 'em. Dean, dad-nab-it, get yourself on across that creek and help Uncle Earl hold them dogs off of me, and I'll jump out."

"Waugh ... Oh my, they're inside my drawers. Augh ... they're eatin' my butt up. Oh, have mercy!"

"Break you a limb off and swat at em," Uncle Earl chided.

"I'm swattin' at em with both hands. Augh ... I'm ... f-a-l-l-i-n-g!" His voice trailed along behind him ... he sped toward the ground.

I was there ... reaching for the dogs, *I gotta help Uncle Earl* ... I was too late.

The dogs lunged toward the spot where Joe Choice was fixing to hit the ground.

Uncle Earl toppled over and he went sliding topsy-turvy down the slick bank toward Caney Creek.

Whomp ... Joe Choice hit the ground right in front of the growling, gnarling dogs.

Instantly they recognized him and licked him all over the face. I could have sworn they were laughing. I parted the dogs and slapped Joe's cheeks and blew in his face. He didn't respond. I looked down at his dull sooty face and chanted ... "Is he dead ... don't let him be dead ... is he dead ... don't let him be dead!"

He just lay there limp.

I cried.

Joe Choice roused up a little and gasped for air; wheezing sounds filled his throat and lungs as he tried to replace the air that the ground had jousted out of him. He was getting his lungs pumped back up, but he still didn't have enough air to talk. He moaned and groaned and rolled around on the ground with one of his big hands on each cheek of his butt. Between wheezes he started to mumble a little.

My pleading eyes met his. "Are you gonna be okay?" I asked.

"Don't know. My butt's on fire ... full of bee stingers. Waugh ...!" His eyes rolled back in his head, and he passed out.

I slapped him and fanned him ... and prayed, like I had heard Mother pray.

He revived a little and got up on his knees. He hollered, "I need air ... where is Earl?"

The dull sooty appearance of the skin on his face was leaving. *He's getting his sheen back ... he's beautiful.*

"I'm coming, Joe." Uncle Earl scampered up the creek bank as wet as a drowned rat and as pale as a ghost. Clawing and scratching, he finally reached the top of the muddy bank and with one jump was by Joe Choice's side. He pulled a Case trapper's knife from his overhaul's pocket, grabbed Joe with one hand, held the knife with the other hand and opened it with his teeth. "Roll over, Joe. I'll dig the stingers out," he commanded.

Pain and fear filled the whites of Joe's eyes when he saw the glint of the moon reflecting from the long, pointed, super-sharp knife blade. They rolled back in his head again. "Whoa ... put it up! You ain't gonna dig them stingers out of me with that thing. Minnie will do it ... y'all just get me home."

The sound of Uncle Earl trying to open the knife with his teeth must've caused Joe Choice to refill his lungs with air ... he ain't wheezing anymore.

It was late, and the fun of the hunt had vanished. I helped Joe Choice gather himself up off the ground and offered my services. "Joe, I'll drive your pickup and take you and your dogs home."

"Trailer and me ... we'll walk home, Dean, so you can get Joe home to Minnie. Dovie and I will come over in the morning to check on you," Uncle Earl reassured Joe Choice. He called Trailer in, waved farewell and then headed up the creek. After he walked a few yards he looked back to see if Joe and me had gotten underway.

"What are y'all waitin' on? Can't you walk, Joe?" Uncle Earl asked in a worried voice.

"I ain't gonna go nowhere without my overhauls, Earl Price. You know me better than that."

"Well, if that doesn't beat a hen a peckin' with a wooden bill. Your overhauls are still on the other side of the creek," Uncle Earl said.

We all laughed as we looked across the creek. There Joe's overalls were hanging on a limb by my big crackling fire. Goose bumps popped out on Joe, and he shivered trying to shake them off.

As far as crossing Caney Creek and fetching Joe's overalls is concerned ... Joe can't, Uncle Earl won't ... I must.

I stood there facing the railroad bridge hole and said a scared prayer for myself: "Lord ... please help me cross over. Help me not make them cottonmouth moccasins mad. Help this night to hurry and get over." It didn't take me long to fetch Joe's overalls.

Joe Choice squiggled down in them and fastened the suspenders but left the side vents open. "My butt needs air," he said.

The dogs knew the hunt was over and raced out into the night toward the pickup. When we got there, the dogs had scrawled out in the bed and were waiting on us. Joe crawled up in the bed with them and lay down on his side.

I crawled in the cab, turned the key on and hit the starter button – nothing. I glanced at the light switch; it was already pulled out. Joe Choice had left the lights on.

Through the woods it was about 3 miles to Joe's house – if there was nothing wrong with you – in Joe's case it was 20 miles.

There wasn't anything we could do. Joe Choice had to get home and get the stingers out of his behind.

"I'll take you," I said.

"I don't need you to take me ... just follow and be sure I get there."

We walked the 3 miles to Joe's house making very little talk.

Joe Choice offered the daybed on the screened-in back porch, but I was content sleeping on the front porch with the dogs. I was too tired to walk around to the back porch and open the screen door. I lay down and propped my head on the woodbox without taking my wet overalls off. I faintly saw Joe come to the door and heard him issue a word of warning.

"You go on to sleep now. I'll not stand for any peepin' through the window."

I thought I heard Joe say, "Light the lamp, Minnie. I got a job for you," but I didn't hear anything else. The snores overtook me; Joe's squeals of pain roused me up a few times, but I didn't dare take a peek.

Joe Choice couldn't sit down for a few days, but he recovered and from that day forth he never clumb a big tree to shake a 'coon out without checking to see if it was a bee tree first.

22
HOMEMADE AIN'T ALWAYS BEST

Dad had fulfilled his "owning a Red River farm dream" and far from his mind was the dream that he had spent so many years dreaming about, floating down Red River all the way to the Mississippi River. The dream that held his attention in the spring of 1957 was getting me through two more years of school. He had resigned himself to the fact that I had dreams other than floating down Red River.

I had dreams of going to work for Safeway and dreams of going to college after I graduated from high school. The one dream I had that Mother and Dad despised and that Mother discouraged at every turn was to own a motorcycle. I wanted a motorcycle so I would have a way to go to work, if I could get a job. That wasn't the reason that I gave Mother and Dad, though. The reason I held up to them was so I would have a way to go to college after I graduated from high school.

The fall of 1957 I ran a trapline every day after school and on Saturday morning. Every Saturday afternoon I went to Safeway in Bonham and filled out a new job application. In answer to the "What job are you applying for" question, I put Package Boy, Grocery Stocker or Assistant Manager. When I came to the question, "Are you willing to transfer and if so where would you be willing to work?" I wrote in, Yes, and then wrote: anywhere as long as it ain't far from Red River.

One cold, drizzly day the postman left a letter in the mailbox addressed to: Dean Price, RFD 1, Ravenna, Texas. The letter was from Safeway in Bonham. Mother knew as soon as she got it out of the mailbox that my persistence had paid off. She rushed home and shoved the letter into my hands.

The note inside said: SUBJECT: Job interview
TIME: Saturday, November 16, 10:00 a.m.

The note didn't have anyone's name on it; it was just signed by the store manager.

I could hardly wait for Saturday morning to come. I was out before daylight running my trapline.

I hope I ain't got a skunk.

I would never leave an animal in a trap, and I suspected that Safeway wouldn't hire anyone who smelled like a skunk. I was thankful that I didn't even catch a 'possum. When I returned from running my traps, Mother had a big breakfast already on the table. I hurriedly ate and got dressed. I wore blue jeans and a white shirt. Mother starched the shirt so stiff that the collar kept my head pointed straight ahead. My hair was slick and plastered back against my head; too much Brylcreem.

I was so excited I could hardly concentrate on driving; it was a good thing there was hardly any traffic.

I sat down across the desk from the Safeway manager. He glanced over his spectacles once in a while as he read my application.

"I gotta opening for a package boy. The holiday season is right around the corner and I could use some extra help. Of course, it's only part-time. You say here that you would like an Assistant Manager's job. There is not one open." He laid my application on his desk and continued, "So, you say here that you're planning on going to college after you graduate. You might just work your way into an Assistant Manager's job, if you study real hard."

Study hard ain't my strong suit ... If I'm gonna have to study hard I might as well study nature things like trapping, fishing and hunting, and if I'm gonna have to work into being Assistant Manager, why, I might as well work myself into jugging minnows or trapping or even becoming a commercial fisherman. I decided right then and there that I was going to have my own business someday, and it was going to involve nature.

I started working at Safeway in Bonham after school on Fridays and on Saturdays. In the 1950s it was against the law for stores in Texas to sell most items on Sunday, so Safeway always closed on Sunday.

When school started back up in the fall of 1958, I faced a choice: quit Safeway or quit trapping. I chose to abandon my trapline; 'possum and 'coon hides weren't worth that much, and I preferred a steady income ... to no, or not much income.

A dream of another sort faced me – the Vietnam conflict was cranking up, and I had dreams of serving my country if the draft got me. I also started having girlfriend dreams. My old dreams of working and college were still there, too. I very rarely thought about floating down Red River anymore; more pressing dreams replaced that dream. Well, maybe not replaced it; they just took precedence over it.

Saturday nights of my senior year in high school were spent 'coon hunting with Uncle Earl and Joe Choice. Mother still reserved Sunday for going to church and getting a day of rest, and she reinforced her stand every time I complained that Uncle Earl kept me out too late and that I wanted to sleep in. "As long as you're under our roof, you will go to church with us," she said.

~

The winter of 1958 dragged by; for the first time since I could remember, I had not trapped during the winter.

Spring had finally come, and things were looking up.

June is the magic month.

Wild plums were getting ripe, and the mustang grapes were just the right size to make green grape cobblers. The wild plums had already shed their wormy fruit, and the ones that were getting ripe were beautiful and tasty. Spring had been wet, and the wild mustang grapes hung from their vines in clusters, their seeds just beginning to form. When Delton and I came in from school, the house reeked with a mixed aroma. Dad was baking a green grape pie in the oven along with a plum cobbler that Mother was baking. We loved Mother's plum cobblers almost as much if not more than Dad's green grape pies. Usually the desert we were having was the best we ever ate. This time we had a pie and a cobbler both to brag on.

Another thing that made June the magic month was the drum run and the flathead spawn. Every year about the time school turned out, around the first of June, the drum started their migration up Red River. It was not uncommon for us to play hooky from school if the drum run happened before school turned out. The drumming sounds that the drum made sent vibrations through the water, and at times there seemed to be droves of the mating drum swimming up Red River. They became ravenous feeders during June, and it wasn't uncommon to catch two or three at a time on a rod and reel. They were easy to hook, and they put up a feisty fight.

Another thing that made June of 1959 special was my class was graduating from high school.

~

After school turned out, I got more hours at Safeway. Monday was Double S & H Green stamp day. Since everyone who traded with Safeway on Monday got twice as many S & H Green stamps, it was a very busy day, and because of that I got a full day's work on Monday. I had more money to spend, and I got serious about owning a motorcycle.

When I started building my own motorcycle is when Mother really got worried.

"Dean's just like you," she told Dad. "Whatever he wants he sets his mind to it, and he ain't gonna give up till he does it. That contraption he calls a motorcycle ain't nothing but a murdercycle."

Dad wasn't all that worried. "It's just a fad ... besides he can't build anything fit to ride to Bonham and Commerce."

Commerce, Texas, was the town where East Texas State College was located. That is where I wanted to go to college because I could work at Safeway in Bonham after school and on Saturday.

I bought a cull Redbone 'coonhound from one of Uncle Earl's friends and traded the worthless hound to JD Overton for a motorbike frame.

No one knew exactly where the frame came from; some thought it had its beginning as one of the FFA boy's projects. Wherever it came from, it wound up being nothing more than a widened bicycle frame, with a place to bolt a motor right above where the pedals had been. The brazing job wasn't the best in the world or the prettiest to look at, but the frame seemed to want to stay together. One of the main design flaws of the thing was the fact that the bicycle's peddles had been removed to make room for an idler pulley, so the thing would have a neutral gear. That doesn't sound like much of a problem. However, without peddles, the thing had no brakes.

JD Overton had fallen heir to the frame and had intended to build himself a motorbike, but he hadn't gotten very far with the project. His part in the project had been to braze two wheel rims together. The rear tire would mount on one rim, and the drive belt from the motor would go around the other rim to propel the motorbike. After he gave up on the contraption, his dad had hauled the frame to their trash dump down on the bluff, where it should've stayed.

I went with JD, and we uncovered the old frame from the heap of trash that had wound up on top of it. We dragged it out of the trash pile, and I took it home. I spent a couple of days cleaning the rust off the frame and rims. When I got all the rust off, I tightened all the spokes and painted the whole thing John Deere green. The motorcycle was far from looking like a Harley, but I thought if I could come across a motor it might outrun a Harley.

After electricity came to the farm, washing machines with electric motors became very popular; now the housewife could wash clothes inside the house. No longer was it necessary to wash clothes outside. The fear of filling the house with carbon monoxide was gone. Whenever a gasoline washing machine engine gave up the ghost, to the trash dump it went; so as often as I got the chance, I checked all the trash dumps in the community. Almost every farm dump held a gasoline engine in some sort of running condition. It wasn't long before I came home toting a Maytag washing machine engine.

The first question Dad had was, "What kind of running condition is it in?"

"It ain't," I answered and added, "yet."

Dad didn't think I would ever get the greasy, gassy smelling piece of junk cleaned up, much less running. Mother knew I wouldn't quit till I did; she became more worried than ever.

I worked on the Maytag engine almost every day. Finally I got the engine cleaned up; the old thing looked pretty good.

Not anywhere like new ... but pretty good.

"It's good on looks," I told JD Overton, "but when it comes to running, it ain't got any fire to the spark plug."

I fixed that; come payday I bought a tune-up kit, which contained new points, a condenser and a spark plug. I soon found that the thing still wouldn't fire off because it wasn't getting gas to the spark plug. A dirt dauber wasp had taken care of that by building a nest in the carburetor. I took the carburetor completely apart and cleaned it in a can of gasoline. When I got the thing back together she fired right off, to my surprise. I threw the parts I had left over in the pigpen.

Mother prayed for me. She prayed a lot anyway, but now it was different. "Dean is weighing heavy on my mind; something dreadful is gonna happen to him," she told Dad.

Mother's "motherly intuition" has proved itself on more than one occasion, Dad thought. He remembered a time, many years ago, when she had a special feeling about her baby Dean going with him to gather corn, and the mules had pulled a runaway; he laughed.

The last hurdle I had to conquer before I could take a test drive on my new motorbike just happened. The old belt that JD gave me to provide power to the bike's rear wheel broke ... beyond repair. The only thing I knew to do was plat one out of net twine. I was bound and determined to get my motorbike running.

Every morning before I went to work I set on the back steps and platted net twine and listened to Mother pray. When I came home in the evenings, she would still be praying. Mother constantly reminded us at the supper table she was worried about me and that she was praying for the Lord to spare me.

"Spare me from what?" I asked Mother.

"I don't know ... something awful," she said.

Her praying continued day in, day out. As I got closer and closer to the day I would have the motorbike running, her praying intensified, if that were possible.

I felt like my life was in limbo. I wanted a full-time job ... but I worked for Safeway part time. I wanted to go to East Texas State College ... but Vietnam was cranking up, and the draft board had first dubs on me.

I finished the new belt, and it was supper strong. It was better than the frayed, rubber belt JD had given me. It fit so tight, it was a strain to get it over the rim. One pull on the starter rope and the Maytag engine fired off, sputtered and died. I didn't let that discourage me; I knew it was out of gas.

After I got off work I stopped in Ravenna and bought a gallon of gas with my last two dimes and rushed home.

By the time I got there it was almost dark and I was going to be off work the next two days, Tuesday and Wednesday, so I sat the can on the porch step and called Amos, Andy and Delton. We went to the river bottom 'possum hunting.

Early the next morning, Tuesday morning, September 2nd, I left out before daylight to go to Red River and get in a good dove hunt. I had to work on the first day of dove season and missed opening morning. When I returned home, I could hear Mother talking to someone.

Probably Mrs. Nixon, our neighbor.

I went inside and found that there was no one there. Mother was lying across the bed talking to the Lord, just like he was there.

"Lord, he's just like in your Bible. Lord, I know you gotta bring him down. Isaiah said you would ... *The lofty looks of man shall be humbled, and the haughtiness of men shall be bowed down.* Lord, spare him ... Lord, you said you'd bring him down ... Please, oh please ... spare him. *For the day of the LORD of hosts shall be upon every one that is proud and lofty, and upon every one that is lifted up; and he shall be brought low:* Oh please, Lord, not too low."

I turned around, went back outside and filled the gas tank on the motorbike. I poured a little gas in the carburetor and went through the starting procedures in my mind. *Put the clutch lever in neutral ... set the choke to the on position and the throttle in the middle.* I wound the starter rope around the flywheel pulley and gave it a quick pull.

The motor burst into action.

I grabbed the handlebars, threw my leg over the bike, and put my foot on the pedal that held the idler pulley. I released the idler, and the belt tightened. The bike just sat there; then the Maytag engine bogged down and died.

The ratio between the pulley on the engine and the wheel rim on the rear wheel is too great.

I started the motor again, jumped on and pushed the bike forward with my left foot as I released the idler pulley. The bike picked up speed. I guided it around and around the house as it picked up more speed. There were no gears to shift and no brakes to push. I sat high and proud on the seat, arms stiff against the handlebars and admired my creation – admired its speed.

"Its dinnertime, Dean. Come wash up, and then let's eat," Mother called.

The motorbike was still gaining speed when I brought it in and parked it by the back steps. I stopped on the porch by the kitchen door and washed my hands in the dishpan before I went inside. I busted through the kitchen door with my excited announcement: "There ain't no tellin' how fast that thing will run. It was still gaining speed when you called me."

That wasn't what Mother wanted to hear. "So," is all she said; she thought plenty more, though.

We sat down at the dinner table.

"Say thanks, Dean," Mother said, then added, "Thank him for your life while you're at it." The tension was so thick, you could slice it like cornbread. I pondered what Mother said, "Thank him for your life." The words were as hard as crow to eat, but what was I supposed to do? Mother was sitting right beside me holding my hand. After I finished asking the Lord to bless our food, I ended my prayer with, "Oh yeah, Mother said to thank you for my life."

I ate like a speed demon and rushed back outside to my motorbike. I fired it off and headed toward the mailbox to pick up the mail.

Our house was at the end of a long lane that led to the County Road. The traffic kept the ruts beat down, but the middle of the lane had grown up with grass. For nearly a year there had been very little rain, and the ruts were ankle-deep in powdery sand. The lane entered the County Road with a sharp curve to the left and a long curve to the right. In the little triangle between the curve left and the curve right and the County Road sat our mailbox.

The curve to the right got most of the traffic; that was the way to town and KB's house. The curve had become banked to the inside over the years, allowing cars to swing out onto the County Road at a pretty good clip. There was hardly ever any traffic on the County Road, and when there was, a trail of dust followed like a dust devil and was visible from the lane.

I picked up the mail. There was a birthday card for Delton from Irma; September 4th was his birthday, and it was two days away on Friday. There was also a letter to me from the Draft Board in Bonham. The notice from the Draft Board sent me into a quandary. It commanded, "Appear in Bonham, Tuesday, September 8th, for a physical." I thought I would pass. If I did, there would be no college for a few years ... If I failed, there would be no Vietnam.

I wanted both.

About halfway home from the mailbox the bike sputtered and died.

I should have gassed her up. I pushed it back to the house. As I pushed the motorbike along in the sandy rut I thought, *I got about 30 miles an hour out of her ... who knows what I can get if I don't stop at the mailbox and go all the way to KB's.*

I poured gas in the tank and struck out for KB's house. The bike picked up speed. As I breezed along the lane, I estimated my speed: 5, 10, 20, probably 25. I entered the long curve leading to the County Road. In my excitement I forgot to look and see if any traffic was coming. It wouldn't have mattered anyway ... the bike had no brakes, and I was flying.

The engine whined.

Mother prayed.

The approaching car and the motorbike faced each other, for an instant. Poised like a bull and a matador engaged in a till-death battle.

Neither the oncoming car nor I had time to dodge – nor could either of us dodge if we had had time – the sandy ruts held us captive.

I extended my left arm over the bike's handlebars and placed it on the car's hood, as if to hold it off. My left foot caught under the car's front bumper – shoes might have helped, but I wore none. The motorbike flipped upside down on its handlebars, and they gouged two long gashes in the car's top. I held onto the bike ... for dear life. The car skidded sideways and threw the motorbike and me into the road ditch.

A terrible putrid smell filled my nostrils.

Broken grinding bones ... like I smelled when the dentist ground my teeth for fillings. But it was mixed with the sweet smell of death and blood scorching on the motorbike's muffler.

The air reeked with the smell of gas and oil from the bike and from the car.

KB's dad, Carl, lived a quarter of a mile away. He heard the collision. "Call for an ambulance, Nickie!" he ordered and rushed to the scene.

Mother heard the "awful rumbling." She stopped praying and ran ... she knew.

I lay topsy-turvy in the ditch.

I propped myself up on my left elbow. My forearm protruded through the back of my hand; the force of the oncoming car jammed my hand down on it.

I was lying on my right thigh, the bone broken in two places. My foot was lying across my shoulder, in my face – *It's still attached to my leg but crushed to smithereens* – I watched my heel dangle, held on only by the skin.

Carl Baker arrived; he knew I wouldn't live until the ambulance got there. He took charge. "I'm taking you to the M and S hospital in Bonham, Dean."

My feet are too dirty to go to town.

"Go find Joe, Sybil ... I'm taking Dean to Bonham ... y'all come on when you find him."

Carl loaded me into the back seat of his brand new Crown Victoria Ford and put his hand on Mother's shoulder and looked into her eyes. "Don't worry, Sybil."

Mother felt an unexplained relief: *The Lord spared him ... he is alive ... he's in good hands.* "Thank you, Lord."

All the way to Bonham, my mind rambled: *What about the Draft Board? What about my physical? What about Carl's brand new car?*

"I'm ruining your new car ... I'm getting the floorboard full of blood."

"I'll take care of it, Dean. You just don't worry about it."

He's saving my life.

I lay critically injured for two weeks, and then I showed some signs of improving. I improved a little with every passing day.

Mother knew that I would live now. She was relieved; the Lord had answered her prayers and spared me. *There will be no going to war for Dean; what a blessing,* she thought.

I went home from the hospital in 14 days and in a little over six weeks I shed my casts. Doctor Joe Stevens took them off and sent me home with instructions to exercise my arm and leg.

"Can I go hunting when I get home?" I asked him.

"Sure you can ... just don't go swimming in Red River until your pressure sores get well."

As soon as we got home, I sat up on the side of the bed. I was dizzy – a shock awaited me – when I stepped out onto the linoleum I discovered I had forgotten how to walk. I fell flat on my face.

"You will be hunting and fishing in no time," Mother told me, then said to Dad, "Joe, it's just like I've told you many times: *Everything happens for the good of those who love the Lord.* The Bible says something to that effect."

The end

AUTHOR'S BIO

The alignment of the stars—No—Red River shaped my destiny. I was born Harold Dean Price in the wee hours of the morning July 11, 1941, in the Red River Valley. Since that humble beginning long, long ago I have felt drawn to Red River like a divining rod drawn to underground water.

I grew up in Dad's footsteps. He taught me how to tie nets, hoop them and fish with them. Dad taught me how to build river boats and how to read Red River. He taught me how to trap mink, 'coon and 'possum. He gave me the dream of making a float trip down Red River. I can still hear Dad saying, "Yep, we're gonna find out why Red River's mouth is at the Mississippi River and her head is in West Texas."

Red River played a big part in my childhood. During my teen years I was instrumental in organizing a club known as "the River Rats." Gaining membership was simple: kill a skunk with a stick. Keeping one's membership was just as simple: go swimming in Red River every month of the year.

After graduating from high school, the farthest thing from my mind was Red River. Dad had accomplished his goal, though; he had gotten me through high school on the wings of a dream, that of floating down Red River. After graduation I moved to Dallas, began a career, married and started my own family. Eventually Red River's gravitational pull on my heartstrings overpowered my rationale. I pulled up stakes, family and all, and moved back to Bonham, Texas.

It took me a long time to create a way to make a living from Red River. In 1986 I began designing and building furniture using dogwood hoops like dad used in his fishnets. I quickly perfected my designs into beautiful works of art. One of my designs was nominated to receive the Texas Forestry Association's annual *Award of Merit for Architectural Excellence in Wood Design.* My Nanny Rocker won the honor.

My lifestyle was the topic of many television productions, including Bob Phillips' *Texas Country Reporter* show, and my furniture appeared in *Southern Living* and many regional magazines, as well as the *Dallas Morning News* and local newspapers.

In 2000 I started writing about Red River. I became obsessed with Red River history, in the history of her people. In 2001 I hung up my hammer, picked up my pen and embarked on a 16-day, 400-mile canoe trip down Red River. My goal: Interview people along the river; study her history and tell her story. *Treasure River* was my first book, and GAP published it in 2006.This book, *River of Dreams,* is my second book, and my third, *Red River Refuge,* is in the mill.

I am obsessed with Red River – I am her most astute scholar.
You can find me on the World Wide Web at redriverscholar.com

www.ingramcontent.com/pod-product-compliance
Lightning Source LLC
LaVergne TN
LVHW050514100826
845148LV00002B/330

9780979808760